Somewhat Saved

Also by Pat G'Orge-Walker

Cruisin' on Desperation

Mother Eternal Ann Everlastin's Dead

Sister Betty! God's Calling You, Again!

Somewhat Saved

Pat G'Orge-Walker

KENSINGTON BOOKS
http://www.kensingtonbooks.com

DAFINA BOOKS are published by

Kensington Publishing Corp.
850 Third Avenue
New York, NY 10022

All Kensington titles, imprints, and distributed lines are available at special quantity discounts for bulk purchases for sales promotion, premiums, fund-raising, educational, or institutional use.

Special book excerpts or customized printings can also be created to fit specific needs. For details, write or phone the office of the Kensington Special Sales Manager: Attn. Special Sales Department. Kensington Publishing Corp., 850 Third Avenue, New York, NY 10022. Phone: 1-800-221-2647.

Dafina and the Dafina logo Reg. U.S. Pat. & TM Off.

Library of Congress Card Catalogue Number: 2007942804

ISBN-13: 978-0-7582-1889-6
ISBN-10: 0-7582-1889-3

First Printing: April 2008
10 9 8 7 6 5 4 3 2 1

Printed in the United States of America

Most of *Somewhat Saved* is dedicated to all those daughters who feel discarded and unloved. It is dedicated to those women who've felt uncovered with their souls unprotected and at the mercy of life. God is able and willing to keep you. We are His heiresses and adopted into His family.

And, to all those men, young and old, who are fathers . . . You are as necessary to these women as the air they breathe. . . . Now step up to the plate.

I share with my readers a portion of a letter. This is the unedited letter I had buried with my own father, for much of Zipporah's story is mine.

Dear Dad,

Over the years whenever the internal need for your paternal covers arose, there were none to cover me; no fitted sheet of fatherly love, no flat sheet of warmth, and no blanket of protection and respect.

I was left to lie naked on this worldly bed to instead be covered with a fitted sheet of secondhand love, often bought on sale, and overpriced. I needed it, so I paid.

I had to settle for the seldom honest flat sheets of warmth. It, too, often came with a price, far beyond my means. I struggled and mentally worked through the muck and mire of my everyday existence to pay for it. I fought with every fiber I had to keep it, though I knew its fabric consisted of never-meant-to-be-kept promises and erratic threads of moral heat.

Knowing I had no blanket of protection and respect of my own, when the harsh cold winters of truth came, I needed and accepted "as is," discounted protection and respect. Its warranties often expired before the dawn came.

They tell me that around the same time I felt an urgency to find my only photo of you and me, eight hundred miles away, you suffered a massive heart attack and died. Were you thinking of me? Did you, somehow, suddenly realize how totally uncovered I was? Was there a reason you never held me, told me you loved me? Unfortunately, I cannot find the photo, so I may never know.

This Saturday, February 15th, just three days before my birthday, you will be buried. Along with the dirt used to cover you, will also be covered any chance we might have had to complete and connect the sides.

However, Father, I want you to know this: also buried with you so that you won't be cold during your sleep, will be my blanket of undying, unspoken love and respect. I can give that to you because I have managed to find and keep a real love, a love that is boundless and unconditional, Love that exceeds and encompasses any and every thing that a love should be. This was a love that helped me to raise three children and blessed me with grandchildren. Such a love helped me to go on and become a wife, an actress, singer, writer, author, and Christian comedian; you see, Dad, I can laugh. This beautiful love, it loved me enough to give me someone to love and to stand beside me, no matter what. That love is the love of God. "For He so loved the world, that He gave His only begotten son, so that whomsoever shall believe in Him, shall have eternal life."

I am told that I look exactly like you and that you will never die until I do. I don't know how true that is, but one thing I do believe. . . . I believe one day, when I cross over to the other side, and you and I can meet again face to face, we will complete this triangle of love.

Acknowledgments

JEREMIAH 8:20–22
20. "The harvest is past, the summer is ended, and we are not saved."
21. "For the hurt of the daughter of my people am I hurt; I am black; astonishment hath taken hold on me."
22. "Is there no balm in Gilead; is there no physician there? Why then has not the health of the daughter of my people been restored?"

I thank God, the beginning and the ending of everything in and around my life.

For their unwavering support, I thank my husband, Robert, my beautiful daughters, Gizel, Ingrid, and Marisa, along with their spouses and children. I also thank my aunts, uncle, siblings, and other family members. I thank my cousin, Delsia Afantchao, of Philadelphia, PA, in particular, who is more like a sister.

I thank Bishop John L. Smith and First Lady Laura L. Smith (St. Paul's Tabernacle City of Lights Ministry), and Reverend Stella Mercado and the Blanche Memorial Baptist Church family. And to Bishop T. D. Jakes and Bishop Noel Jones, two constant sources of inspiration, I thank you.

To all the churches, book clubs, media, libraries who not only embraced the Sister Betty Comedy ministry but assisted in propelling my books to award levels and entry onto the Essence Best Sellers List, I thank you.

I also thank my editor, Selena James, and all the Dafina family, and my attorneys, Christopher R. Whent and Christian Alfaya.

I must thank my prayer partners, author Jacquelin Thomas and Intercessory Prayer Warrior Kizzie Sanders of San Antonio, TX. Whew, if only folks knew! And my third-grade teacher, who inspired my writing journey, Mrs. Bobbie Madison-Mackey of Williamston, SC.

And to all the residents of Pelzer, Belton, Greenville, Anderson, and Piedmont, SC, I thank you for the memories and a lot of material. ☺ Thank you, Brotha Smitty, a constant source of laughter. And my friends from coast to coast, I thank you.

I'd like to also thank Sister Marvella Brown and the Dale City Christian Church drama club, Dale City, VA, for their continuing support in adapting my stories into wonderful and hilarious events. To Sister Vivian Dixon; Mt. Pisgah AME Church, Columbia, MD; the Lofton family and So Bold Entertainment, Anderson, SC; Cheryl Questell and our Quest-Walk Production Company; the Richard De LaFont Agency. I offer a special thank you and abundant love to Pastor and Co-Pastor William and Shirley Mangum, Fort Pierce Christian Center of Port St. Lucie, FL. And to those whom I've omitted, please blame it on the head and not the heart.

To all the fathers who have daughters: Your daughters need blankets of love, security, wisdom, and your prayers; step up to the plate now, or you'll pay for it later—we all will.

Prologue

When a town has a population of less than twenty thousand folks and about fifteen thousand of them were jammed into a ten-mile space, fights and feuds were bound to happen. And when that town was as small as Pelzer, South Carolina, these incidents were often listed in the entertainment section of their one and only newspaper rag, the *Daily BLAB*.

The *BLAB* was an acronym for Braggarts, Liars, and Busybodies. Every Pelzer reader knew that the news was hardly, if ever, accurate, but it was downright entertaining nonetheless—unless your name was in it.

Of course, the day Sister Betty saw her name in that town rag, she fell on her knees kicking, and screamed as much as a seventy-something-old woman could. She couldn't believe that her God— the same God she'd prayed to at least six times a day, the same God who'd seen to it that she became wealthy in her old age, and the same God who'd called her on the telephone many years ago— was now allowing the old devil to defame her good name by having it on the front page of the *BLAB*.

What had she done to deserve such a thing?

A copy of the *BLAB* arrived at Sister Betty's mansion earlier that morning. And in bold misspelled print it read: GOODIE TOO SHOES SISTER BETTY SEEKS TO UPSEAT MOTHER SASHA PRAY ONN . . . "continued on page two."

"In a bid to bring new life and some morality into the Crossing Over Sanctuary Temple's decrepit Mothers Board, newly wealthy Sister Betty will run for president at the Mothers Board conference to be held in Las Vegas, Nevada. She'll pit her salvation against the encumbered Mother Sasha Pray Onn. Hopefully, she'll be wearing the whole armor of God. Because if not, when the election is over this newspaper plans to have a 'pull-out' section detailing the life of the late Sister Betty. Mother Pray Onn is sure to kill her."

1

In a posh home located in the wealthiest section of Pelzer, South Carolina, where worries were left to those on the poor side of town, was where Sister Betty resided.

Sister Betty was something of an enigma. She always wore a white ugly-looking hat around town with a strange fluffy white and black feather that waved like it was possessed when she walked. She also wore a large gold cross and carried a Bible with her initials embossed along its spine.

Sister Betty hadn't always lived high on the hog, as some referred to her. She, too, once lived on the other side of the tracks. However, due to the untimely and embarrassing death of one of her longtime friends, wealthy Mother Eternal, her station in life had changed dramatically. Mother Eternal had succumbed to a heart attack while clutching a cash register. It was attached to the pulpit. Her generosity left Sister Betty with more money than she'd ever had, and more problems than she'd ever imagined.

Sister Betty had lived in Pelzer, South Carolina, since her early twenties. And ever since that time, with her well-documented though mostly self-proclaimed experiences with God, she'd also gained something of a reputation as God's go-to woman. So eventually she became Pelzer's moral compass. She was the official, though barely appreciated, chief negotiator with heaven.

Just barely five-foot-two, she'd gained some weight over the years, and only old photographs testified of a younger Sister Betty who'd been a well-proportioned, brown-skinned beauty. Now her shoulders were slightly stooped as she struggled to bare the burdens of others.

She was also the chief prayer intercessor in her church prayer team of two. Just her and her longtime friend and neighbor, Ma

Cile, were left. Out of what started as a team of five women praying, three had dropped out from exhaustion. So Sister Betty and Ma Cile would double up on praying and, of course, they'd do it on a daily basis. Now Ma Cile, hospitalized by a stroke, was no longer available. But Sister Betty pressed on as she stood in the gap for her people.

So, when she saw her name and the lie about her running against a woman who some believed was truly a spawn of Satan, she wanted to know, where was her God?

Sister Betty didn't have to wait long for hell to break loose. If she wasn't going to it, it would come to her. And hell had no problem coming to church; it never had.

It all came to a head the following day after the church service. No matter how saved she claimed to be, things got so bad that morning, it was all Sister Betty could do not to put down her Bible and pick up a brick in defense. She'd barely put her hand down from repeating the benediction when it happened. She'd thought that since no one had mentioned the headline in the *BLAB* that God had taken care of the situation. But if He was going to do it, He hadn't yet.

Current Mothers Board president and resident terrorist Sasha Pray Onn, nicknamed Mother Terminator, and Vice President Bea Blister, called Mother Rambo behind her back, confronted Sister Betty in the downstairs fellowship hall. They'd read the *BLAB* and took offense to her running for the office of president of the Mothers Board. They'd planned on attending the upcoming Mothers Board Conference in Las Vegas unchallenged.

As they blocked her exit, the two old women reminded Sister Betty that even before the Ain't Nobody Right but Us–All Others Goin' to Hell Church disbanded and was absorbed into the Crossing Over Sanctuary Temple diocese, *they'd* created and made the Mothers Board what it was.

Mothers Bea and Sasha had headed the chaotic, geriatric auxiliary and had no intention of relinquishing their positions—ever. "We aren't stepping aside for you, the Reverend Leotis Tom, the Taliban, or the United States president," Sasha boasted.

"And you can believe that!" Bea added.

Those two old she-warriors were serious. They would've gone so far as to ask God for His I.D. before they'd move aside. Sasha and Bea were so cantankerous that even old Satan wouldn't battle them without the Lord on his side.

With a toss of their heads, Bea and Sasha backed out of the fellowship hall with their eyes still trained on Sister Betty.

Sister Betty had not gotten a chance to refute the *BLAB*'s falsehood. Instead of speaking up when there was a moment of sanity and silence, she didn't; she had a chance to leave the hall in one piece, so she took it.

Arriving back at her home, Sister Betty changed clothes and went into her living room to think and pray. Seated in her favorite recliner, her feet propped on an ottoman, she laid her head back. She tried to meditate, hoping it would help her come up with a plan. She shifted her legs on the ottoman and her boney, arthritic knees crunched like they were made of aluminum foil. And, of course, she knew that those aching signs always preceded a mission from God. She was tired. The last thing she wanted was another battle with those hardheaded church folks, as she liked to call them, because she didn't use profanity.

The young people weren't nearly as difficult to minister as those staunch never-gonna-change-their-minds older ones.

"Why would You let a lie like that be printed?" Sister Betty looked toward the ceiling, waiting for God to answer. "The Mothers Board, Lord?"

She'd dealt with the Mothers Board before. There was always something the women didn't agree with. If the pastor asked for a donation, they'd fuss about the amount. If he said something was going to be free, they'd want to know why there wasn't a charge. Nothing pleased them.

However, as long as the current president and vice president Sasha and Bea led the fray, Sister Betty's ministry life would always be one long, unending roller coaster.

She'd never understand Sasha and Bea. Earlier they'd banded together to confront her and yet the two of them had occupied the same pew each Sunday for the past twenty-something years and couldn't stand one another. The Mothers Board members always reelected Sasha and Bea. It was as though the other women just loved the chaos that followed their rule.

Sister Betty rose and went to her kitchen. She brewed a pot of her favorite cayenne pepper tea and carried it with her into her

bedroom. She needed to do some serious praying and the hot peppered tea always gave her a lift in both her spirit and her imagination.

For two weeks after the confrontation, Sister Betty fasted,
prayed, travailed, and even rolled around like Hannah, thrashing
floor-style in her bedroom. Sister Betty had cried until her eyes
bulged trying to convince God that He shouldn't put her in the
midst of another one of Bea and Sasha's messes. However, God
being sovereign always had the last word.

In this case, however, Sister Betty wanted the last word.
"Heavenly Father, just once, can I please go to some third-world
country or even the Middle East and spread your message? Please
don't put me in the middle of another one of Bea and Sasha's
messes. . . ."

Suddenly, Sister Betty's left knee crunched and shot forward
as though she were twenty. She howled. "Okay!" She'd have
said more but experience taught her that her arms were just too
short to box with God.

So she got up from the floor as quick as she could. It wasn't
only God that spurred her to move. That cayenne pepper tea was
doing it, too.

Sunday rolled around again. Only this time it was the fifth
Sunday. Many of the members used that particular Sunday to do
other things. They felt their heavenly service was done by attending the other four Sundays. Sister Betty could only hope that
Sasha and Bea would be among the missing.

As she dressed and prepared to leave her home, she recalled
the dream she'd had the previous night. Lifting her pageboy-styled
gray wig about an inch, she scratched her head and pondered.
Why would I dream about *Rambo*? She'd not been a fan of such
violence, so she'd only seen the first three movies. In her dream
Rambo wore a dress and walked with a cane. Somehow, even
with the silly disguise, she still knew it was supposed to be Rambo.
She couldn't recall the entire dream, but one thing she knew for
certain—Rambo was about to fight the Terminator. Only in her
dream the Terminator wasn't Arnold Schwarzenegger. The tall
figure was slightly bent, with very dark skin, a natty dark wig,
muscles that resembled silly putty, and, like Rambo, it wore a
dress. The two superstars were about to rumble. That's where
her dream ended.

Sister Betty went to church and praised God like her life depended upon it. Her feet moved faster than usual as her dance of worship became more like a tap dance. She shouted, "Hallelujah" and spun until almost woozy.

"I'm praising and glorifying Your name, Father. You said when the praises go up the blessings will come down. I need a blessing, now!" Sister Betty's body resembled a switchblade as her arms shot up and out. "Victory, victory," she screamed while she continued to praise God and shake her head. The shaking caused her hat to lean gangster-style and that ugly feather to bounce uncontrollably. Now emboldened with supposed power, she stared at Sasha and Bea. Holding her Bible across her tiny chest as a shield, Sister Betty said accusingly, "God's not pleased with the Mothers Board."

Before Sister Betty could finish her revelation, Sasha and Bea shot up from their pews. Each woman had a revelation for Sister Betty.

"Don't say another word," Sasha snarled, while she pointed her cane at Sister Betty's still bouncing hat feather. "Whether you say it's a word from God or whomever, I will still stick that ugly feather in a place you won't like," Sasha promised, before heading back to her seat.

On her way back to the pew, Sasha used her Bible to tag team Bea who'd moved closer to Sister Betty to deliver the verbal coup de grâce.

"And you're gonna need someone to drag your meddling butt to a Healing service," Bea added, as she pointed a bent finger at Sister Betty's hat feather and hips, "'cause you gonna be crippled for life!"

Knowing Bea and Sasha didn't make empty threats caused Sister Betty to stop prophesying and retreat from the church. Suddenly fearful, she'd forgotten God's word never returns void.

2

Five hours hadn't passed since that morning's Crossing Over Sanctuary Temple's spirit-filled fifth Sunday service when Bea and Sasha ran across one another in downtown Pelzer.

When faced with a common enemy, the two old women were an unbeatable force. But when it was just the two of them, each woman went into self-survival mode.

So, with the sun setting peacefully, the crotchety old women squared off. As she clutched her Bible, Sasha's beige-colored complexion darkened as she glared at Bea. Her five-foot frame stiffened on legs shaped like parentheses, which made her look like she were about to leap. Instead of a Rambo headband, she wore a little white pillbox-shaped hat pinned to a steel gray bun.

Bea "the Terminator" Blister wouldn't give an inch. She exuded venom with equal ferocity as her dark wrinkled face turned into a mask of defiance. If she had not had a curved spine and could stand straight, she would have towered over Sasha a full nine inches.

Bea had spent a portion of her younger years thugging and mugging in the countryside of nearby Belton, South Carolina. Those criminal tendencies had finally sent her to several jails to reconsider her ways. It was during those years in the prison system that she'd learned how to bend people to her will. She simply knocked them out and threatened to do it again if they told. Very few did and those who did only did it once.

"Ain't you afraid this last little bit of sunshine will melt your evil old behind?" Bea grimaced and then pointed toward Sasha's tiny hips, which resembled two old boxing gloves dangling from Sasha's waist. "You just couldn't let me enjoy the rest of the

Lord's day without having to look at your wrinkled tail, could you?"

Sasha's back hunched as she hissed like a cobra. With spittle flying because of her loose-fitting false teeth, she did some pointing of her own. She lifted her cane directly at Bea. "Is there ever a moment in my saved life that I don't have to run across you in the path of my salvation?"

"You ain't on the path of salvation. You're on the road to hell!" Bea shot back. "You're wearing those horn-rimmed magnifying glasses and still can't see where you're going."

"I betcha I can see well enough not to bring a pan of macaroni and cheese to church with the bottom all black and crispy." Sasha tapped her cane hard against the sidewalk to make her point and to show just how hard that mac and cheese were. She continued, "If you live to be a hundred, nobody will ever eat your cooking again." Sasha stopped abruptly to check her false teeth, which had begun to slide away from her gums. Confident they wouldn't betray her by falling out, Sasha continued her tirade. "Oh, I'm so sorry. You *are* already almost a hundred."

Not one to be outdone, Bea lit into Sasha loud enough for anyone within ten yards to hear. "Don't worry your skinny behind about my cooking. You just make sure you wearing those magnifying glasses the next time you accidentally stick an Odor Eater insole inside your raggedy drawers instead of a Depend pad!"

"You're a liar," Sasha hollered. She was indignant, although somewhere in the back of her mind she did remember doing something akin to the accusation. "God ain't judging no liars. I guess you'll be absent from heaven's court on judgment day and gone straight to hell."

Bea pushed a strand of her cheap, natty red wig out of her face. She inched closer and then yelled, "I'm sorry. You're right. I did lie. I said you did it by accident. I gave you too much credit. You probably needed that odor eater pad in your old granny drawers!"

Geriatric Rambo and Terminator were about to go into round two when the approaching sound of howling police sirens stopped them. Not fully sure if someone hadn't called the cops on them, they retreated a few feet from each other. They stood like statues and smiled as though they hadn't let a single mean word flow.

When the sirens suddenly stopped, both women turned to see why. They saw a crowd suddenly gather down the block.

"I wonder why the police are raiding old Pookie's on a Sunday evening," Bea said, her face suddenly looking as sweet as a cherub's.

"Hmmm, it does cause one to wonder," Sasha replied softly with a mischievous grin.

In an instant, the old women temporarily forgot their bickering. They started giggling like old friends.

"You called those cops, didn't you?" Bea asked with a twinkle in her beady eyes.

"Yes, I guess I'll take the credit." Sasha laughed. "He snookered me out of that bingo money we won on that cruise."

Several months earlier, Bea and Sasha were duped into sharing a cabin on a cruise by Sasha's equally mean-spirited niece, Ima Hellraiser. Ima had done so in the hope that the two old women would cancel each other's birth certificates by killing one another. It was during a week of on-again-and-off-again memory lapses that the two had temporarily bonded and scammed a bingo game by feigning heart attacks. To keep the old women from sinking the ship with their antics, they were declared winners and shared the huge bingo pot.

Sasha hadn't meant to admit to Bea that she'd let ole Pookie outfox her. But it was out there and she couldn't take it back.

"That reprobate cheated me out of my money, too," Bea sheepishly admitted. "Pastor preached from the Book of Second Chronicles and the seventh chapter. It was the fourteenth verse. So I played seven hundred fourteen. It came four seventy-one. But he said I didn't box my number. You know I always box my number."

"Well, I'm sure you did," Sasha agreed. "Everybody in the church who plays numbers knows you always box your numbers." She stopped and peered up the block, before continuing. "That pocked-face demon had it coming. They should snatch him up by his raggedy boxers for cheating us poor old women out of our hard-earned money."

"Do you think he's learned his lesson?" Sasha asked with mock concern. "I don't think he'll try and pull nothing on us poor old folks again."

Their false commiseration was interrupted by the sounds of

glass breaking and Pookie's cussing from inside the store. The women saw one officer suddenly snatch down a couple of old dusty album covers and posters announcing an upcoming Louis Armstrong concert from the storefront window. Pookie hadn't changed anything in his store except the winning numbers for losers in years.

The flashing lights from the two police cars and the ruckus inside the store were enough to draw several more onlookers. When they saw what was happening to Pookie, a few of them, still with Bible in hand after leaving evening services, started to cheer. Pookie had managed to finagle many of the good gambling church folks in Pelzer. And he never paid tithes on his money, either.

"I've always known Pookie was a liar and a blind one at that," Bea said.

"What are you babbling about?"

"I've known Pookie probably longer than you. So the first time he told me he thought your legs were shaped like a Barbie doll's legs, I knew his eyes were going bad."

"I do have legs like a Barbie doll," Sasha snapped as she raised the hem of her white skirt, showing knobby knees that resembled an anorexic baby elephant's. "Jealousy is so ugly on you."

Bea crunched her nose and pointed. "Unless Barbie has legs shaped like a pair of needle-nosed pliers, you don't have legs like her."

Their peace pact had quickly crumbled.

"Quiet down, they're bringing him out," Sasha warned, intending to return the insult later. "You gonna mess around and get us in trouble again." She couldn't remember what trouble it was she was trying to avoid so she turned and hobbled away, switching her hips at Bea. *Here's my last word about that*, she thought as she put a little extra switch in her tiny hips.

"Good riddance," Bea called out and then cheerfully added, "Are you coming to prayer meeting on Wednesday?"

"Of course, I'll be there," Mother Sasha hollered, while continuing to shake her hips. "I'll keep coming and praying for your sorry self until you get saved."

"I hope you shake it and break it," Bea hollered back with laughter.

Sasha had barely turned the corner when Bea saw the squad

car finally pull off with Pookie handcuffed and ranting. She giggled as she watched him grimace. He was popping up and down like a jack in the box and the police gladly beat him down every time he tried to raise up to scream some more. They drove past Bea. As much as she wanted to remain an innocent bystander, she just couldn't help it. She smiled as she waved and winked at them.

And that's when she saw a familiar figure walking carefully around the crowd that gathered to watch. "Sister Betty," she murmured. Taking on Sister Betty with Sasha by her side was one thing. Bea wasn't about to do it alone, so she moved on.

3

Sister Betty took her time coming out from among the crowd in front of Pookie's. She'd spied both Bea and Sasha moments earlier as she walked down Left Street, where she always went to pass out her Bible tracts on Sunday evenings. Even before she'd moved into her palatial home, she'd done so.

"You know that you need Jesus," she'd say as she offered a tract. She always made it her business to stop by Pookie's place to get the church crowd as they came and went.

She didn't need to be right up on them to know that Bea and Sasha were having one of their regular fights. She purposely took her time handing out her Bible tracts and holding a prayer vigil as the police escorted the numerical engineer, as Pookie liked to be called, into the waiting patrol car.

She didn't stop praying until she saw Bea walk away in the opposite direction. "Thank you, Jesus."

Bea, who had hurried about a block away in the opposite direction, stopped to rest. She was so tired that as she began to move again, she actually looked like a turtle walking through tar.

Bea thought about returning to her empty apartment and quickly dismissed the thought. Since she'd stopped dating eighty-year-old Slim Pickens because of his infidelity, she was lonely. For a moment, she stood there wishing she'd married or had children so she'd have a reason to go home.

There's got to be another way of making some more money. My rent is due and my pension ain't, Bea thought. Then she heard the ripples of laughter.

Lounging around at a bus stop farther down the block were

several other old people. It seemed as though the only people on the street that night were the senior citizens. Bea saw that most were leaning on canes and she swore she could smell them reeking of Bengay. They were huddled in front of a closed grocery store, smiling and just glad to be alive.

As Bea approached the crowd, she called out to an old man she thought she recognized. She believed his name was Buck or Chuck. She decided to call him Buck.

"Hi there, Buck," she whispered. "What's going on?" His appearance made her think of an old pervert she once knew. With such nice weather, no reason for him to be wearing an overcoat.

Buck didn't answer right away when he heard Bea call out his name. Instead, he blew his bulbous nose into an old, wrinkled handkerchief.

"Good to see you tonight. You are Bea Blister, aren't you?" He wiped his furrowed brow and squinted before continuing. "I'm just trying to see if I can add a couple more dollars to my pension this evening."

The words *more dollars* made Bea's arthritic knees straighten, carrying her quickly to Buck's side. "What's that you say?" she asked.

"We're on our way to the bingo game at the church over there on Shameless Avenue. The game's supposed to begin in about thirty minutes, and that doggone church bus is running late. If it don't come soon we're gonna miss the game and the nursing home will know we're gone and send out security."

These weren't just seniors on a mission. They were a few old folks who'd walk barefoot into a flaming volcano for a chance to add a dollar to their small pensions. They didn't feel too guilty, since the church that held the game sanctioned their innocent gambling habits and provided transportation.

"What church is holding it?" Bea asked suspiciously. What was left of her survival skills caused her to question a lot of things.

"I can't give out that information without some incentive," Buck said, licking his crusty lips as he leered at Bea.

"Why don't I just take a rock and hit you?" Bea replied while pretending to look for a rock.

"It's the No Hope Now–Mercy Nevah Church," Buck answered

quickly. He'd have quoted the church history if the rumbling of the old bus approaching hadn't interrupted.

The dimly lit bus approached with a cockeyed, redheaded driver with skin the color of rancid beef draped over its wheel. The bus shook and sputtered dark fumes as its brakes squealed like it was in pain.

She didn't see a destination sign displayed, but Bea decided to trust Buck, hoping that it was the bingo bus. She followed him and the others onto it.

4

While Bea went off to play bingo, Sister Betty returned home. After changing clothes, she knelt beside her couch as she often did, and prayed.

She'd barely gotten into her praying when the persistent ring of the telephone caused her to stop.

The telephone was on its fifth ring by the time she finally made it off her knees. Normally, she'd take the phone off its hook before praying. This time she'd forgotten.

"Hello."

"How are you, Sister Betty?"

"Who is this?"

"It's Reverend Leotis Tom."

"I'm sorry, Pastor. I didn't recognize your voice." She had no idea what her pastor could want with her. "What can I do for you?"

"I read the headlines in the *BLAB* a few weeks ago, and I've been meaning to speak to you."

"I'm so sorry," Sister Betty began to explain, but she was cut off.

"No need to apologize. I've chatted with a few of the other women on the Mothers Board and, against their concerns, I've decided that I want you to run for the office of president. I'll let the board nominate a vice president."

"Say what . . . !" Sister Betty's mouth flew open.

"I normally don't read the *BLAB*. But I'm glad it was in the bathroom and I did. God is so good. I've prayed that someone would come in and take the Mothers Board to higher heights. Everyone knows there's no one higher than you when it comes to God's business."

"I don't wanna . . ." Sister Betty pouted, sitting down with the phone still stuck to her ear. Her eyes were wild with disbelief as the reverend continued chatting up a storm.

The more reasons she gave for not wanting to enter into World War Three with Sasha and Bea as well as the others, the more reasons the reverend gave as to why she should. They went back and forth for almost thirty minutes. He quoted scriptures, visions, and almost offered her a salary. Almost, but he didn't. He was about monies coming in, not going out.

"Don't be so modest," the reverend chided. "I've already taken up a collection and purchased your ticket to the Las Vegas conference. I haven't told either Mother Sasha or Mother Bea yet."

"You won't have to because I ain't going!"

And while the reverend and Sister Betty played word tennis, each trying to one-up the other with their own rationalities, all hell was about to break loose on the other side of town.

Arriving finally at the church, the old folks piled off the mysterious bus. The last rider had barely stepped safely away before the bus and its cockeyed driver disappeared under the cover of darkness. Everyone checked their pockets and purses to make sure they had their ten-dollar entry fee. They huddled, counting their pennies, dimes, quarters, and taped-together dollar bills.

One by one they entered. Some of them shuffled, a couple of them griped, and one limped while a few others maneuvered their wheelchairs and canes onto an elevator and descended into the windowless subbasement of the No Hope Now–Mercy Nevah Church.

Minutes later, they got off the elevator and lined up against a wall, fidgeting to try to avoid the chipped and peeling paint that began sticking to their clothes like lint. From nowhere three spry female ushers appeared. With one arm held behind their backs for propriety sake and nothing else, each usher zipped through the line with a collection plate for the fees and then quickly disappeared.

Once they found their seats, the seniors talked competitive trash. "I hope you've put aside some cat food for your dinner, 'cause I'm taking this pot," Buck chided one of the seniors, whose seat kept sliding from under him every time he tried to sit.

"You must be goofed on stink weed if you think you're winning tonight," the old man responded as he finally plopped down, almost breaking a brittle hip as he did.

The others said nothing as they concentrated on rubbing arthritis salve and alcohol into their elbow joints and flexed their gnarly fingers to get the blood flowing.

Ten minutes later, their clothes splattered with ink and a magnifying glass in one hand, the old folks were ready. The rousing once-a-month bingo game sprang into full swing. It was seniors night and no holds barred was the rule.

The pastor and founder of No Hope Now–Mercy Nevah Church was the Reverend Bling Moe Bling. His ill-fitting snowy white toupee looked like a cloud hovering over his pointed head. He sported a shortened crippled leg supported by a bicycle kickstand.

Now in his late seventies, the reverend had first started preaching in his early seventies. He claimed that God had called him on his cell phone and told him to spread the word. He'd divorced his first wife after she'd insisted it was just static or probably a wrong number. He was determined to do God's work for a price and so he started the seniors' bingo night.

The reverend, who was dressed in his traditional bright red Nehru-collared long robe, stood lopsided behind a rickety picnic table. Smudged bingo boards were stacked high on the table. Off to the side, Pepsi-Cola bottle caps took the place of real bingo chips.

As the reverend called out one number after another, he leaned to one side, grasping the table for support with one hand. By the time one of the senior citizens, stuttering as if his lips were hummingbird wings, finally called out, "Bingo," the bicycle kickstand the reverend used to support his shortened and useless left leg fell over. With his hands flailing as if he were trying to fly, he accidentally knocked over the table. The fall caused all the previously called and uncalled numbers to fall to the floor.

Every number from B1 to O75 shot off the table. It took a moment before it occurred to the seniors or sunk in that there was no exact way to tell who really had bingo. Echoes of "bingo" rang out at the same time as the players all inched and then clamored toward the table. By the time reasonable order was established, the only things distinguishable were the odor of Bengay and pieces of somebody's wheelchair.

It took another fifteen minutes for the ushers and anyone

able-bodied to round up the seniors, and to lift the Reverend Bling's shriveled leg back onto his kickstand.

"I want my money and I want my money now," Bea screamed from the back of the room. She stood shuffling from side to side, the hem of her long blue dress bustling as though it were alive and ready to do damage. As her eyes widened in anger, she moved her hands back and forth as though she were competing on a ski slope. "I just spent the last fifteen dollars of my pension money trying to win that one-thousand-dollar bingo pot and I'll knock out anybody who gets in my way and then pray 'em back on my way to the bank."

Her tirade had forced her dentures to move forward in her mouth. While Bea stopped and adjusted her false teeth, to argue her point further, more drama was unfolding in the rear of the room.

The drama inched its way forward, making a *rat-tat-tat* sound with the tip of its cane as it emerged from a table in the back. Snickering, it spoke up and took advantage of the momentary silence from Bea's challenge.

"Y'all know she's crazy. She's probably having another Alzheimer's episode, because it was me who yelled out bingo first," Sasha cackled.

Sasha was still dressed in her all-white linen gown from earlier. As she inched along, the dress billowed about her elfish brown frame. She used her walking cane to part the sea of other angry seniors as she limped up to the table.

"What tha . . . ? In all the rush to play bingo, Bea didn't know that Sasha was even there. She became so angry she started trembling.

"That woman wouldn't know bingo from Scrapple," Sasha hissed, forgetting to continue her charade of humility, and that scrapple consisted of meat parts and was not a game. Shooting an angry look back at Bea, she continued to inch up to the table. She used the tip of her cane to poke at the Reverend Bling's chest. "That money belongs to me and if you don't give it to me right now, I'll tear you asunder."

"Ain't you a woman of God?" the Reverend Bling asked as he bravely tried to maintain a vertical position.

He didn't want to appear weak but it was hard to do when he used a kickstand for leg support. "The Almighty wouldn't be pleased if you tore me *asunder*," he said in a mocking tone so that the others wouldn't think he was afraid.

He could've saved his energy. The others didn't think he was afraid; they knew for certain that he was.

"If God didn't want me to tear you asunder, He wouldn't have put it in the Bible," Sasha answered carefully. She never took her beady eyes off the reverend as she used her cane to drag a dust-covered Bible toward her from the end of the table. In her rush she'd left hers back at her table.

Before Sasha went on to further prove her Bible knowledge, she glanced over at Bea to make sure the woman didn't sneak up on her. Bea was still trying to collect her wits and didn't pose an immediate threat. Sasha picked up the Bible and didn't even open it, choosing instead to quote the passage while she held the book.

"It says in the book of Matthew, the twenty-fourth chapter, the fifty-first verse—"

Sasha stopped suddenly and turned to the others to make sure that all eyes were on her before she continued. " '. . . And shall cut him *asunder*, and appoint him his portion with the hypocrites.' " She stopped again and pointed her cane to the others scattered behind her and particularly at Bea. "That would be y'all. Y'all, the hypocrites." Then she turned back to the reverend, glaring. "There shall be weeping and gnashing of the teeth."

Sasha laid her cane across the table and hung her head. Suddenly speaking softly and humbly, she added, "So saith my God." She clutched her heart slowly and looked at the others as though they all didn't share the same God.

"Well, Mother Sasha, I guess you do know your Bible." The reverend snickered, nervously. He quickly looked over his shoulder to see if any of the ushers were going to help him.

They weren't.

"Of course I know my Bible." Sasha nodded with confidence and then added her own interpretation. "As you can see, God has said that I can beat you into a ball of Silly Putty if you don't give me my money."

Sasha would have said more but suddenly she felt a sharp pinch on her shoulder and cried out, "Ouch!"

"If you try and take my money, you'll be the one looking like a ball of gray-haired Silly Putty."

The voice was strong, determined, and of course, familiar.

When Sasha turned around, rubbing her bruised shoulder, she stood face-to-chest with Mother Bea.

While her longtime foe had spouted customized Bible verses, Bea had snuck up behind Sasha and, with her own false teeth in her hands, had reached down and used them to nip Sasha's boney shoulder.

"Got a Bible verse for that?" Bea taunted, pointing toward Sasha's bitten shoulder. "How about Psalms one twenty-nine, verse four? Do you know that one?" She laid a finger to her lips to silence the others in case they wanted to butt in. "Let me quote it for you." She lifted her head toward the church ceiling and proceeded. " 'The Lord is righteous: He hath cut asunder the cords of the wicked.' " Bea looked down and pointed toward Sasha. "And that's where you come in. You are that wicked heifer in the book of Psalms."

The reverend took advantage of the face-off between the two mothers and beckoned two of the ushers, Sister Judah and Sister Israel, to his aid. "Why didn't you two come and help me while I was being attacked?" he whispered angrily when they arrived.

"I was waiting for Sister Judah to move. She was closer to you," Sister Israel replied. She was still grasping the collection plate and felt secure that the reverend wouldn't want her to drop it to save his hide.

"I don't know what she's talking about," Sister Judah said in a huff. "I don't understand what the big deal is," she added while pointing toward Sasha. "She's just an old lady talking about a sunder. I don't even know what a sunder is or what it looks like."

"Well, let me explain it so you and Sister Israel understand—" The reverend gripped the table for more support. "Zechariah. The eleventh chapter and the fourteenth verse says, 'Then I cut asunder mine other staff.' " He nodded towards them. "That's you two," he said as he continued quoting. " 'Even Bands, that I might break the brotherhood between Judah and Israel.' " The reverend stopped abruptly and through clenched teeth, said, "Now in your case, it will be sisterhood."

Sasha interrupted the discourse, barking, "Can we possibly get back to giving me my money?"

"It's not yours. It's my money. You're always trying to take what's mine," Bea snapped.

Mother Sasha became so mad her bun appeared to be twisting like a helicopter propeller. "When we were younger and she was much uglier than she is now, if that's possible, Bea Blister kissed my boyfriend, Jasper, behind the bleachers at the homecoming game."

"She's a liar!" Bea screamed, spittle flying from the corners of her turned-down mouth. "She's just jealous. She's always been jealous."

No one said a word, as they waited for the rest of the sordid tale to come out.

They didn't have to wait long because Bea was just getting started. "It was her ugly butt that kissed my boyfriend, Jas, at the tennis match when we were living in Williamston, South Carolina."

Old Buck knew that they were both wrong. As hazy as his memory was at times, he'd never forget that debacle. It had started at a home-going service of one of their high school teachers. Her name was Miss Lizzie Crow. It was immediately after the service and folks had gathered to eat in the field behind the church and chat about the service.

Buck, at that time an award-winning sprinter, had dashed across the field to use the outhouse. When he came out, he saw Sasha's own sister, Areal Hellraiser, displaying her curves against an old juniper tree. She was using her pink tongue, letting it dart in and out, as she licked a young man's willing face, almost devouring his mouth. And, because Buck, even back then, had been a lurker, he'd watched with fascination.

Old Buck couldn't remember what Areal wore, only what she'd done. But he did remember that the fellow wasn't Sasha's boyfriend. It was just some guy that she and a whole bunch of girls liked. His name was Jimmy or perhaps it was Jasper. He smiled at the memory and shook his head as he watched the two old women go at each other. *She was close,* Buck thought. *At least the man's name had started with a J.*

Buck's smile grew almost maniacal as he also remembered that he saw that same Areal Hellraiser later that same week kissing Bea's boyfriend, too. It happened at a baseball game, not a tennis match. And, Bea's boyfriend's name was also Jimmy or maybe it was Jasper too.

Old Buck placed a hand inside one of his torn pants pockets, looking angelic as he let his mind recall other details from his youth, both real and imagined. Of course, his memory was just as faulty as Bea's and Sasha's. It was a good thing he'd kept his mouth shut because he'd only fuel the eternal flame.

It was an instant replay. Bea and Sasha had fought off and on over the past twenty years, mostly over accusations that neither had witnessed but had been told by someone they couldn't even remember. Sadly, there were other times when they just fought because they both existed in the same place and for no other reason.

"I have an idea." The Reverend Bling excitedly snapped a finger to get everyone's attention. He'd finally decided that he needed to take charge, particularly since he saw that most of the other seniors led by Buck had taken the opportunity to sneak away. He didn't blame them. He'd have left, too, but his desire to live another day and not be arrested outweighed a bingo pot.

By the time the reverend finished snapping his fingers, the only ones left in the basement were the two old mothers, the two ushers, and himself.

"Obviously, it's my fault that the numbers got mixed up when the table overturned. Therefore, my solution is to give a consolation prize that can be shared by the two of you."

"I don't want a consolation prize. I want my thousand dollars," Sasha barked. She was livid and was about to snatch a hat pin to stick him and make her point.

"I don't want any consolation prize either." Bea became so mad with the reverend's shameless ploy that she handed Sasha's cane to her and then pointed toward the reverend. She shouted, "Go ahead, Sasha. Handle your business."

The reverend's self-preservation went into overdrive. His eyes grew large like an owl's as he scanned the room trying to come up with a plan. Then he saw a plan come together.

Behind the bingo table was an old bookcase. The reverend saw something there that he took as a sign from God. Sticking out of one of the reference dream books was the plane reservation ticket for his upcoming trip to Las Vegas. He had received it about a month ago after turning in his frequent flyer miles and had placed it in the book for safekeeping.

His pastoral anniversary was coming up. He'd planned to fake humbleness and take cash from the congregation, along with one of its female members.

He wouldn't tell the Pastor's Aide Auxiliary that he'd already paid for his trip by cashing in his mileage. Instead, he'd pocket the church's money to use in the casino playing the nickel slot machines. At the time he'd purchased the tickets he hadn't known about the upcoming Mothers Board Conference.

However, at that moment, he'd give his only good leg just to get out of that church's basement without harm.

Just as Sasha was about to lift the sharpened business end of her cane with the help of her temporary ally, Bea, the reverend spoke up again, quickly.

"Mothers, come. Let's reason together," he said with false confidence.

"Isn't that term, *reason together*, from the Bible?" Sister Judah quickly leaned over and asked Sister Israel.

"I'm not sure. If it isn't, it sure sounds like it could be." Sister Israel made a mental note to look it up in the dust-covered Bible she'd bought some time ago from the Family Dollar Store.

"What do you have in mind?" Bea asked with a hint of suspicion as she gently placed her hand on Sasha's scrawny shoulder to temporarily stop her from harming the reverend.

"Out of the goodness of my heart and, of course, being led by a spirit, I want to send the both of you to the upcoming Mothers Conference in Las Vegas, Nevada. You'll be in Las Vegas and out of my sight for almost a month!"

His smile was broad and insincere. The dim light in the basement beamed upon his twenty remaining teeth mostly crowded in the front. The brown-stained teeth looked like he had about twenty malt chocolate bits sticking out of his gums.

It only took a moment for the two old women to understand the offer. It took less time than that for them to forget that moments before he was the common enemy who'd made them the best of friends.

"I'm not going on no trip with this old hag," Sasha snapped as she shoved away Bea's hand. "Keep your sinning paws off me."

"I know you didn't think I'd share a room with you and your bursitis. And you smell like week-old corn chips and spoiled cabbage juice," Bea chided with her voice steadily rising. "I'd rather sip cold olive oil and soak my teeth in hot orange juice."

A mask of concern covered Sasha's normal nastiness. It was as though she and Bea were suddenly the best of friends again.

"You know, they say that a mixture of cold olive oil and hot orange juice is good for the digestive system. It'll make you regular," Sasha said sweetly as she reached for one of Bea's swollen hands.

"You think so?" Bea asked. Suddenly she, too, felt a foreign tenderness to the little sprite, who usually gave her indigestion. Concern spread over Bea's face. She leaned closer and continued sharing with her temporary best friend.

"I've been a little on the backed-up side recently. Sometimes, when I go to the bathroom, I feel like I'm about to sprain something." Bea's cheeks inflated as she patted the fatty tissue on her plump rump and stomach for emphasis.

"T-M-I," the Reverend Bling interrupted, and covered his ears. "That's too much information! Have mercy!"

"Oh, God will if you let Him," Sasha turned and said. She could taste the sweetness in her voice as her eyes traveled slowly upward and over toward the huge white cross hanging between the bingo and the exit signs.

Unlike Sasha, whose sweetness seemed content to stay around a bit, Bea's mind teetered dangerously between sweet and surly.

"Should we make the call for the flight and hotel reservations or will you do it, Reverend Bling?" Bea asked softly, choosing to be sweet.

Bea didn't wait for the reverend to respond. Her touch was almost genuine as she then bear-hugged Sasha. "I can't wait to take a trip with my best friend. I could use a little R and R."

I bet you could use a little rubbing alcohol and roulette, the reverend thought as he continued grinning, appreciating his own genius.

Unfortunately Bea, in her temporary state of sweetness, had hugged that still-sore spot where she had just nipped Sasha with the false teeth. The pain was enough to wake the demons in Sasha and she let loose.

"She's attacking me," Sasha cried out as she tried to extricate her tiny body from Bea's clutches. She spun and raised her cane, pointing it toward Bea's shocked face, and screamed, "Reverend Bling, did you see that?"

It was loud enough to take Bea's demons off pause. "She's a liar. She tried to steal my thousand-dollar bingo pot," Bea yelled as she hopscotched in a circle, trying to avoid Sasha's cane.

The reverend felt his blood pressure soar into upper triple digits. He couldn't take it any longer. *Doggone Alzheimer's gonna make those two old crones destroy my place of business.*

He forgot his own disability as he tried to defy the law of gravity by attempting to stand. Without giving another thought to the absence of his kickstand support, he placed the thumb of one hand in his robe pocket, looked straight at them, and orated. "Leviticus, chapter five and verse eight, 'And he shall bring them unto the priest, who shall offer that which is for the sin offering first, and wring off their heads from their necks, but shall not divide it asunder.'"

He surprised himself again. Until that evening, the only verse he could quote from memory was, "Jesus wept."

With the fat under his chin hanging and flapping like a deranged turkey's wattle, he raised his voice to almost falsetto. "You two old women are going on that trip to Las Vegas and you're going together or I'm going to carry out God's word and wring your wrinkled necks."

Bea and Sasha quieted and watched the reverend try to reclaim his composure. As they waited, they hung their heads in remorse, temporarily forgetting they weren't afraid of the reverend. Suddenly, they saw the reverend as more manly and authoritative as he ordered them around. Even his ugly chocolate brown teeth didn't look so bad.

"Of course, if you say so, we'll go together," Sasha replied, as she batted the remaining five eyelashes on her right eyelid.

Bea innocently stepped in front of Sasha, completely covering the woman's view of the reverend. "Will you be traveling with us, Pastor?" she asked with a broad smile. She hadn't remembered putting her teeth back in but there they were. She knew because she could taste the residue from the Fixodent paste.

"Oh, hell no!" the Reverend Bling shot back, and then quickly repented. "Oh, Lord, I'm sorry," he said. "I didn't mean to say no." He then calmed down enough to add nicely, "Just go pack and don't tell anyone."

"Oh, we won't tell anyone," Bea replied, lying.

"Can we ask which airline we'll be flying on?" Sasha asked. "I'm just a bit curious."

The reverend picked up the reservation form from between the pages of the dream book and smiled. "The Closet Airline. You'll be on flight fifty-fifty." He stopped and fingered the tickets inside the manila envelope, suddenly remembering that he would have to pay extra to get the names changed on them. It would be well worth it, and anyway, he definitely didn't need them knowing that he'd planned on taking along one of the other female church members. "Y'all are leaving within the coming week. I'll call you as soon as I get home and make your reservations."

"The Closet Airline, it sounds small, intimate, and a lot like fun," Bea said as she turned to Sasha, adding, "By the way, I've flown many times."

She was lying.

"So have I," Sasha replied. She was lying, too.

Bea wouldn't leave well enough alone. She had to take it further. "I'm actually used to flying either in first or in business class. In case you didn't know, that's located in the back of the plane like those seats in a limousine."

"Of course I knew that," Sasha answered with a huff. Turning to the ushers, who still hadn't moved, Sasha confessed, "Bea and I like to tell the truth just like Ananias and his wife did in the Bible days."

Neither usher responded. Instead, Sister Judah whispered to the other, "Didn't they fall over dead because they lied to the disciples?"

"I believe I have heard or read about that somewhere," Sister Israel replied.

Sister Judah looked around quickly and added, "Lightning just may strike those two. I think we should be safe standing over here. If they fall they won't hit us by accident."

While the two ushers stood safely, so they imagined, a few feet away, the two old women continued with their minds temporarily relaxed by senility.

Still grinning like a mouse hiding the last piece of cheese, Bea said nicely, as she walked back to where she'd left her pocketbook, "That's wonderful that you've flown before. I should've known that you had because you're so modern. Why don't you come by my house tomorrow and we can discuss what we'll pack."

"I'll be there," Sasha replied. "Where do you live, again?"

Bea stopped moving and with the hem of her long blue pleated skirt still swirling about, she pulled out a pen from her pocketbook to write down her address on the back of an old bingo card.

Sasha took the card gingerly and smiled at Bea. She winked and folded the card in half, tucking it down between the folds of her breast.

Not sixty seconds passed before Sasha forgot where she'd placed it and patted her lower front pocket to make sure the card hadn't fallen out. Her breasts were so long she didn't know where her bra ended and her front pocket began.

It was almost nine o'clock. Completely exhausted, the Reverend Bling gave the benediction and a few more warnings of secrecy to the mothers.

Five minutes later, the church doors closed and the remaining people scattered. The reverend limped off into a waiting car, leaving the two old women standing on the sidewalk. He'd had enough drama for one night. Offering them a ride was out of the question, and although killing them might be the only way to gain peace of mind, he wasn't ready for a prison ministry.

Ignoring the apparent slight from the reverend, Bea laid a finger between the folds of her two bottom chins and asked impishly, "Do you think he was serious about us not telling anyone about the trip?"

"It's hard to tell. I don't think he's ever serious about much," Sasha answered. "But he'd better be about this trip." She stopped and shifted her Bible and cane from hand to hand before continuing. "It don't matter if he was serious about us keeping quiet; I can't. I have a couple of folks I need to brag to."

I can't wait to tell that know-it-all Sister Betty how God blessed me tonight. She ain't the only one He blesses. The smile crept across her face as she reveled in the moment of bringing down one of her oldest church enemies.

"I wanna tell her, too." Bea chuckled. As another wave of hot outdoor air enveloped her, she fanned her face, only stopping long enough to wave for a cab. One finally pulled up and the women decided to share the ride and split the cost.

During the cab ride the two old women shared further thoughts and space without bickering. That was until they got about two blocks from the adjacent streets where they lived, and Alzheimer decided to let them know that he was riding along, too. They suddenly started fighting about everything from what was the best brand of bladder control diapers to whether or not they would be among the 144,000 caught up in the rapture.

5

The plane trip from the Greenville-Spartanburg Airport to Las Vegas was uneventful. Sasha and Bea were so exhausted from the previous week of packing, arguing, and other senior-related issues, they'd fallen asleep immediately after boarding. By the time they'd landed, they were well rested and ready for their adventure.

"G'bye," repeated a stewardess with a creamy-colored Barbie doll body and teeth white enough to rival the color of new fallen snow. She stood at the aircraft door and said over and over, "Thank you for flying Closet Air. Please come again."

"G'bye to you, too." Sasha smiled and waved.

"Isn't she just too pretty?" Bea giggled and pointed back.

"Yes. She's just as pretty as a picture," Sasha cooed. "I betcha you were probably that pretty, too, when you were younger."

"Much prettier," Bea replied, laughing again.

As they walked away, they shifted the pocketbooks in their hands and locked arms for support.

Between the temporary memory lapse of their feuding relationship and the Las Vegas scenario, the old women were suddenly behaving like the Christian women they claimed to be.

They were deep in conversation as they oohed and aahed over the airport sights. Even as they passed crowded rows of nickel slot machines with ever hopeful tourists' imprisoned hands glued to the levers, they oohed and they aahed but kept their change in their pockets. They looked like mismatched cherubs dressed in white, clutching their pocketbooks and Bibles in the busy baggage area.

"How are you holding up, Bea?" Sasha asked as she reached up and gently patted the clammy arm of her current best friend.

"I'm doing just lovely, Sasha dear." Bea chuckled. "I can't wait to see what wonderful transportation the reverend arranged for our ride to the hotel."

"If it's anything near as grand as the plane ride, I'm sure we will enjoy it."

As soon as they and the skycap ventured through the revolving airport doors and onto the sidewalk and into the warm sun, they saw a tall, thin, young man with mocha-colored skin and acne clusters holding a placard with their names. He stood several feet away between a late-model, white stretch-limousine and a dark blue 1998 Beetle.

"Pray Onn and Blister," he called out slowly, several times, as the shadow from the hot sun silhouetted his pocked face.

"Oh, listen, Bea," Sasha gushed. "That young man standing over there is calling our names."

"I see," Bea replied. She then turned to the skycap and pointed to the man with the placards.

"Good, please follow me." The skycap pushed the luggage car and the women followed.

"You see, dear, the reverend took care of everything," Sasha said softly, pointing straight ahead. "Don't you just love that white stretch limo at the curb?"

"Sure do. I can't wait to get inside with all that cool air-conditioning," Bea said as she slipped a five-dollar bill to the skycap and directed him toward the limo.

The women donned their sunglasses and strutted, as best they could, like movie stars with plenty of attitude to make folks think they were.

At the same time the young man with the placard approached the old women and the skycap started pushing his luggage cart toward the limousine, as the passenger door to the limousine opened.

And the old adage *never let the devil ride 'cause he'll wanna drive* took on a new meaning.

6

While Bea and Sasha were trying to gain entry to the limo, squads of airport security police dashed through the Las Vegas airport terminal with their weapons drawn.

"Get down!" the police yelled, causing droves of screaming passengers to dive for cover, knocking over trash cans and rushing to the restrooms for safety.

Four police officers crashed through the revolving doors leading to the front of the passenger pickup area.

With rifles shoulder high, they screamed at the old woman hunched over with one knobby knee placed firmly on the back of a fallen man wearing a dark uniform. The man was screaming and clutching a placard.

"Madam, release the man and step away," one of the police officers demanded. "We'll take it from here." She was close enough for him to forgo using a bullhorn.

"Oh, thank the Lord, you've arrived," Sasha responded while clutching her heart. She let her fingers spread wide as though she were trying to prevent her heart from escaping her scrawny chest. She nodded toward the curb. "That's my best friend, Bea. She's been holding that craggy piece of flesh until y'all arrived," she explained.

"Madam, please move back. We'll handle it," repeated one of the officers, a portly black man in his twenties who looked unattractive both physically and mentally. As he approached Sasha, he pushed his gun back into the holster, then quickly but gently took her by the elbow, attempting to pull her to safety behind a nearby column.

He had no way of knowing that all his actions would send hell into overtime.

* * *

Three hours later, they all stood before a judge in a Las Vegas courthouse. The judge was a stoop-shouldered, elderly Caucasian man with paper-thin hair. He wore an ill-fitted black robe, no doubt from his days before legal burdens forced his shoulders into submission.

"Unbelievable," the judge said as he leafed through the mound of papers placed in front of him by the law clerk. His eyes grew wide and then narrowed, making it seem as though he thought he must've done something wrong in his previous life to deserve the chaos now in his courtroom. "I'm too old for this crap." His supposed muffled declaration traveled loudly around the courtroom because of the mounted microphone.

"Is there an attorney present for the accused?" The judge continued to let his head rest in his hands as his elbows slid back and forth across the bench.

"Sammy Coch, of the Coch, Roach, and Spray Esquires, located at One-oh-six Strip Row, Las Vegas, Nevada." His voice was deep, and yet a bit effeminate. He was a tall, middle-aged, Asian man whose courtroom antics and the amount of cases won were legendary in the Las Vegas legal community. Just like any good legal hound dog, he'd followed the smell of money and another opportunity to embarrass the court when he thought the old women were wealthy movie stars.

Neither Bea nor Sasha knew who the man was who'd stood up for them and at that moment, they didn't care. Instead, they stood like misunderstood angels with their hands cuffed in front. They were so much in sync that even raising a cuffed hand to dab at an invisible tear was done at the same time.

"I'm misunderstood," Sasha sobbed softly. She stopped suddenly and leaned on her cane for sympathy. Somehow the security personnel wrongly thought the cane was not a problem.

Sasha even went so far as to let her bottom lip quiver. But that only lasted a few seconds because those false teeth were about to make an involuntary court appearance, too.

"He misrepresented himself," Bea added haltingly, with loud sobs accompanying each word.

The judge was so put out he'd not raised his gavel once to silence them.

And then Sammy Coch did his thing. By the time the attorney

finished explaining the situation with a bunch of "to wits and ergo's," he was treading on the judge's last good nerve. "Whereby, your honor, with the court's permission, I plan to prove that these poor old women are the victims of a simple misunderstanding."

"Didn't I just say that?" Bea was trying to whisper to Sasha and was doing a miserable job of it. A stern look from the judge caused her to shut up.

". . . When these sweet elderly women arrived in Las Vegas . . ."

He's got one more time to call me old, Bea thought angrily, *and I'm wrapping his behind in a wonton.* But she was smart enough to keep tears in her eyes, the same eyes she kept trained on the judge, who had his trained on her as well.

". . . they thought they were about to be kidnapped," Sammy Coch droned on, ignoring the look of confusion on the judge's face. "They reacted appropriately by beating the accuser. They thought a limousine was to pick them up and instead that man—"

Sammy Coch stopped and dramatically pointed his finger at the chauffeur who stood with bloodshot eyes, mentally tattered, and still clutching his placard to cover his torn pants zipper.

"That man, a man much younger, much stronger, and with a much longer criminal record." Sammy Coch really didn't know whether there was a criminal record involved, but the accusation usually worked. He continued, "He physically tried to force these innocent old women into another car, which was obviously too small. Naturally, the women tried to defend themselves."

The judge had seen and heard enough. He bucked forward from his chair, letting it rock loudly, and banged his gavel. He'd made up his mind, which was prompted by the fact that he had a golf game shortly. He rustled a few papers, which included the arrest record of the driver. He shook his head in disgust and blatantly ignored the fact that the long criminal record was actually just one charge, and a sealed one at that, and went ballistic on the poor driver.

"How dare you take advantage of a tourist?" The judge banged the gavel again and raised his voice. "These poor old women without knowledge of the streets were just putty in your hands. Weren't they? Thirty days in county!"

The driver looked around to see if another case had started and he just wasn't aware.

The judge summoned the bailiff. "Cuff this criminal and get

him out of my sight. And I'd better not see you back in my court."

By the time the driver caught a clue that he'd been railroaded by two old women, only the back of his behind, and his cuffed wrists, could be seen.

And, instead of thanking the judge and their attorney, Bea and Sasha sucked their teeth and admonished them for calling them "old" in public. As usual, Bea waddled away with her back bent over, making her look not only like a darkened Quasimodo, but an angry one as well. Sasha did what she always did when she wanted to have the last word. She grasped her cane, snatched her Bible off the bench, and shook what used to be her "money maker," and was now only worth a few pennies, at the judge and left.

"Ow," Bea winced, "my back is killing me."

"I'm in pain, too," Sasha shot back. "Putting a li'l sumpthin' extra in my switch caused a shooting pain up my hip bone."

So the two old women who dared anyone to refer to them as such hurried off as fast as they could, to find some salve and heating pads.

During the time it'd taken for the court procedures to happen, Sister Betty had also arrived in Las Vegas. Two representatives from the Las Vegas Crossing Over Temple met her at the airport. In between, the several hallelujahs, church greetings, and her need to hurry out of Sin City and back to Pelzer, Sister Betty rode sulking to the Luxor Hotel.

7

The Luxor Hotel and Casino with its 350-foot pyramid stood out in mock elegance with its Egyptian decor on Las Vegas's South Strip. At the base of the pyramid, with temperatures in triple digits, swarms of people with cameras in hand, tourist maps, and anxious cash for the slot machines stopped to gawk at the two elderly black women carrying suitcases followed by a three-man camera crew.

"Are they celebrities?" someone from the crowd asked.

"I don't recognize them," a voice responded.

"I think the heavier one looks like that actress who played the role of the grandmama in that movie *Soul Food*."

Another voice chimed in. "Irma P. Hall?" The man strained to focus his camera to take a picture. "I think you're right."

"So who is the smaller woman with the cane?" a female voice asked quickly.

"I heard someone call her Mother something. I couldn't get it all."

"Wow!" another voice added. "I'd heard Mother Love lost a ton of weight, but she looks like she almost melted away. I hope she's all right."

And just that quick Mothers Bea and Sasha became celebrity impersonators. The camera crew had followed them from the courthouse, hoping for an interview with the two feisty out-of-towners who had thrown the airport into a frenzy. But the crowd in front of the Luxor proclaimed them otherwise, and many wannabe paparazzi took pictures that would later give undeserved, negative attention to Irma P. Hall and Mother Love.

* * *

A young woman watched all the hoopla going on with the old women and the camera crew. Their appearance seemed to stir things up a bit, as if the Luxor, or the Vegas Strip, needed it.

During the past eighteen months, thirty-year-old Zipporah Moses had lived inside several crowded homeless shelters. On this particular day she'd come onto the strip to get away from all the doom and gloom a shelter often provided. She lived several miles away from the Luxor where some of the neighborhoods weren't quite as affluent.

She'd sometimes spend time reclaiming her sanity inside air-conditioned Las Vegas movie theaters. During moments of fantasy she'd honed from years of foster-home-to-foster-home living and trying to survive, she'd seen movies both good and bad. Although she had not recognized either of the elderly women, she certainly knew they were not Irma P. Hall or Mother Love.

Zipporah felt a sharp push and spun around. She was small boned and stood only five-foot-six. It would take no effort to shove her from her spot. Life did it constantly. No one in the crowd gave her a sign of culpability. With no one to lash out at, she turned back to refocus on the two old women.

Zipporah shook her head in disbelief at the crowd snapping pictures and gabbing about things they knew nothing about. *This should be for me. They should take my picture,* she thought.

For a moment, she indulged in her lifelong dream of having that kind of success, a dream that served as her respite from life. The shelter she'd found in fantasizing often proved to be her saving grace. Though fame and happiness were constantly out of reach for her, she believed only that kind of recognition and that kind of money would deliver her out of the loneliness and homeless shelters. In her fantasy, she would command these adoring and now misguided people from a stage such as New York City's Radio City Music Hall or perhaps even the Los Angeles Universal Amphitheater.

Above the din surrounding the old women's appearance, she imagined how it would be.

Now, ladies and gentlemen, put your hands together and show some love for the incomparable voice of a young lady who the Queen of Soul, Miss Aretha Franklin, has dubbed, "my rightful successor." Stand on your feet for Lady Z . . . Zipporah Mosessssssssss. The crowd would chant her name as she took the stage. She'd wear a sky blue dress on her shapely, size four frame. That color always came alive against her mocha-colored skin. Her long, shoulder-length, ash brown hair would fan her heart-shaped face and accentuate her lively hazel eyes. . . .

"Are you okay?" Zipporah heard someone ask. She turned to see a young security guard about her age ogling her. When she didn't respond, he seemed to look past her in a dismissive way as though his lot in life were better than hers. "You'll have to move along. You can't just stand here. Either you're going in or not."

She tried to rally by returning to her daydream against the backdrop of the continued noise, pretending he'd not interrupted. She'd hoped to retain a small piece of her daydream. However, she couldn't dismiss the security guard's nonchalant demeanor. It had quickly brought down the curtains on her dream without effort. "Excuse me." She'd said it politely, trying to offer him another way to express his wishes for her to move on.

He caught the attitude, so he used his baton to indicate what he wanted her to do while adding, this time politely, "I'm sorry but you must move along. The show's over. Those two old women have gone."

And that's when she realized they had.

He didn't wait to see if she moved or not. Instantly, he'd moved on to a few other stragglers, urging them to vacate the front of the Luxor lest they give the hotel a bad name. Among the onlookers, Zipporah suddenly recognized two of the other women from her current shelter, so she rushed away before they called out to her. She didn't want to be associated with homelessness, even though the nondescript building gave her free shelter at night.

There must be something better in store for me, were the words she repeated every day. Zipporah held her head proud and shifted the weight from a beige knock-off Coach pocketbook that only seemed to make her faded lemon yellow short set more noticeable. With her mind still on a better life, she walked a few yards past the Luxor and then noticed a ten-dollar bill lying next to a trash receptacle.

Quickly, Zipporah let the bag drop from her arm onto the sidewalk. She stumbled slightly to give the impression the bag fell by accident. With skills honed by finding only fleeting pieces of happiness in her young life, Zipporah hurriedly stooped and snatched up the ten dollars along with her bag.

As she blended into the crowd of the well dressed and the fortunate, Zipporah's mind raced. Yesterday was the last time she'd eaten, the memory causing her stomach to growl loudly. She'd hurried from the shelter early that morning, as she did most mornings. Months ago, she'd decided to forgo the unappealing and almost nutritious breakfasts and gamble on finding something better in the streets. There was always a church buffet happening or something akin to it.

With a grumbling empty stomach and clothes clean but outdated, she'd also gone on unsuccessful job interviews. Twice within a year's time, she'd found temporary work that was much too temporary for her to show off her office skills. Pretending to diet so as not to go out with the other employees and spend her limited funds on lunch became her norm.

An accidental shove from a passerby again interrupted her thoughts. With the ten dollars she'd just found and the twenty dollars she had pinned to her brassiere, she felt a sudden purpose to her steps. Thirty dollars would have to last.

She was also on her way to audition. She sometimes sang at a few local dives that only paid tips. Today, she had a real chance, a better opportunity to get a job with one of the hotel musical revues that paid weekly.

If I land this job, I'll only have to make this last until payday. It's Monday, I can hold on until Friday. Lord, please allow me to get this job. She purposely omitted asking God if it was His will, because she couldn't imagine a God that would continue to let her linger in her present state when she was trying so hard to get out.

Another loud rumble stirred in her stomach as she approached the side entrance to the Luxor Hotel. A quick look at the large clock in the corner told her that she was ten minutes early. At the very least, it would show them that she was dependable and serious.

Zipporah retrieved her sheet music from her bag. She smiled and carefully straightened its overused edges. Entering the hotel, she found where she needed to go and pushed the elevator button to the fourth floor. She allowed herself to relax as she stood against the back wall of the elevator and waited for the doors to close.

8

Bea and Sasha registered at the front desk without incident. Given their room numbers and personal keycards, they left their luggage for a later delivery and headed toward the elevators.

Several people from the anxious crowd, moments before attracted to the mysterious celebrities, had managed to sneak into the lobby. They crushed and circled the women, blocking their entry onto the elevator, and shamelessly asked them for autographs.

Of course, Bea and Sasha, as tired as they were, fell prey to their own egos and forbade the hotel security from dispersing the crowd before they gave them what they'd asked. They scribbled, "God bless" and "Thank you" on pieces of paper and tossed them to the crowd while smiling and posing for pictures with a few who insisted that they do so.

Although the deluge only lasted a short time, it was exhausting. When Bea spied the elevator, she snatched Sasha and pushed her toward its opening door. They were already inside before Sasha could protest.

"Bea, have you lost your doggone mind?" Sasha's words were halting but the venom was direct. "You won't be satisfied until I pray for God's strength to swat your annoying behind with my precious cane!"

"Mind ya manners, Munchkin," Bea hissed and pointed over toward a young lady whose eyes were wide with fear. She was huddled against the back elevator wall clutching papers.

Before Bea could apologize for their rude interruption, the elevator bell rang and the young woman departed in a hurry.

"Are you satisfied?" Bea barked. "After that fine welcome we received now people will think we have no class."

"Bea Blister, put your wrinkled claws on me again and I'll teach you a lesson you never learned in class."

They'd gone from celebrity back to prize fighters between the first and sixth floor. The old women fussed, hissed, barked and threatened along the hotel corridor as they searched for the room number.

After circling the corridor twice, Bea was tired. "This is crazy. I cannot find that room anywhere on this floor."

Sasha peered over her glasses at her keycard and, with resignation, added, "Where in the world would they put nine-oh-nine?"

Temporarily in one accord, they were ready to return to the hotel lobby and tear someone apart at the registration desk. In a snit, the women headed back toward the elevator. On the way, they saw one of the hotel room maids, a young Hispanic woman dressed in a light green uniform.

As nice as she could, Sasha smiled and said, "We're looking for our rooms. It's nine ninety-nine and nine nineteen." She held up her keycard for the maid to see.

Balancing towels on one arm and a bag of toiletries in her other, the maid, who was about to enter one of the rooms, placed the items back onto the cart.

The maid returned the smile. "No problema, senora," she replied and reached for the keycard in Sasha's hand. "You should be looking for room six-sixty-six. This is the sixth floor. You looked at the card upside down." There was just a hint of superiority in her voice.

"That's what I told her," Bea blurted out. She tried to hide her embarrassment and failed as she quickly turned her keycard around in full view of the others.

"Sasha Pray Onn, is there any place I can go where you will not be an embarrassment?" Bea asked, shaking her head.

"Bea, I'm in no mood for your foolishness."

The maid, having seen all types of crazy both back in her country and in Las Vegas, hurried off. She was getting as far away from the old women as she could.

9

Zipporah's interview had finished before it began. An hour later and she was back to dealing with defeat. Before she interviewed, she'd already accepted the odds of her getting the job. She was only courageous in her daydreams. Predestining defeat was a mind game she'd played for quite some time.

Stepping back onto the sidewalk in front of the Luxor, Zipporah blended in with the crowd. Zipporah slipped quietly into one of the fast-food restaurants. She'd made sure it was one of the restaurants almost two blocks away from the Luxor and around a corner off the strip.

After deciding how much she could afford off the side-item menu, she paid and left the counter. She'd spied a worker clearing the clutter off a table next to a bathroom. The table was small and the chair lopsided, much like her life. It took her a moment to balance the chair as well as what had transpired during the interview and audition. Idly picking at a side order of french fries so cold the grease had already started to congeal on her plate, Zipporah let her mind retrace that afternoon.

"Zipporah Moses, number thirty, Zipporah Moses, you're next." The pasty-colored, thirty-something woman called out. Seated on her high-back throne behind her desk, she'd let her coral-colored glasses rest on the tip of her pointed nose and pursed her lips.

"You're Zipporah?" she'd asked with a touch of sarcasm. Her tinny voice was unapologetic as she let her blue eyes travel over the mismatched ensemble hanging for dear life on Zipporah's hidden and shapely body.

Without so much as a note sung or another question asked, the pasty-colored snob on the throne with the tinny voice, outdated glasses, and no decorum announced that magically the position was filled. To further her insult, she tossed Zipporah's application into the wastebasket. A quick flip of the woman's hand dismissed her without ceremony. She hadn't even bothered with an introduction. Zipporah felt lower than a street curb.

Adolescent giggling from the next table interrupted Zipporah's dismal replay. A young girl of about fifteen wearing too much makeup and not enough clothing flirted with a man several years older. To whatever the older man said, the young girl responded with over-the-top laughter while under the table she stroked his upper thigh, teasingly along the inside seam of his pants.

Zipporah fought the urge to go over and drag the stupid girl away before her youth betrayed her, as Zipporah's had done. Her inexperience and lust for a singing career had led her to entertain men she wouldn't have normally shared the same air with.

The sound of trays slamming took Zipporah's attention away from the young girl and her destiny of disappointment. She put her head back down and picked at the cold french fries.

"We didn't come all the way to Las Vegas to eat at a low-class place like this!" Sasha had fussed all the way from the hotel to the spot where they now stood.

"Sasha," Bea snapped, "we need to save what we can to play bingo and gamble."

The reference to her favorite pastimes calmed Sasha. "Okay, Bea. Let's find a table and eat this crap so we can get on with our vacation and keep our Mothers Board positions."

Bea and Sasha's loud bickering suddenly invaded Zipporah's attention. She slowly looked up. It was just in time to recognize the two old women from the elevator and the fray outside the hotel. *How much worse can this day get?* she wondered, quickly turning her head slightly toward the wall to avoid eye contact with the crabby old women, or anyone for that matter.

Sasha stopped sniping for a moment and nibbled on the crust of her tomato, okra, and mustard sandwich.

Meanwhile Bea, trying to gnaw at a hamburger that oozed more oil than sauce, leaned forward suddenly and found Zipporah in her view. She focused intensely as she tried to recall where she'd seen the young woman seated at a table nearby. *I've never been to Las Vegas before so where do I know that young lady from? And, if I don't know her, then whom does she remind me of?*

Something about the young woman caught Bea's attention. She suddenly became agitated. She hadn't come all the way to Las Vegas to do anything but retain her Mothers Board position at the conference, and add some monetary blessings to her purse. Yet, she felt compelled to stare at the young woman.

"Bea!" Sasha hissed, shooting bits of tomato and okra from the corner of her mouth.

"What?" Bea barked, wiping the dripping oil from the cuff of her sweater and glaring. She didn't know how long Sasha had tried to get her attention and she didn't care. There was something disturbing about that young woman seated against the wall. She clicked her false teeth as she tried to recall why.

"It's your turn to pay for the meal," Sasha announced.

"I'm not paying twenty dollars for some dry bread and veggies and a hamburger with enough grease to fry a bucket of chicken." She flicked the tiny speck of slimy okra back at Sasha. "I've got something else on my mind. . . ."

But when Bea turned around the young woman was gone.

10

The National Missionaries and Mothers Board Convention started late the next morning but it didn't matter. Most of the five hundred attendees were well past the age of worrying about showing up on time. They were happy just to show up at all.

Outside, the morning air was muggy with a rare thunderstorm threatening to kiss the arid Las Vegas atmosphere with much needed moisture. Inside one of the Edna Jaeger Hotel and Conference Center's banquet rooms the ongoing praise service was hot.

The Edna Jaeger was a new facility built less than five years ago and named for one of Las Vegas's leading Afro-American female entrepreneurs. There were four floors of opulence with two of its floors completely enclosed in glass. The Jaeger, as it was called for short, also had a top-of-the-line sound system and a grand stage for small performances or events. It had the added attraction of having its own casino and first-class first aid center. The latter two features explained why the Jaeger was chosen for the Mothers Board Convention. Gambling and the acceptance of Medicaid were a plus for most of the seniors.

Bea and Sasha stood beaming behind the podium. All the attendees were dressed in white from head to toe. Bea and Sasha looked well-rested despite their action-packed afternoon and their constant bickering. Sasha had even managed to forgive Bea for suggesting that her room number, 666, was prophetic. They'd managed to take a break by going to their respective hotel rooms to regroup for the election battle.

"This is lovely," Bea whispered as she waved to several of the women she knew. She let her dark, weathered-skin hand drop and rise, as though the audience would receive an anointing by her action.

"We can't lose with this much love in the room," Sasha added with a low chuckle.

As if on cue the other attendees started clapping and then one by one they stood.

"Oh my." Sasha blushed as she pretended to be embarrassed by all the applause.

Bea was about to go into her humility routine when someone from the crowd hollered, "Praise the Lord, Sister Betty's here."

Bea's wig slid off to the side as her head quickly twisted toward the door.

Sasha's jaw dropped and so did her false teeth. If the crowd wasn't so involved in greeting Sister Betty, they'd have heard the partials clang when they hit the floor.

All the attention caught Sister Betty by surprise. It was her intention to arrive and just sit in the back until the nominations and other festivities were over.

While the other mothers and missionaries flocked toward Sister Betty, Bea and Sasha fought the urge to rush over and tackle the woman, the sanctified thorn in their sides. But they stood and smiled using the correct amount of decorum because they were there to represent their church. And, more so, they wanted the reelection.

Bea and Sasha gave one another a quick glance. The sneers hidden behind the false smiles silently conveyed their collective plans to get rid of Sister Betty.

"That old heifer has got to go," Bea hissed.

"I agree." Sasha had raised her cane out of habit but quickly let it drop. "Let's get together after we go to the casino and pray about it."

It was much too hot, even for a Las Vegas morning. But for Zipporah, weather conditions couldn't be a consideration for her first day on the job. It wasn't something she'd wanted but the homeless shelter mandated that each occupant had to search for work. So when the director handed her a list for possible employment openings, she had to take it. Especially since the musical job hadn't panned out.

She had her application folded neatly in her pocket as she made her way to the employee administration area in the rear of the Jaeger Center.

A nondescript woman wearing light blue eye shadow sat at a small desk outside an expensive oaken door. The door had a gold-edged plaque reading HUMAN RESOURCES DIRECTOR.

"Just have a seat. I'll let you know when you can go in." For the next few minutes the woman kept her head down, which allowed her blue-tinged silver locks to thankfully hide the ugly blue eye shadow.

"Thank you." Zipporah waited for the woman to indicate where she should sit. "Is there any particular place?" Zipporah finally asked.

The woman still didn't respond, so Zipporah found an expensive red leather chair and allowed her weary body to succumb to its comfort. Until that moment, she hadn't realized how tired she was. But of course she was. How could she not be tired? Her tiny room certainly didn't offer a tenth of the luxury contained in the small space in which she now sat. Without thinking, she allowed her head to lie back. She fought the urge to close her eyes but she'd already lost the battle as soon as she sat down. The luxury where she now sat, compared with where she'd laid her head for the past few months, rushed past her fatigue and took over.

The rooms inside Zipporah's West Strip Homeless Shelter were small. Each room resembled a cramped prison cell, containing only a narrow cot with a thin mattress and a dresser. Comfort was not a consideration for short-term accommodations. A clock radio's alarm sat among the clutter on a small dresser. Every morning it screamed as if in pain to wake Zipporah from restless sleep.

That morning Zipporah was robotic as she prepared to leave the confines of the shelter for another day of searching for work. There were small scratches on her arms that confirmed she'd clawed and scratched at invisible demons during the night. Self-mutilation had almost become the norm for her. She dabbed a little cocoa butter on her skin to quicken the healing. Singing was the dab of healing she used for her inside wounds.

Zipporah had no sooner signed the residency clipboard meant to track the comings and goings when she heard the voice she'd assiduously tried to avoid.

"Miss Moses, can you please step inside my office?" Miss

Thompson's words were soft and sympathetic but official. Taking a file off a cabinet, she walked toward her office, not bothering to see if Zipporah followed.

To visitors, the fortyish Miss Thompson appeared as an overweight yet genteel woman. She had cinnamon-colored skin and snow-white hair that cascaded past her shoulders. To the residents of the shelter, she was a nosey woman who always seemed determined that they would never overstay their allotted time unless it was at her whim.

"Close the door, Zipporah." Miss Thompson still hadn't turned around, choosing instead to flip switches on her standing fan. She seemed pleased as the fan blades hummed louder.

Zipporah closed the door. She shuddered slightly despite her effort to remain calm. Almost thirty days ago, she'd asked Miss Thompson for an extension on the measly but necessary living arrangements. She was almost three days past the time she was supposed to leave.

"I think I know what you're about to say—"

"I doubt it." Miss Thompson hadn't bothered to sit, choosing to lean over her desk as if it gave her more authority.

"You're past your discharge time and I don't have to remind you that there are others who need shelter, too."

Zipporah was determined not to let one tear fall. She failed.

"You're young, very pretty, and I'm sure you have talents you haven't tapped into yet."

Miss Thompson let the word *talents* linger as though it was a term to which she could attach all sorts of meanings.

"I don't want you to say a word. I need you to listen. I've a friend who can use a woman with your *talent*."

Zipporah's heart raced. She'd heard those words before, spewed from her then supposed boyfriend, Lonnie. With common dreams of producing their own Broadway-styled show, they'd arrived in Las Vegas full of hope. He was thirty. His tall, muscular build and pecan-brown complexion were disarming once he lit his charm fuse. A slippery tongue and large innocent brown eyes, he had; money he did not.

Within two months, they were broke. Lonnie decided he would earn a few dollars performing one-nighters as a bassist with whoever was hiring along the strip. Despite her protests of doing anything illegal such as shoplifting, he'd beaten her and then smiled before depositing her from their used Odyssey van onto the unforgiving streets of Las Vegas.

"You're talented. Do on the street what you do to me at home. Figure it out."

"Zipporah, figure it out." Miss Thompson stood with her arms folded as though she expected Zipporah to drop and give her several push-ups.

"Excuse me?" Zipporah spoke with indignation. She'd finally figured it out.

"Did you understand what I just offered?" Miss Thompson's voice was no longer soft. It seemed to rise with annoyance as she again asked, "Have I made myself clear?"

The answer wrapped in a string of expletives lay trapped inside Zipporah's dry mouth. Her eyes tried to escape the intense gaze emanating from Miss Thompson's cherublike face. The balance between hunger, homelessness, and the possibility of escaping both seesawed within her mind.

While Zipporah's mind raced, the buzzer on the intercom caught Miss Thompson's attention. She glanced away quickly to answer the call and to write a quick note. It was long enough for Zipporah to rush out of the room.

Without a thought of the meager belongings in her room, Zipporah fled the shelter. She sprinted for two blocks without stopping until she arrived at the bus stop. It didn't matter where the bus was headed, she just needed to escape.

And that's when she realized she'd left her bag inside Miss Thompson's office.

That was yesterday. She'd managed to talk the night supervisor into retrieving her bag from Miss Thompson's office. She'd made the excuse of having cramps and just needing to go to her room and lie down. The night supervisor, a kindly woman and the total opposite of Miss Thompson, sympathized and took the bag during a time when the office was empty.

About the same time her head nodded off to the side again, Zipporah's name filtered through her involuntary nap. How many times had her name been called?

"Miss Moses, you may go in." The annoyance in the receptionist's voice was palpable and the ugly blue shadow seemed darker and uglier. "Perhaps you'd like to go home and rest before you commit to a possible job here."

Zipporah's head snapped as though held by a rubber band. Aggravation accompanied each word the woman had spoken, but not without reason.

"I'm so sorry," Zipporah answered sheepishly. "I was praying." The lie had rolled off her tongue too quick. Her face twitched from guilt. But it wasn't enough to take the lie back.

From the sour look on the receptionist's face Zipporah wasn't too sure if she had even a chance of getting the job. The woman's face suddenly softened as though she understood the need to pray.

"Have faith," the receptionist whispered and smiled.

A man opened the door and politely invited Zipporah to come inside and have a seat.

"Good afternoon, I'm Mr. Lamb." She could tell his smile was genuine and inviting when he didn't immediately look away. His speech had a hint of a southern twang and it sounded almost like he was teasing her, although he'd not said anything that would indicate that he was.

"Miss Moses, have you had a chance to look over our manual and familiarize yourself with our particular needs?"

"No, I haven't. I've only completed my application."

"Let me give you one to look over."

He hadn't said it but he seemed to indicate that the job was hers, if she wanted it.

"Thank you."

Mr. Lamb walked back and forth between two cabinets selecting several manuals and papers. He walked like a professional model displaying a well-proportioned body. His waist was small but definitely manly. His skin was olive brown, smooth and hairless in the places she could see.

She noticed that they had something in common. It was in the eyes.

Mr. Lamb was at least a head or so taller than Zipporah. He acted a bit older than he appeared and she guessed his age to be in the early to mid-thirties.

He was gorgeous and she wasn't quite sure what to do with her observations. But her angst suddenly dissipated as she determined that whatever Mr. Lamb was selling, she was buying.

"Tell me a little something about yourself." The accent tantalized her as she drank in every inch of him. He'd asked about her, wanted to know something personal.

And then she remembered. Her clean but faded floral-print dress revealed more than she'd wanted. Her black pumps that set her back twelve dollars, which she revered as though they cost a million, said that she was Zipporah Moses, a homeless woman. Las Vegas's best-kept secret—a woman who could out-sing Aretha and hit notes that Mariah couldn't reach with a ladder.

Her shoulders slumped as she scrambled to find a way to evade the question. She didn't have to. The telephone on Mr. Lamb's desk rang. "Chandler Lamb speaking, how can I help you?"

Chandler . . . She now had a first name to go with her first impression. She tilted her head slowly, letting her eyes drink in what she now could call Chandler, although not to his face. But it didn't take a second for her to return to reality. She was sure he would never associate with the likes of her beyond this office.

Zipporah shuddered slightly as she pretended to remove an imaginary piece of nothing from her skirt. She needed to get a grip; she didn't have time for frivolous daydreaming. She sat up a little straighter and focused on several pictures adorning the office wall.

It was of no use, her eyes were immediately drawn back to him.

He sat and then pushed his chair back, letting it lean against the wall. He tugged at the telephone cord until it extended to its full length. With his free hand, he drummed a fast rhythm with a pen.

His face was still handsome despite the sudden look of chagrin. "Mandy is out to lunch, so have someone handle it until I can get security there." He stopped and scribbled something on a sticky note. "I'm in the middle of interviewing a new employee—" He lay the receiver down harder than he'd wanted, then turned and gave her a look of exasperation before he continued to write.

He pressed another button on the phone bank while trying to hide his aggravation behind a smile. He was evidently embarrassed by the momentary show of unprofessionalism. "I'm sorry for the interruption, Miss Moses. Please give me another moment."

"It's not a problem." That was the best response she had. What she really wanted to do was to place his head on her shoulder. She'd cuddle him while saying seductively, "Don't worry. I'm here to make things better."

Again, she'd allowed a fantasy moment to visit. For the next few minutes she did everything she could to avoid eye contact and pretend she wasn't listening to whatever the problem was. From snatches of conversation she'd learned that the problem was in one of the conference rooms and that it involved several church women. She wasn't sure how serious it was but it caused Mr. Lamb to order security to the room and hold those involved until he got the building manager there.

". . . I'll decide what to do once security gets there. Just calm the women down. The last thing we need or want is bad press or a lawsuit."

After hanging up, again Mr. Lamb started scribbling, but this time he handed the paper to Zipporah. "Give this to the receptionist when she returns. She'll tell you where to go for your uniform and have you fill out the remaining paperwork. I'm placing you on the eleven in the morning until seven in the evening shift. If things work out, then I'll see about a permanent shift for you. You'll need to come back inside my office before you leave." Without waiting for her to reply, he rose and extended a handshake before escorting her out of his office.

"Mandy, you're back. Good. Please take care of Miss Moses. She has the paperwork for you to get her started. She's starting tomorrow."

"Yes, sir, Mr. Lamb," Mandy replied. "I'll take care of things."

Mandy waited until the door closed behind Chandler Lamb before she addressed Zipporah.

"I see your prayers worked." She gave a half smile before turning away.

So Mandy was her name. So what happened to the smiling woman with the ugly blue eye shadow? This one still wore the ugly eye shadow but the encouraging personality was gone. This one in less than ten minutes had returned as an uppity woman with an uppity name.

Zipporah watched as Mandy strained to remain dignified. She pushed her rimless glasses down on her nose and looked again at Zipporah, this time with disapproval. She looked as though by Zipporah's very presence Zipporah had taken the building from a five-star rating to a one. Her disdain was apparent. Her true reasons for disliking Zipporah were not.

After giving Zipporah detailed instructions, Mandy led her back inside Chandler's office.

Inside the office Chandler was busy trying to do the job of human resources and guest relations. He was still rapping the pencil as he gave orders into the telephone.

"I also need you to get in touch with a Reverend Leotis Tom. Here's his number." Chandler gave the numbers hurriedly. "Apparently, several of the conference attendees have started a row in our Billie Holiday banquet room." He put down the phone and got up. He started gathering papers from his desk.

"Isn't that where the National Missionary and Mothers Board Conference is being held?" Mandy tried to suppress a smug smile at her knowledge of everything that went on at the Jaeger, but failed.

"Yes, I don't know all the facts. I sent security over there before things get completely out of hand."

"I see you have your briefcase. Are you leaving early when you finish with Miss Moses?"

"No, Mandy, I'll be back." He could tell by the way she just stood there that she needed more information. "Just so that you know, my godmother is visiting for a few days. I'm going over to her hotel to surprise her with a visit."

Zipporah listened as Chandler gave further instructions and explanations regarding what she thought should've been his personal business.

To Zipporah, the mention of the church mothers acting unseemly reminded her of the two old women she'd witnessed cutting up at the Luxor. *Whatever these women were doing in the conference room would pale compared to the antics those old women were capable of doing,* she thought. She placed a hand over her mouth to muffle a laugh. At least she didn't have to worry about running into them again. She hadn't gotten the singing job at the Luxor and she certainly wouldn't be staying there, so there was no reason their paths should ever cross.

Chandler Lamb left quickly, before Zipporah had a chance to regroup and thank him for the job. She sat mute as Mandy lay down Mandy's law. If she hadn't known better, the way the receptionist acted, Zipporah might have thought Mr. Lamb worked for Mandy.

She suddenly felt uncomfortable at the thought of Mandy being a bit overprotective of a man who looked young enough to be her son. But she needed a job and this was the first opportunity she'd had in months. Whatever the relationship between Mr. Lamb and Mandy, Zipporah's need for work was more important.

Zipporah's new job as a casino cocktail waitress was what it was, and she'd make the most of it. She'd watched other casino hostesses in their skimpy outfits with fishnet stockings and painted faces. With forced painted smiles they pranced around on aching feet and tried to ignore the unwanted touches and alcohol-laced come-ons from the big-time pretenders.

She was certain she had the figure to compete, and with a bit more makeup, she was sure to pull in enough tips. If she was intimidated by anything more, it was the idea of balancing those trays while sashaying from aisle to aisle in stilettos.

11

Sister Betty couldn't get back to the Luxor Hotel quick enough. She'd never been so embarrassed: Bea and Sasha elbowing one another and acting like common heathens. Bea's ranting. Bea comparing Sasha to the munchkins in the *Wizard of Oz* and threatening to kick her behind all up and down a Las Vegas yellow brick road.

Other indignities displayed by Bea and Sasha replayed in Sister Betty's mind. Again, she couldn't believe how unseemly they'd acted. She hadn't been that upset in quite some time. Right in front of the other National Missionary and Mothers Board members, they'd done everything to prove they were not worthy of their seats on the board.

If it weren't for the sudden appearance of the security guard, Sister Betty was certain someone would've gotten hurt during the shoving match. The proverbial straw broke when one of the female servers toppled over a chair and landed with a bowl of fruit on her head like a hat. The server's screams then brought down the head of security, who joined the other security personnel.

The head of security was a portly, middle-aged, white man. He stood erect with a scowl as he surveyed the conference room damage. His eyes narrowed while he opened and closed his fists. He looked as though he'd be adept at punching cows with his bare hands or doing likewise to the Mothers Board. He promptly informed the members that their conference luncheon was officially over. He wouldn't commit as to whether he'd recommend that the Jaeger honor their contract for the remaining two weeks. And he was bound to inform any other facility where they'd planned to hold their conference finale about their behavior.

While Sister Betty and several other women slipped out, he was still snipping away at Bea and Sasha. The two old women had stood huddled together as the head of security blasted away with spit flying everywhere. With their invisible, lopsided halos spinning, they'd tried to look pitiful. They somehow managed to look guilty, still, despite the phony tears.

While the church mothers were dismantling the conference room on the fourth floor, Zipporah took her paperwork to the departments Mandy had directed before she returned to the shelter.

Zipporah tiptoed inside the shelter and scribbled her name on the sign-in sheet. She'd made it illegible on purpose, hoping it would allow her time to make her next move. Whatever came next, she hoped it wouldn't be Miss Thompson.

Sister Betty thanked the Lord that through the goodness of a couple of strangers who had helped her to secure a cab, she'd made it back to the Luxor.

One of the first things she did was to take a quick shower. She was still tired and decided to lounge in her robe instead of dressing. She remained so put out she didn't place her cross around her neck. It lay on the dresser, but it didn't stop her from kneeling to pray.

"Lord, what is this all about? I still don't know why you have me here with all this confusion going on. You said in Your word that You were not the author of confusion. Please give me an answer before these folks make me lose my testimony."

She prayed until the tears ran down her cheeks and seeped into the corners of her mouth. She drank enough of the salty tears to elevate her high blood pressure. "I need an answer, Father God. I need an answer now."

She was about to thrash around on the hotel room floor for the third time when she thought she had finally heard God answer her. She dismissed the thought when she realized that what she'd heard was a series of light raps on her hotel suite door. She rose and for modesty sake, clutched her robe so tight only her tiny chin peeked out.

"Who is it?" She'd risen too fast and had started feeling a bit heady. She wasn't completely sure if she'd completed the sentence. She asked again, "Who's there?"

"It's me, Auntie Betty. It's your godson."

The voice sounded familiar. It was almost like hearing music playing. She tightened the grip on her robe collar and asked again, softer this time, "Who is it?"

"Auntie Betty, it's Chandler."

Without thinking she flung open the hotel door. In her excitement, her small hands let go of her robe collar as she reached out to hug him.

"Oh, my Lord." Her eyes widened as did his. Only Chandler's wide-eyed expression was followed by a loud gasp. As Sister Betty reached out to hug her godson, her robe parted. All the nakedness Eve tried to hide from God behind a fig leaf, Sister Betty exposed to the young man she'd not seen in a long time.

While Sister Betty tried to hide her embarrassment from her godson inside her Luxor Hotel suite, Sasha and Bea were on the way to bring more.

Bea and Sasha were tired. The Las Vegas heat seemed to sap every bit of energy they had. However, they kept just enough to continue arguing in the taxi ride back to the Luxor.

"Do you believe how that man spoke to you?" Sasha complained bitterly as she pointed her finger at Bea.

"He was fussing at you 'cause you started that mess." Bea swatted at Sasha's accusing finger.

Bea and Sasha argued back and forth for the entire ride. Each accusation tossed around was more unbelievable than the other. They bickered in the hotel lobby, although not as loud. Elderly or not, they had enough sense to hide their fussing behind smiles and the sunglasses they'd picked up earlier in the day. After all, they didn't know if someone would, again, want their autographs. They stood for a few moments posing in the lobby, but no one asked for their signatures or took pictures. So they continued chiding one another on the elevator. Each accused the other of bringing shame to their newly found, supposed, celebrity status.

"I'm gonna pray for you, Bea." Sasha leaned against the elevator wall as well as her cane. So much quarreling had left her wheezing as though she were having an asthma attack. She'd add more but she couldn't.

"Make sure you remove that log from your own eye before you start complaining about me to the Lord." Bea was in no better condition.

Sasha was the first one to get off the elevator. As usual, she waddled her tiny behind directly in Bea's direction. Tired or not, Sasha was always determined to have the last say so.

All Bea could offer was a weak, "Make sure you have your butt downstairs on time this evening. We're supposed to lead the prayers if they change their minds and let us back in the conference center."

Of course, things only got worse. Bea had forgotten her room number, and of course, her perpetually weak bladder wasn't cooperating or trying to wait until she remembered. She searched her pockets for her keycard and then finally remembered that Sasha was holding it. She'd given it to her earlier so she wouldn't lose it. Now she was about to lose her dignity if her Depends pad didn't hold out. Somehow she'd managed to remember which room Sasha was in. Why she could remember 666 and not remember her own room, she didn't know.

Her eyes were immediately drawn to a small figure down the hall. It was Sasha. She was fussing and knocking at the hotel door with her cane. She was so mad she didn't care that Bea was suddenly standing next to her.

It was another few minutes before they finally figured out that Sasha was trying to enter her room with Bea's keycard.

Bea was about to snatch her keycard from Sasha's hand when she actually had a lucid moment and lied her way out of her own situation. "I knew you'd need my help. You looked so tired so I decided to offer my assistance." Bea fumbled her words trying to make the lie work.

Sasha was too tired to argue with Bea's silliness. Instead, she kept quiet and used the correct keycard to enter her room.

If Sasha hadn't been so exhausted and had paid closer attention, she'd have noticed that Bea was now hopping around like a bunny on crack. But she didn't. So when Sasha pulled the keycard out and the little green light on the door clicked and opened, Bea spun into action.

The clicking sound was all Bea needed to hear to send her bladder into overdrive. Bea shoved Sasha aside and raced inside Sasha's bathroom. She'd forgotten or didn't care that Sasha didn't offer folks the use of her own bathroom back in Pelzer. Bea depositing anything other than money in her hotel bathroom was unacceptable.

When Bea sheepishly came out of Sasha's bathroom it was on.

"You old cow, who told you that you could use my bathroom?" Sasha's eyes grew large as she, as usual, raised her cane in Bea's direction.

"Well, heifer, would you have rather I raised one leg and squirted your door?" Bea's energy was renewed by the visit to the bathroom even if her clarity wasn't. She swatted Sasha's cane aside like she would a fly.

"You couldn't even raise anything if you tried."

Sasha was wrong. Bea could raise something and so could she. They were at it again. Only this time they raised more hell.

If they didn't have separate hotel rooms, they'd have torn down the Luxor.

12

"Have mercy, I'm so embarrassed." It took Sister Betty several tries just to get her slip over her head. She could've stepped into it but she was still upset. "Lord, I've shown him parts of me that no man except You has seen since my youth."

No matter how much Sister Betty babbled from inside the other part of her hotel suite, it didn't matter. It'd taken her almost ten minutes trying to get over her embarrassment of having her godson see her nakedness. As for Chandler, he wasn't sure if he ever would.

While his godmother struggled in the other room to put on clothes and a straight face, Chandler stood at the hotel room window and looked over the Las Vegas skyline.

It was no sense trying to pretend he didn't feel embarrassment; he certainly did. However, he also felt love for his godmother. She and his grandmother, Ma Cile, had been friends since his mother's youth. He smiled as he recalled the time he and his cousin Lil Bit argued over whether or not Sister Betty had received a telephone call from Jesus. He'd argued that she hadn't and of course, Lil Bit said she had. Ma Cile dispensed a whipping that day. She'd set their little butts on fire and threatened to burn the ashes. It made whether they believed the telephone story or not a mute point.

"I'm back. Sorry it took me so long."

Chandler turned around slowly just in case she'd forgotten to close a clasp or left something unbuttoned.

They chatted as though everything was fine although the cloud of embarrassment still hung. She offered to order room service and fussed about him as though he were still that young boy she'd affectionately called June Bug.

"So, June Bug, tell me how you've made out here in Las Vegas."

"I hope you don't plan on calling me June Bug when we're in public," he teased. "I'm a grown man and you might give the ladies the wrong impression."

"Wouldn't wanna do that." Her eyes finally twinkled as they always did when the two of them were together or chatted.

"Why are you visiting Las Vegas? You didn't give me any particulars in the voice message you left," he said.

"I know you must be surprised that I even learned how to leave a message on one of those answering machines. Ever since I moved into that la-di-da neighborhood, I don't do too many things on my own."

"I saw the pictures of the house. It's fabulous and I'm so happy Mother Eternal loved enough to provide for you and my grandmother."

Sister Betty and Chandler spent the next hour or so reminiscing over some of the childhood pranks he was famous for or blamed for committing. It was the first time in several days when her mind wasn't focused on the Mothers Board or her main nemeses, Bea and Sasha. She was also delighted that he had finally settled down after seemingly losing himself as a promoter in the music industry.

"Didn't you work for one of those record companies?"

"Yes, I did. I almost sold out to the devil," Chandler declared sadly. "It's a business where truth seldom wins and it's the first one to the crap pile who eats less of it." He sounded angry and ashamed, and he was.

"Well," Sister Betty finally asked after hearing his story, "are you still saved?"

"Somewhat." That's all he could say. "I guess I'm just somewhat."

Some other time she would've used this opportunity to preach to him. She'd let him know that God always welcomed the prodigal son and that he was justified by his acceptance of Jesus. She'd remind him that God was married to the backslider. Opening her Bible, she'd have pointed out how in the book of Psalms, when David ran to God in worship and confession, God always forgave him. But all she could do was sit and listen to Chandler talk about what had occurred in his life over the past several years.

"And, forget about marriage or much of a dating life. . . ."

He hadn't realized that her mind had momentarily drifted until she'd yawned and asked him to repeat what he'd said.

"I was talking about women." He laughed, knowing that he probably made her feel a little uncomfortable mentioning something so worldly.

"You'd better hurry up and get a wife. You know Ma Cile wants great-grandchildren." She winked and stifled another yawn at the same time. She didn't realize how tired she still was.

The poor attempt at disguising her tiredness hadn't escaped him. "Listen, I left a mess of a situation back at the conference center. I need to see about it." He stood and offered his hand to help her to her feet. Ignoring her feeble protest about wanting him to stay, he kissed her on her cheek.

Suddenly, she was grateful she hadn't mentioned that she'd been a part of that mess. She'd repent later. "Okay, if you must leave, you make sure that we get together again."

"We'll get together and have dinner, I promise. I'd love to show you Sin City." His voice grew deeper as he mentioned the word *sin*.

"You need prayer." She couldn't resist giving a playful tap to his hand to show her supposed disapproval at his choice of words.

Chandler laughed at her rebuke and made sure he heard her lock the door before moving on. He had already pushed the elevator button before he realized she'd never said why she was in Las Vegas. The elevator door opened and he promptly forgot about it.

For an unknown reason thoughts about the young woman he'd interviewed earlier took over. She wasn't particularly his type. She was pretty enough, so that wasn't it. However, she'd be working as a cocktail waitress in the casino. He didn't have time to wait for a woman to arrive at his station in life, or at least to make the type of money he now earned. He didn't want to take the time to see if there were any other ambitions. He was a "right now" man. By the time the elevator landed at the lobby floor, he'd decided Zipporah Moses was just another pretty face and nothing more.

13

Sasha took her time nibbling on a cracker and drinking the hotel's weak tea she'd made. Her mood was considerably better after a night's rest. She wore a wide grin as she looked in the mirror. She'd showered and put on the hotel-issued robe. It was much too big, although the tag read, "Small." It was the first time she'd had an opportunity to look around her hotel room. It was lavish in comparison to the scantily furnished home she owned in Pelzer.

It didn't take long before Sasha found herself bored. The Bible she carried but seldom read lay abandoned on the coffee table. She tossed about the idea of whether to carry it to the conference center or use one of the Bibles she saw in a pile there yesterday. She then remembered that she didn't know if the conference would continue there. What could she do to pass the time? Before she could decide, she heard soft taps at the door and someone say, "Hello, I'm here to clean your room."

"And it's about time." Sasha stood slowly as though opening a door took great planning. After Bea had used her bathroom she refused to use the toilet in it until it was cleaned again. Of course, she wasn't about to do it herself. So she'd had hotel services send a maid. She'd claimed the maid had done a poor job earlier, and she wanted it redone immediately. How her lie impacted the job of the already overworked maid wasn't a consideration.

"Come on in so you can get started." Sasha barely looked at the woman. If the woman had robbed her she couldn't have given a description.

"How are you, today? Can I get you anything, Miss Pray Onn?"

Sasha didn't answer, preferring to ignore the woman, as if replying would break the maid's concentration.

Whether Sasha answered or not didn't seem to faze the maid. She went about her work, ignoring Sasha, too. To pass the time while the woman worked, Sasha picked up her Bible from the table. When she thought the maid was not looking she'd peer over it and watch.

The woman looked almost as old as Sasha. She was certainly as thin. Everything the maid did seemed to be methodical. If nothing else she was organized.

When she was finished, she again asked Sasha if there was anything further she needed. "Do you need an extra towel or anything?"

"No." Sasha didn't look up. She kept her eyes upon the page of her Bible.

"Well, you have a blessed day," the maid said as she suddenly started humming a hymn. And then she stopped.

"Miss Pray Onn."

"What?"

"Bible is upside down." And with that said she walked out of the hotel room still singing the praises of God.

Sasha's face turned red, almost dark red. Her blood boiled from the embarrassment. The maid was right. The entire time she'd tried to make herself seem superior her Bible was upside down in her hands.

In the meantime, down the hall, Bea was keeping out of trouble by sleeping as much as she could. She'd tried experimenting the night before by mixing several different herbal teas she'd discovered in the room. Like a bad dream those teas had started to return like the gift that just kept on giving. It was like a chain reaction. Every time the tea returned and caused her stomach to growl, she rushed to the bathroom. Now she was starting to feel a sense of normalcy, and it was almost noon.

One of the first things Bea noticed when she finally got herself together was the blinking light on the telephone. She wasn't sure what it was for so she ignored it. There was a note slid under her door that informed her that the housekeeping services would be offered again later. Apparently, she'd slept through any knocking on her door.

In the meantime, things for Sasha had worsened. The embarrassment of pretending to read a Bible upside down, a blow to her ego, was nothing compared to the phone call she'd just received from the Reverend Leotis Tom. His words did nothing to soothe her surly mood. He spoke to her as though she were a child and not the president of the Mothers Board. And how dare he insinuate that the conference was about to be cancelled and it was hers and Bea's fault.

"I resent the implication that Bea and I would do anything to sully the reputation of Crossing Over Sanctuary Temple," she'd told the reverend. "I imagine no one mentioned the fact that your beloved Sister Betty was also there."

She'd hoped he'd taken it just the way she'd meant it. He did and she didn't like his response.

"Just like Jesus told Peter when he asked about John—what's it to you? Everything you do is a reflection on me and this congregation. Mother Sasha, I'm surprised that you would bring dishonor on us."

Sasha had listened, half-heartedly, to the reverend as he continued his telephone sermon. He'd droned on and on about morality, and hers in particular. All the while she'd bounced her cane softly on the floor as if she were pounding him. It wasn't until he'd mentioned the possibility of her and Bea returning early, if the conference center decided to cancel the event, that she'd paid full attention. With that last threat she'd promised to make Bea behave. She still hadn't taken responsibility for her actions.

They'd barely been there two days and already Sasha and Bea were on the verge of giving their home church and Las Vegas a bad name.

When Sasha and Bea met up later Sasha gave her edited version of the warning call from Reverend Tom. In the end, each promised that they needed to do whatever was necessary to keep from bringing more trouble to the already troubled National Mothers Board Conference.

And for some reason known only to them, they decided to go to the conference center and apologize to see if it would heal things. They also made a decision that they would stop in the conference center casino—after all, healing had its cost. According to them there would be souls that needed saving and even

Jesus went to the sinners. That was their excuse and they were stuck with it.

Zipporah tried to rest but the excitement of finally having a job was too much. She'd also discovered quite by accident that Miss Thompson would be away for several days. For that Zipporah was grateful.

She styled her hair, applied her makeup carefully, and rechecked her bag to make sure everything she needed was packed. Her new uniform, the stockings, and her orientation book lay neatly folded inside.

Earlier, Zipporah had decided to forego the usual shelter breakfast of cardboard-tasting no-frills cereal. The meal seldom varied with the exception of an occasional two-day-old bread and cheese sandwich and coffee thick enough to sop with a biscuit like molasses. The combination often left her feeling bloated and quite often confined to her room and/or a bathroom.

Giving God another quick prayer of thanks, she checked the time. Her schedule required her to be at work about a half hour early but she decided to make it a little earlier to be on the safe side.

She'd soon discover that there was nothing safe.

14

It was barely four o'clock in the afternoon. False hopes of big fortunes permeated the air inside the conference center's noisy casino. Daydreams of hitting the *big one* hovered over every player. Every so often an excited squeal was heard over the *clang-clang* sound of a winning slot machine. Folks dressed in everything from couture to shorts were two to three deep around the roulette, craps, and poker tables.

Every method from kissing the dice to playing a supposed favorite number, no matter how many times it didn't come through, was used. The banks of slot machines were the noisiest. Blue- and silver-haired seniors commandeered the nickel slots. Most of them weren't above pinching and fighting if they thought their hard-earned pensions were threatened. The imaginary threats generally followed someone accusing someone else of taking a lucky seat or a machine.

That particular afternoon many couples were seated at the bank of slot machines playing side by side. So far, there was harmony even among those who scrambled off from their planted positions to get more coins to use. Customarily one of the couple would play his or her own slot machine while trying to keep an eye on the partner's, until he or she returned.

However, it was Bea and Sasha who arrived as a threesome; they'd brought Armageddon along, too, as they sat down to sermonize and witness while playing the slots.

Two lemons and a cherry had barely made it to one of the winning lines when all hell broke loose inside the casino. It started when Bea sat down and then immediately had to get up to use the bathroom. She'd already dropped in her five nickels and asked Sasha to watch her machine until she returned.

Unfortunately for Bea, Sasha didn't feel in the mood to watch the machine. She purposely kept her back turned as Bea walked away, not noticing another woman sit down at Bea's unattended machine. The elderly woman who'd commandeered the machine had a pasty complexion and dyed blue hair. She was long and lean and wore a pair of white-rimmed, octagon-shaped frames that she immediately yanked off. She narrowed her eyes until they almost sank into her pudgy, freckled face. Like an owl with a tic, her head swung back and forth. She'd realized that there were several unplayed coins in the machine. So she did what anyone would in that situation . . . she pulled the lever.

That woman might as well have pushed the button on the red phone in the Oval Office. The results were just as deadly.

A musical rendition of "We're in the Money" rang out from the slot machine. The ticking sound of a winning money voucher printing from the slot machine caught the attention of several nearby players. The old woman stared at the machine with her jaw dropped as the alert light on its top flashed. Finally she cried out, "I've won! I've won!"

Dashing over from the left side, one of the casino attendants, with a fully loaded keychain dangling from her hand, parted the sea of onlookers. She was a young woman whose smile seemed as practiced and as sincere as a used car salesperson's. She'd barely gotten within a few feet of the winning slot when her grin shifted to horror.

And Sasha barely had enough time or room to shift her weight on her stool when she, too, started to squeal.

Bea sprinted by with her white skirt billowing about her hips and ankles like a storm cloud. Her back hunched over, looking like the Jets running back Curtis Martin, Bea rushed the slot machine. She snatched her unattended cardboard coin cup and was about to go to work. She was about to do some serious damage.

The woman's laughter stopped. Her heart almost stopped, too, at the sight of the big, black woman, with the killer eyes and attitude to match barreling down upon her. Bea towered over that woman like a female Shaka Zulu and the coin cup was her lethal spear.

"Drop my money or die!" Bea hissed as she suddenly straightened her crooked spine without feeling the pain. "I ain't asking twice."

The woman didn't hang around long enough for Bea to ask

twice. She not only left Bea's bucket with the quarters but left her own as a tribute.

In the meantime, the casino worker inched her way closer to Bea and without so much as a "congratulations," she switched off the alert sign, opened the slot machine, and wrote down some numbers on a pad. "I'll be back with your winnings."

"The heck you will," Bea snapped. "Doggone thieves around here won't let you have nothing. I'm coming with you. You're gonna give me my money and it'd better be correct."

All the time the drama was unfolding, Sasha looked on. She was trying to see exactly what the machine paid without being obvious. But she couldn't. She was too short and nearsighted to do so without giving away her intention. Instead she used her cane and poked Bea.

"Bea, sweetie, how much did you win?"

And that's when Bea realized that she didn't know. She tossed her head to the side, back and forth. "How much do I get from this machine?" she asked the casino floor worker.

The young woman looked down at the pad in her shaking hands and said, "You've won fifty dollars in this nickel machine."

"Fifty dollars," Sasha barked. "You raised all this Cain over fifty dollars?" Sasha started cackling. "That's a doggone shame."

And that's when Bea saw another stranger lean over from his stool next to Sasha's now unoccupied seat. The stranger hurriedly placed some coins in Sasha's machine so he could play two of them at one time.

"You are absolutely right, Sasha." Bea grinned and immediately apologized to the still-frightened casino floor worker before turning back to Sasha and adding sarcastically, "I know you wouldn't act the same way if someone tried to steal your machine and money."

"That's right. I wouldn't act crazy. I'm too saved to act so country and undignified." Sasha gave a mock grin and acted humble to add further validity to her claim of salvation while gambling.

Once again, the *clang-clang* sound of a winning machine rang out. Sasha's head spun around quicker than the rest of her body, almost giving her whiplash. The man was about to start scooping the receipts from the well of the machine when he felt the wrath of Sasha descend upon him like a plague.

Sasha squealed, "Give me strength, Lord."

The poor man hopped around howling, "Help me, Jesus."

Sasha snatched her coin bucket and whipped that man so bad that when she finished the poor man looked at the machine and thought he saw fruit salad. His eyes were so swollen all the cherries, oranges, bananas, and dollar signs looked blended together.

And that's when the same head of security from their earlier fracas appeared.

And while Bea and Sasha were in the casino doing what Bea and Sasha always did, Sister Betty was on her way down.

An automated voice announced, "Casino floor," inside the elevator.

As Sister Betty started to exit the elevator she turned and saw the look of disapproval etched on the faces of the other mothers from the Mothers Board who'd ridden with her. Their collective looks of disapproval embedded within the folds and lines of crowfeet, feminine whiskers, and latent menopausal tendencies were sobering. She was so embarrassed she told them that floor had the closest bathroom.

The brocade fabric wall outside the casino bathroom was the only support Sister Betty felt, as she crept along. She'd promised Chandler that she'd meet him for an early dinner and now felt sorry she had. He'd never mentioned that she'd have to go through the casino in order to get to the restaurant.

Why in the world would she jeopardize her good standing within the church by going inside a casino? As many times as she'd thrust Bible tracts into the hands of wayward people as she stood guard outside bars, strip joints, and other places of ill repute, she'd never entered any of those places. But now she had to go through the casino to get to the restaurant on the other side, and the church folks, the real church folks, had seen her. Her feet seemed mired as though she were walking through mud. In her mind, her spiritual body would be like a magnet. Sin would cling to her very essence.

"Do you need help?" Zipporah had only arrived at the casino floor twenty minutes before when she saw the elderly woman. The old woman looked lost. Zipporah knew that lost look when she saw it. She'd worn that look practically every day, for most of her adult life, in the place of makeup.

Sister Betty looked pained as she looked up to see where the voice came from. Her body, without her permission, took an authoritative stance. What kind of outfit was that she wore? Sister Betty wondered. The young woman was wearing a tiny piece of pleated black fabric that was supposed to cover her hips but did not. And, why did she wear fishnet stockings? Sister Betty knew what they were because there was a time in her life when she had worn them, too. She also thought the young woman wore too much makeup. Everything about her caused Sister Betty discomfort.

And there was something else. The young woman looked familiar, yet Sister Betty was certain they'd never met.

Zipporah's attention was drawn away by a not-too-subtle hand wave from one of the gamblers at a nearby craps table. Whatever the old woman's problem, it couldn't come before her job.

Zipporah sauntered toward the man. Her walk held a promise that she had no intention of keeping. Of course, the gambler knew it but the view was worth the tip he'd give her.

Zipporah took his order and gave him a complimentary smile. When she brought back his drink she used the stirrer in a seductive manner to further mix the drink before handing it to him. He'd let his fingers linger just a second longer than she'd have liked but it was quickly followed by a five-dollar tip. She placed it slowly in the little waist pack she wore in such a manner as to let him know that she'd be happy to bring him another.

No sooner had Zipporah turned to answer the beckoning hand of another gambler than she was almost knocked to the ground. She'd been accidentally tripped by an elderly man who was fighting with an elderly woman. Zipporah fought to retain her balance. Gripping the side of a stool, she immediately recognized the old woman. She was one of the pair of seniors posing as Hollywood actresses in front of the Luxor the day before.

I knew those old crows were trouble, she thought. Her mind raced. Was the world completely occupied by troublemaking old folks? Her first day on the job and already she had unwarranted attention. And that's when she saw the rip in one of her fishnet stockings. The tore went from her knee to her upper thigh. Cuss words spew from her mouth before she could stop them. She hadn't spoken loud but she certainly made an impression on the man standing behind her.

"Never lose your professional cool. It never works."

Chandler saw embarrassment replace the anger on Zipporah's

face as she jerked around. No doubt she'd been prepared to cuss him out. "Don't worry. Your first-day goofs, if not too serious, are always forgiven."

"Thanks." That was about as much as she could say without following it with expletives. She accepted his hand as he extended it to help.

Zipporah tried to pull together the netting on her hosiery. It was useless. "I can't believe those old women can be so much trouble."

"I can." He smiled as he crossed his arms, admiring the area on her thigh where the hosiery was torn. Not wanting to embarrass her any further with his wanton stares, he turned around. It was just in time for him to come face-to-face with security as they were leading the old woman toward the casino's exit.

Sasha struggled against the grip of the younger man. "You'd better let me go. I'll pray for God's vengeance."

"Has that ever worked for you before?" the guard replied. He was foolish enough to think he had the answers and the upper hand.

From a few feet away Sasha heard a familiar voice. She suddenly stopped struggling. With her free hand, she adjusted her glasses to see clearly.

"Oh, my goodness," she shouted. "Bea, come here."

"I'm coming, Sasha." Bea was hustling faster than she would have if she'd had the urge to use the bathroom. "Oh, my goodness, I can't believe it. It's June Bug."

Bea descended upon Chandler, pawing and kissing him. Zipporah stood mute. She couldn't move or believe what she saw. Those two old women knew Chandler Lamb.

With the agility of a much younger woman, Sasha yanked her other hand from the grip of the stunned security guard. She did it so easily it took a second for the guard to recover. He wondered who had been holding whom.

"June Bug, baby, is this you?! Oh, my Lord." Bea was beaming as she hugged him to her breast. "I can't believe it's you."

"Mother Blister, you're squeezing me." He wasn't sure if her calling him June Bug was what embarrassed him, or the massive hug. Either way, whatever embarrassment he felt was about to be kicked up a notch.

Sasha managed to step on the poor security guard's foot as she strutted and parted the sea of geriatric onlookers with her cane.

"Is this my June Bug?" She knew exactly who he was but she wanted the crowd to think they were closer than he and Bea.

"Praise the Lord, Mothers." He tried to prod them toward the side exit door. But they wouldn't budge.

Instead, they circled Chandler. "Your Aunt Betty didn't tell us you were here in Las Vegas," Sasha scolded. "You'd think her and your grandma, Ma Cile, were the only ones who cared about you."

"That's right," Bea chimed in. "You know everybody loves June Bug."

But everybody didn't always love June Bug. Chandler remembered there were many times when both Mothers Blister and Pray Onn would lie in wait by the church exit. The two feisty old women would ambush him. They'd accuse him of doing things both imaginary and often real that would require they lay hands on him. There was one time, in particular. Mother Pray Onn, barely taller than him at his age of twelve, whacked him so hard across his shoulders it caused him to cry out to God. It was the first time he'd done so and meant it.

The sight of Sister Betty's shocked look as she stood just outside the casino exit stopped Chandler's momentary visit to his past. All he could do was shrug his shoulders and give her a half smile showing his amusement and concession. He'd done the same to Zipporah but she'd left. He didn't know why but at that particular moment, he was more concerned about Zipporah's image of him. Had she heard the old women call him June Bug?

"You handle your business, June Bug." The taunt came from two tables away from where they stood. There was no longer any doubt that most of the casino had heard him called June Bug. He was almost ashamed to admit that while he had Bea and Sasha in his grasp, he wanted to wring their necks.

One look at the pretended innocence on Bea and Sasha's faces confirmed Chandler's secret desire. He definitely wanted to wring their necks, just not in front of more than three hundred witnesses in the casino.

What Chandler didn't realize was that he could've done it and gotten away with it. There wasn't a patron there who didn't want to do the same thing to Bea and Sasha.

15

While Chandler dealt with the craziness inside the casino with the old women, Zipporah had slipped away into the restroom. She was glad to find it empty. There was no need in looking at the hosiery. They were ruined. Every six weeks, she was supposed to receive a uniform allowance in her meager check. She'd only started working three hours ago and already she'd have to find a way to replace a part of her uniform.

Zipporah didn't think twice about rebuking her thoughts of strangling those old women until the sun set and rose again. And, if she had thought twice about it, it didn't last long. No sooner had she looked up than she saw Bea's reflection in the mirror over the sink. The old woman was staring at her, not in a mean way but in an odd one, nonetheless.

"You okay?" Bea stared, still trying to remember where or if she'd seen the young woman before. "It looks like you got a run in your stockings."

Zipporah looked at Bea. She didn't return the woman's kindly look with one of her own. Instead, she was about to light into a litany of reasons why within the past couple of days she considered the old woman to be stalking her. Everywhere she turned, she and that other ball of gray-haired spitfire were there descending upon her world.

"I'm all right." Perhaps if she kept her response to a minimum the old woman would just disappear.

But this was Bea Blister. The only thing disappearing in her life was her monies and much of her memory.

Bea had become so preoccupied with the young woman she'd forgotten why she came into the bathroom. She went over to the sink and started washing her hands as if she'd completed her bathroom mission. She was certain it was the same person she'd seen at the hotel, the restaurant, and now the casino.

"I don't mean to intrude, honey." She did mean to do it but she had manners, and it was such a small lie. "Have you ever been to Pelzer, South Carolina?"

Zipporah didn't want any further discussions but once again, she deluded herself into thinking that a one- or two-word answer would make the old woman disappear. At the very least, make her quit asking questions. "No."

"Well, do you have any family there?" Bea was persistent. There was something familiar about the young woman. "I've seen you somewhere."

You're everywhere I turn, Zipporah thought. She didn't bother to answer. She grabbed her small bag to leave. She needed to go to her locker and change into her one extra pair of fishnets. She threw a disapproving look at the old woman, who just stood there with a quizzical one of her own.

Just when Zipporah thought things couldn't get any worse, they did. She stepped through the door and straight into the path of Chandler and the other old woman.

"I think you should take your break now." Chandler had spoken before he'd meant to do so. Something about the pretty woman was getting to him. He'd only met her less than twenty-four hours ago and already their paths had crossed more than he'd liked. "I'll let the floor manager know I authorized it."

"Thank you." Zipporah was in a one-word response mode. Without thinking, again, she tried to clutch the torn area covering her thighs.

"And don't worry about replacing those with your own money. I'm sure the ones responsible will see that it's covered." He glanced down at Sasha.

Sasha turned and looked around. She wanted to know who Chandler was referring to. "June Bug, why are you looking at me?"

His face reddened and he clenched his fists. It was as though all his diplomacy was about to exit, leaving the door open for a little *street* to come in. Why didn't they stop calling him by a name he hated even when he was young, and still did?

Zipporah saw Chandler's embarrassment. For a brief moment she felt hers paled in comparison. *June Bug,* she thought as she stifled a smile. What kind of name was that and why in the world would someone place it upon him?

"Thank you, Mr. Lamb. I'm okay. But I think I will take that break," she said somewhat stiffly. If she stuck to her rule of distancing herself, she'd survive. He was way out of her league and she had enough problems. No way she'd leave herself open to more.

That's the excuse Zipporah told herself. The truth was that she really didn't want to have anything to do with anyone connected to those old women. She knew trouble when it came and those two women, no doubt, invented pandemonium.

Sister Betty was still watching from nearby. She wasn't quite certain if Chandler, Bea, or Sasha had seen her. If they hadn't that was fine with her. She wasn't comfortable being so close to a casino and she'd let Chandler know that when they dined.

Sister Betty continued her watch while resting against the far wall. She concentrated on the young woman standing in a bit of disarray in front of Chandler. There was something eerily familiar about the woman. She knew her godson. Although she couldn't hear what was said, she read his actions clearly. *Chandler likes her,* she thought. And for a brief moment, the thought made her smile.

If Zipporah wanted to spend another moment in Chandler's presence, it was cut short by the reappearance of the other old woman, Bea.

"Oh, you know June Bug?" Bea had barely stepped out of the ladies' room before heaping more embarrassment upon Chandler.

Zipporah almost couldn't help it that time. She gulped, forcing down the urge to laugh. She felt torn between her need to escape the perpetual mayhem the old women tossed about like a game of ping-pong and her pity for Chandler.

Zipporah chose to walk away, leaving them to work out whatever dysfunctional relationship they had. She needed to keep her job.

"That was just plain ol' rude," Bea hissed. And that's when it hit her. She knew why the young woman looked familiar.

"Sasha," Bea snapped. "Didn't that young gal look like somebody we know?"

"No." Sasha's eyes squinted, causing her face to twitch and

her glasses to slide down upon her nose. "She don't look like nobody I know."

Chandler hadn't seen those two old women in quite some time but he'd known them long enough to know that Sasha was lying. He'd seen that same look upon her face when she used to lie during testimony service and at other times.

For a moment, Chandler forgot his own embarrassment as he spied Sister Betty leaning against the far wall.

"I've got to leave. Do you two promise to behave?" Chandler followed his request with a quick wink to take the sting out.

"She promises." Sasha, again, tossed Bea under the proverbial bus as she feigned innocence.

"Ooh, I can't wait for the meeting to begin," Bea snapped. Her threat to Sasha was real. Her only problem would be in remembering what she was going to do at the meeting later that evening if indeed it was going to happen. No one had made a decision or shared it with her. But whenever she got the opportunity she'd get Sasha with whatever would cause Sasha pain.

16

Zipporah managed to change the torn hosiery and return to the casino floor just in time to catch the beginnings of the late afternoon gamblers.

Trying to make up for the hour she'd lost as well as the tips, Zipporah strutted up and down the banks of slot machines. The aisles became her catwalk as she modeled her desperation, hidden by forced smiles and pleasantries. She even returned smiles and nods as many of the men offered their own false promises with bold leers. It wasn't just the old men acting ridiculous, the young ones were, too.

Several of the young men got out of hand, seeming to feel as though it was their duty to grant themselves access to her. They shamelessly grabbed at Zipporah with an unsolicited or an "I'm ready for you and my drink" accidental touch.

She wasn't a stripper with pasties or an enormous fan of feathers peeking from behind her, but Zipporah felt as though she were. But in the entertainment business the show *must* go on. So Zipporah tucked away the shame she'd begun to feel in the recesses of her mind, perhaps for another day. She moved to the throbbing rhythm of a headache. Already the job was becoming a love-hate relationship, at best.

Chandler and Sister Betty sat at a table for two off to the side away from the patron traffic. Chandler leaned across the table and moved aside a slender crystal lamp offering only enough light for the diners to read a menu. The lighting was meant to underplay any imperfections or to give privacy to some who might need it.

"I'm sorry," Chandler whispered. He'd apologized several

times between bites as he dined with Sister Betty. "I wasn't thinking. It never occurred to me that you'd be uncomfortable walking through a casino."

He tried to add a little humor to his apology. He smiled and said, "After all, didn't Jesus walk through a casino when he chased out those money changers?" From the look on her face, he'd failed.

"It was a temple," Sister Betty hissed. She surprised herself with her curt reply. "Don't try changing the Bible to get out of this mess."

"When she's better you're not going to tell my grandmother, are you?" Chandler was determined to turn around the situation even if he had to stand on his head and sing.

"You know she'd kick your behind if she weren't in that hospital." The thought of Ma Cile before her stroke standing over Chandler when he was a young boy with a switch caused her to chuckle. Laughter was the blanket for their pain whenever they talked about Ma Cile. "You remember that time when you and your cousin Lil Bit argued over whether or not God had called me on the telephone?"

"How could I forget?" Chandler laughed. "I couldn't sit or hardly stand for several days. Ma Cile beat the black off me."

"I know." Sister Betty chuckled. "That's why you have such a smooth brown complexion now."

The mood had lightened. His mission was accomplished, almost. Although, the thought of Ma Cile languishing in a hospital was always a lingering cloud he'd learned to live with.

"I need a favor." Chandler placed down his fork and gently reached for one of Sister Betty's small hands. He looked lovingly, like the good little godson he was, into her eyes and kissed the hand.

"You're about to set me up, aren't you?" She knew it and at that moment, she'd have given him anything. Chandler had always been the son she'd lost at an early age. "What do you need?"

"Will you please—" He stopped to look around. He didn't want anyone to overhear his request.

"Go on, Chandler." She was starting to get a little nervous. He seemed very serious.

Turning back to her, Chandler continued. "I need for you, Mothers Blister and Pray Onn . . ."

"What do those two have to do with me?" Sister Betty didn't realize she was trying to yank her hand from his. He held on tight.

"I'm not trying to put your salvation in the same vein as theirs." He knew what she was thinking. "I just need for all of you to please stop calling me June Bug."

"Say what?"

"Aunt Betty, I'm a grown man. When y'all call me June Bug in public, it's embarrassing."

"Is that it?" Sister Betty started laughing so hard she almost lost her dentures and was drawing attention to their table.

"What's so funny?" Chandler asked as he looked around at the other diners now focusing on his table.

"I'm okay. I just thought you were going to ask me to do something with Bea and Sasha." She stopped chuckling long enough to wipe her mouth with her napkin and then emit a sigh of relief.

"Well, there is just one more, tiny thing. . . ." Chandler leaned in closer to Sister Betty and continued speaking.

When Chandler finished, Sister Betty's eyes grew wide. Without meaning to do so, her tiny fist hit the table. She was surprised at her anger but not able to stop it.

"June Bug, have you lost your mind? I'm not investing in the Devil's music."

And just like in the television commercial, most of the other diners stopped in midbites as the name *June Bug* echoed around the restaurant.

Chandler's smile slid and his shoulders sunk. Suddenly, he felt like the little boy who always seemed to be in trouble. However, now he was a grown man, and when it came to trouble, not a lot had changed.

17

The next morning, Bea laid aside her anger with Sasha and called her. Together, they'd contacted some of the other church mothers and apologized for their behavior and that it caused a small setback in their conference plans.

They'd already decided that they'd apologize to the conference center manager, too. They would return, early, to the conference center and eat however much crow was needed to put things back on track. In their minds, it wouldn't be good business for the conference center to cancel the conference after their performance. Bea and Sasha were confident that their apology would be successful, so they told the other mothers that the conference was back on even before they'd left the hotel.

Knowing that nothing ever went as planned, Bea and Sasha also decided that if they didn't arrive in time to see management and apologize, they'd act as though they thought the conference was still on. And, if the management insisted it wasn't, they'd act like the crazy old women they were.

Bea arrived alone. No matter what she'd told Sasha, she was still a little miffed and didn't want to share a cab with her.

Bea sat on a small red velvet sofa that looked like a replica of a sombrero, inside the conference center lobby. She was dressed in her proper Mothers Board attire. Her skirt was white but not the same shade of white as her blouse. For Bea it was typical. If she ever wore anything that matched or complemented her plus-sized figure, it was by accident. There was even a slight run in her stocking that had the shiny evidence of clear nail polish. It was an old trick most of the older women used to repair a snag or a run.

As the other members of the Mothers Board arrived and went

through the lobby, Bea nodded appreciatively toward some and completely ignored others. And the same was done to her. Every one of the women had her own agenda.

A few of the mothers actually came to network and see how they could improve their ministries. They were the newest members and stood out immediately. They were mostly in their early sixties and full of hope. "Ain't God good?" they'd asked, clutching the straps of their Bible tote bags, inscribed with the words WOMEN OF GOD, stitched with bold-colored threads.

Then there were some mothers and a few missionaries who wanted the other women to know that they were avid Bible readers. Their Bibles had bookmarks placed throughout the pages. They'd come prepared with the appropriate Bible verses memorized and just the right amount of indignation to use readily on anyone or any situation they didn't deem appropriate. The one thing they all had in common was the Mothers Board member war kit.

The war kit always contained a small Bible for practical use and a larger one for show. The kit also had small vials of blessed oil.

Only Bea and Sasha carried their precious demon chaser and blessing enhancer liquid in a spray can. It was something they'd decided to do before they'd left Pelzer. In their minds the spray canister would serve a dual purpose. They could spray away evil spirits, ensure blessings, and spray any ashy ankles they saw, with just a few squirts of the flammable liquid. With their quick tempers the spray canisters were lethal weapons. Bea and Sasha were more than capable of setting a place or person on fire while ignoring their own particular sins.

Bea kept looking around for Sasha, but she wasn't there, and by now it was too late to find management and apologize. *I could apologize without her,* Bea thought as she sat on the edge of the sofa, *but it's her fault we're in this mess.* With her mind set on Sasha taking the blame, Bea didn't budge.

While the other mothers laughed and heaped their sage advice upon each other, Bea continued to ponder. Earlier, she'd finally realized why the strange young woman looked so familiar. She didn't know why she hadn't seen it before. She also didn't know why Sasha would lie about not noticing the same thing. It was so obvious. The young woman looked like she could've been Sasha's niece Ima's twin sister.

Sasha's niece, Ima Hellraiser, had that same mocha complexion, the same beautiful almond-shaped hazel eyes, and both young women had shapes that rivaled any Victoria's Secret model. However, there was a huge difference in their demeanors from the little Bea had seen.

The true carrier of Sasha's DNA, Ima Hellraiser, was a witch on wheels. True to the Hellraiser genes, Ima wasn't happy unless she was causing pain. At one point in her life Ima could've taught S and M to the Marquis de Sade. During their recent cruise vacation Bea had witnessed another side to Ima. Ima had met a young man, a minister, aboard the ship and obviously fell head over heels. Of course, true to form, Ima had doused the romance fire before it'd barely ignited. Ima couldn't keep a man if she and the man were Siamese twins.

"You're too good to ride in the same car with me?" The voice was snippy, almost venomous, and definitely unapologetic.

Bea looked up slowly. She had not seen Sasha come in. "I thought you'd left already." The lie rolled off Bea's tongue effortlessly.

"I see," Sasha replied. "I thought it might've been something else."

"Like what?" Bea struggled to stand. Her hips seemed to lock from sitting so long. "What else could be wrong?" There, she'd opened the door for Sasha to acknowledge the obvious.

But Sasha, being Sasha, simply strutted her tiny hips and walked away.

Like Sasha and Bea, Sister Betty had arrived, too. One of the other mothers had contacted her and feigned surprise that Bea and Sasha hadn't told her about the meeting. Not having Sister Betty at the conference was like not having rain in a desert; it'd be dull and dusty. Besides, when the three old women came together it was always entertaining—a bit dangerous, but entertaining.

Sister Betty gave hugs and quick pecks on the cheeks to some of the other Mothers Board members. She wasn't used to politics and didn't know whether to linger or just move on inside the room.

"Mother D'Claire had to leave so suddenly," one of the other women said.

Sister Betty didn't know much about politics but she knew the signs of gossip. Instead of responding, she smiled at the woman's feeble attempt to engage in idle chatter.

The rebuke in Sister Betty's silence and her smile hit its mark. The woman moved on. A moment didn't pass before Sister Betty heard that same woman make the same remark to another. When she saw the other women gather around the gossipmonger, she sighed.

"Why didn't you tell us that June Bug worked at this conference center?" Sasha's question was more of an accusation as she approached. She tapped her cane slightly and refused to take her eyes off Sister Betty. "Where's your Jesus love?"

"That's a good question. It's where it's always been." Without giving it a second thought, Sister Betty turned and walked away. She was shocked and saddened by her response. Why had she let Sasha back her into a corner? Back in Pelzer, that would've never happened. She'd have prayed and smiled while not giving the devil an inch.

Only the third day in Las Vegas and she'd found out her salvation and love wasn't as strong as she'd thought. But why would God cause her to come to Las Vegas to discover it? Why didn't He do what He always had?

Again, she'd found something in common with the Bible's Jonas's disobedient spirit. Jonas had fled rather than preach to those he considered heathens. Except, in her case, she'd have gone voluntarily into the belly of the big fish, rather than deal with Bea and Sasha.

All the while Sister Betty, Bea, and Sasha were stewing in their personal dramas, the other Mothers Board members observed. For most of them, the new and the old, Bea and Sasha's behavior was no surprise. However, seeing Sister Betty teeter on the brink of her precious relationship with God was shocking.

The women finally entered the conference room and were surprised that no one told them to leave. Of course, there wasn't food, or water, or pencils and pads either. Yet, Bea and Sasha claimed a victory refusing to believe that their meeting hadn't been discovered yet. They'd preferred to believe that they had favor. They weren't aware that management discovered that Chandler Lamb's godmother was a part of the group. Management needed to figure out what to do, so until then, they'd do nothing.

* * *

Later that evening, long after others had gone home for the day, Chandler was still upstairs in his office.

With his suit jacket thrown over one of the chairs instead of hung up and his shirt and tie unbuttoned and loosened, he poured over a pile of papers. Frustrated, Chandler closed the folder full of paperwork that lay atop his desk. He'd done everything but concentrate on its contents.

A vision of torn hosiery revealing creamy thighs invaded his concentration. "Zipporah Moses," he mumbled, not in an angry way, but in amazement. In two weeks he'd have to give the "talk" to Zipporah. He'd have to tell her whether or not she could keep her job. There'd be polite conversations before then, hopefully, if he had any grievances or suggestions on how she could improve. He could only imagine she'd do her best not to snicker as he tried to act professional.

"Okay, June Bug," he imagined she'd say, "if you feel that I can do better." She'd probably stifle her laughter as she fought for control. "And you want me to take you serious, June Bug?"

Chandler's hands were shaped like a church steeple supporting his chin when Mandy walked in. He'd forgotten she was still there.

"Yes, Mandy." By the look on her face he wasn't sure if he'd spoken quietly or shouted at her. He had to get Zipporah Moses out of his mind before he completely lost it.

"I was trying to wait for you to give me the last report to type." Mandy stretched out her hand, indicating he should place the folder in it. "I'm starting my vacation tomorrow and I'd like to get a head start."

"I'm sorry, Mandy. I'd completely forgotten." He reopened the pages and thumbed through them. It was all an act. He couldn't remember what he was looking for.

"I know you said that you didn't need an assistant while I'm gone, but if you don't give me those papers, right now, you will," Mandy predicted.

Without meaning to do so, she'd handed him an excuse. "Mandy, you're absolutely right. Don't worry about this report and go home. I'll get one of the other girls from guest services to type it. It's no big deal." He didn't know if that was something that was appropriate or not. He'd never asked anyone in guest services to perform something not in their job description.

"Good luck with that." Mandy didn't know what Chandler's problem was, but she wasn't about to let it interfere with her vacation plans. It was going on eleven o'clock, way past her six o'clock quitting time, and she had an early morning flight.

"I've got packing to do," Mandy said. She was still watching him struggle with whatever had taken his attention. He hadn't bothered to ask where she was vacationing, so she told him, "I'm going to beautiful Hawaii, the island of Kauai to be exact."

Chandler didn't look at her but he did respond. "Make sure you pack a coat." He hadn't paid attention and thought he'd covered the fact very well.

"I'll do that." Mandy shut the door hard as she left his office. He was her boss but that didn't mean she couldn't let him know that she wasn't pleased with his lack of attention.

Thirty minutes later Mandy was gone and Chandler had turned off the office lights. During that time he'd had no further thoughts about Zipporah or his embarrassing old nickname, June Bug. But by the time he'd entered the underground garage and turned the key in his 2007 Avalon Limited, thoughts of Zipporah had returned.

It had taken one look at a bra advertisement. It was the Victoria's Secret model Selita Ebanks. The creamy, coffee-colored complexion, well-proportioned body, and inviting smile; it all reminded him of Zipporah. All that was missing from Selita was Zipporah's sexuality and enticing hazel-colored eyes. He had hazel eyes, too, but he wouldn't call them sexy. He stuck his head out the car window and peeked again at the billboard. His smile was appreciative. "Beautiful." Selita's eyes were dark brown but gorgeous nonetheless.

It was well after one in the morning. Zipporah wrestled with sleep. She'd arrived back at the West Strip shelter before the midnight curfew. If she was grateful for anything else, it was that Miss Thompson was supposed to be away for another week. The woman watched her like a hawk and Zipporah had already stayed beyond her time. If she could manage to pass her two-week orientation, she'd have the job permanently. She ran down a laundry list of things she needed to do better than just survive.

If she combined her salary with adequate tips, which she was determined she'd earn, she could move into a cheap kitchenette or a studio. She craved a place with her name on a mailbox and a key that she controlled. She'd rent a place where she didn't have to hear the sound of another person's voice, if she didn't want to. She wanted out of that shelter.

A small hum emitted from Sasha's hotel room air-conditioner. It was a low sound that somehow had joined in harmony with a whirring sound coming from the bathroom. Sasha could've stopped the annoying bathroom sound but she didn't want to sleep without a light. Keeping the one on in the bathroom was the least invasive but she'd have to endure that buzzing sound.

It wasn't hard to fall asleep the first couple of nights in Las Vegas. Sasha's tired body had claimed sleep the moment her head hit the oversized pillow, but not tonight.

She couldn't sleep because she'd seen the same thing Bea had. There was no doubt about it. The young girl working in the casino could've passed for her niece's twin.

Sasha's mind raced back to reclaim memories. Some of those memories were forgotten on purpose and others due to aging.

Sasha, in her youth, had lied to save the honor of her family. Back then, if an unmarried girl became pregnant, it meant unbearable banishment by the community.

And, if a church girl became pregnant, then she was banned from all church activities as well. It would start by her being called out by the pastor or the mother of the church. Each auxiliary would follow the lead and as they called it back then, she'd be "sat down." As the months would pass, her belly swelling with the promise of life inside, the woman's heart would fade and shame would surely kill her slowly.

And so shame came to Sasha's family and it came without apology.

Sasha Hellraiser wasn't the oldest child but she was the tiniest of the three girls and one boy, and she had the most gumption. Even back then, almost sixty years ago, in Anderson County, South Carolina, her nickname was T.T. They'd called her Tiny Terror and she tried effortlessly to live up to the nickname. Whenever trouble came to their doorstep, she'd answer the knock, armed for battle.

By the time she was a young adult, her temper was well known in the church, too. Had the Hellraiser family members committed acts that should've had church doors shut in their faces? Of course, and no matter how destructive their behavior, they always did it with style. Hardly anyone was permanently hurt by their little acts of indiscretion. A little embarrassed or inconvenienced, perhaps, but never physically hurt unless deserved. However, nothing was ever done that actually caused them the embarrassment of being asked to leave the church. Until . . .

Sasha's hands grabbed at the bed sheets as she tried to turn over. Her tiny body ached from lying in one position so long. It also ached from knowing that if she didn't do something quick, a secret could come out. But what if she was wrong and it was a coincidence that the young woman looked like her niece, Ima? What if she was losing sleep for nothing?

Sasha could feel her heart beat faster. She could almost hear it as it joined the combined chorus of the air-conditioner and the whirring sound coming from the bathroom.

To her surprise, Sasha got off the bed and heard herself praying aloud. "Lord, what can I do? I haven't heard from You in quite some time, but I need to hear Your voice, now."

For the first time in quite a while, Sasha actually knelt to pray. She'd not done so in the past few years. She used her various ailments, specifically arthritis, to deprive God of His most humble due. But this night, trouble could come in such a manner as to cause Sasha to skip rope, double Dutch, if necessary. She needed to hear from heaven and true to her tenacity, she'd not get up until she did.

Down the hall, Bea looked over at the clock with the huge numbers and too many buttons. She saw that it was almost two o'clock in the morning. She'd lay down around midnight and two hours later, she still couldn't sleep. The only thing she'd managed to do was run to the bathroom a few times. But that's something she'd do whether she'd been sleeping or not.

It wasn't the strong resemblance between the young girl in the casino and Ima Hellraiser that bothered Bea. She'd always heard that everyone had a twin somewhere. But this girl looked so much like Ima that even a blind person would've agreed with her. So why did Sasha lie and then walk off? Sasha's denial was what caused the sleep to stay away.

Two more hours passed and the alarm clock buzzed as it

struck four o'clock. Why Bea hadn't heard the alarm the past two nights, she didn't know. She struggled to find the right button to turn it off. It was two more trips to the bathroom and several more tries before she was able to disarm it by pulling out the radio power cord from the wall socket.

Bea's mind was kidnapped by Sasha's lie. Sasha lied; that was nothing new. But why this lie? They were in Las Vegas, miles away from Pelzer. No need for Sasha to lie about something as small as a family resemblance.

Suddenly, Bea sat straight up in the bed, no easy task for her curved spine.

"There's a family resemblance!" If she weren't absolutely sure about it before, she was then. There was no reason for her to speak, or shout it out, since she was in the room alone, but she had. Just hearing those words sent her mind into overdrive. She didn't know how yet, but she was determined to see that young lady again.

A sly grin appeared on her chubby face. Of course, that meant she'd have to revisit the casino. A good detective always went back to the scene of the crime.

18

The next morning came and neither Bea nor Sasha showed signs of tiredness. They even decided to share a cab to the conference center. But they rode in silence, not out of anger but a need to gather their thoughts. Each had a mission and one had nothing to do with the other.

"Mothers, please take a seat."

Standing at the podium in the conference room was an elderly woman with a lemony complexion and teeth to match. She rocked side to side trying to adjust the microphone. The woman, named Mother Lizzie J. Borden, was dressed in yellow, which was the color for the morning, so she thought. She wore thick glasses that made her look like an owl tangled in a sunflower patch as she continued her fight with the microphone.

"I'm trying to get this thing adjusted," she laughed nervously, as she finally positioned the microphone.

"This morning, I'd like to thank all of you, again, for coming. As you all know, this morning we must finish the nominations for the Mothers Board presidency positions for all churches involved. And, we will also vote for a national president."

The rest of the mothers did the appropriate amount of clapping—thirty seconds and no longer, along with the appropriate amount of two "hallelujahs."

Had they been at their home churches, no doubt, there'd be two or three of them shouting. The shouting would be followed by a good amount of them just passing out from sheer exhaustion, although they'd claim to be in the spirit. But today, they were in Las Vegas. Most of them just wanted to get on with the meeting so they could go and witness the other sinners downstairs inside the casino. Of course, there were some passionate

Bible toters who had their tithe money and a little extra inside their Bible. The money would be folded neatly and prayed over as it lay in the nineteenth chapter of Numbers.

Bea and Sasha had arrived together but sat seats apart. Counting them and Sister Betty, they were the only three from Crossing Over Sanctuary Temple. Yet they all sat as far apart as possible. There wasn't a hint of fellowship between them.

Each woman had an excuse. Bea and Sasha didn't want to sit next to one another. That was their excuse; they just didn't want to.

Sister Betty, on the other hand, told herself that she'd be more comfortable seated in one of the cushioned folding chairs. She was still in denial and growing bolder in it, day by day.

"As you know," Mother Borden announced, "we're doing a new thing this year. The home pastors have nominated the person they wished to see as president of their respective Mothers Boards."

Mother Borden lifted a typed sheet of paper from the podium and stepped out. She began to call off names.

Sister Betty heard the words, "I decline." She recognized the voice. After all, she should know her own voice. But she felt like she was having an out of body experience. She was supposed to say, "I accept." That's why Reverend Tom sent her. More importantly, she knew that's what God wanted her to do.

Disobedience was out of character for her and yet, her own will had interfered with the plan. All she could do was rush from the room in tears. Again, like Jonas in the Bible, she just didn't want to deal with the likes of Bea, Sasha, and some of the other board members of her home church.

The truth was, she'd become too comfortable, physically, financially, and spiritually. She just didn't seem to have the old soul-winning, demon-fighting energy and driving determination God had given her years ago. And she couldn't remember when it'd stopped.

Sister Betty had barely left the room when the buzz started.

"Hmm," one of the mothers whispered. "I always thought she was just too good." Her comment was one of many that echoed throughout the conference room. Women who'd have never said anything bad, aloud, about Sister Betty suddenly seized the opportunity to do so.

The moment was all that Bea and Sasha could've hoped for. Sister Betty had embarrassed herself. They were poised to take advantage of such a situation whenever it would occur. Yet, at that very moment Bea and Sasha only wanted to do one thing. Each, separately, wanted to walk out of the meeting and look for the young woman working in the casino.

So in silence, they slipped out. Not together but with the same purpose, they headed to the casino.

19

The elevator door on the Jaeger Conference Center's fourth floor opened. It took Sister Betty by surprise when Chandler walked on.

Immediately, Chandler saw signs of tears and his smile left. "Aunt Betty," he said softly, "what's wrong?" Except when she was praising God and overjoyed about it, he'd never seen her cry or get too upset. She was everyone's Rock of Gibraltar. She was the go-to woman of God, the one who God used for everything.

Chandler's stepping onto the elevator caused Sister Betty to lose control. Until that point, she'd only had tears in her eyes. His appearance brought about sobs.

Chandler immediately ushered Sister Betty off on the next floor. Fortunately it was the same floor as his office, so he took her there.

"What's wrong?" He was grateful that Mandy wasn't there and no one from the human resources office had arrived to take her place.

Sister Betty couldn't speak. Her small shoulders heaved and her spiritual wall built of "God is good all the time and all the time God is good," collapsed.

"I'm just tired." She said each word as though it were made of concrete and just too heavy to carry. "I'm just tired."

"God's always given you strength." Chandler didn't know why he said that except it was what came to mind. "You've been saved, sanctified and filled with the Holy Ghost for as long as I can remember. I've never seen you like this." His concern was genuine and seeing her like this was unsettling. If her burden was heavy enough for her to throw in her spiritual towel, what chance did anyone else stand? After all, God had called her personally.

Chandler didn't ask any further questions. Instead, he took her small hands in his and lowered his head. He found himself doing something he'd not done in quite some time. Chandler prayed. He didn't pray the quiet little prayer that some would out of habit or custom. Chandler prayed like he'd heard his grandmother, Ma Cile, do when rough times visited.

When Chandler finally finished praying both he and Sister Betty were exhausted. He'd even gone so far as to lay one hand on her head and invoke God and heaven to come immediately to her aid. He didn't pray for himself, only for her.

And, Sister Betty felt her strength and resolve start to return. Her complexion appeared brighter as though it had visited heaven and returned with its light.

Chandler's complexion appeared the same. The feeling he now felt was a familiar one. It was an emotion he'd not experienced since leaving his prayer life back in Pelzer, South Carolina. Like so many others, he'd grown up in the church. His home life was rich in spirituality. Between the guidance of his grandmother and Sister Betty along with several other church members, he should've never succumbed to the bright lights of the big city. Yet he had.

"You look different, June Bug," Sister Betty finally said as her color returned to normal and the tears dried up.

"So do you." Chandler's handsome face beamed as the Sister Betty he so dearly loved returned. He laughed and shook his head knowing that it was of no use to mention that she'd promised to not call him June Bug in public.

He would've continued laughing but Sister Betty's expression had suddenly changed. He quickly turned and looked toward the office door. He was shocked to see Zipporah standing in the doorway.

"I'm sorry to disturb you, Mr. Lamb. I'll wait outside." Without waiting for Chandler to speak, she turned to leave.

"See what praying will do?" Sister Betty whispered. "She's very pretty."

"I think that's evident," Chandler said as his sudden smile betrayed the words he spoke. He hoped he sounded professional and aloof about her observation.

"Too bad, though," Sister Betty said softly, "it's really too bad."

"What is?"

"She looks just like Mother Pray Onn's niece."

"So she looks like her niece? So what if she does?"

"I've forgotten you've been gone from Pelzer for quite some time. You've probably forgotten about Ima Hellraiser."

At the mention of Ima's name, Chandler fell back in his chair. "No way!" Even if he didn't want to admit it, he suddenly realized that there was a strong resemblance to the woman who'd made life miserable for so many.

"It took me a few minutes to see it but the resemblance is very strong. Heaven knows we don't need two Imas."

"We really don't need the one we have," Chandler added. "Her name is Zipporah and I believe that's a Biblical name. So you know there's no connection to the Hellraiser family."

They laughed a while longer. They'd forgotten Zipporah was seated in the outer office.

But she wasn't seated for long. She'd heard the mention of her name and the laughter that followed. She didn't know why they were laughing, but it had to be about either something she'd done or the way she looked.

So Zipporah left feeling Chandler was no different than the other people she'd met. As for the old woman who sat with him, the Bible clutched in her hand, she could care less about what she thought. The old lady couldn't be much of a "woman of God" if she gossiped and laughed at people she didn't even know.

Zipporah tried to convince herself that she didn't care, but she did. Her face was a mask of anger as she dashed onto the elevator. She moved so fast she couldn't stop herself from stepping on Bea's foot.

It was Bea's thimble-shaped pinky toe. The pain shot up from the toe through her thick thigh, straight up the curve in her spine and almost knocked her eyes from their sockets.

"What the . . . ham and cheese!" Bea yelped. "Lawd, help me!"

Zipporah's eyes widened and the apologies flew. She couldn't stop apologizing all the way down to the casino floor. A part of her apology was because she was truly sorry for stepping on Bea's foot. The other part was because she was afraid she'd now lose her job if anyone found out that she'd assaulted one of the patrons. And the fact that it was the same old woman she'd seen cause a ruckus from the first day wasn't lost on her.

Bea's mind fought to gain control over the pain. This was an opportunity she couldn't resist. She'd never have imagined she'd have to suffer to make the young woman's acquaintance, but if it gave her leverage on Sasha, it was worth it.

"Oh, honey," Bea said softly between the grimaces from the

pain, "it was an accident. I shouldn't have been standing all the way against the back wall, minding my own business, when you ran onto the elevator."

Since Zipporah was fifteen minutes early for her shift, she figured she'd use the time to humor the old woman. She needed to keep her job.

"I'm still so sorry," Zipporah said. "I don't know what else to say."

"Well, you started off the right way," Bea explained. "You said you were sorry." Bea suddenly smiled and added, "Ima would've never apologized."

"Excuse me?" Zipporah's look of confusion suddenly turned to fear. *What if this old woman was truly dangerous? And who is Ima?*

"I didn't mean to call you that," Bea said politely. "I'm Mother Bea Blister from Crossing Over Sanctuary Temple out of Pelzer, South Carolina. You remind me of someone I know."

"No, she don't!" The words were as welcome as a fox in a hen house.

It was Sasha. She'd just arrived in time to hear a little of Bea's explanation. Sasha chose not to explain her outburst. Instead, Sasha just waddled her little hips down the aisle of slot machines. As she turned the corner she looked back at Bea with a warning stare.

Bea shot back one of her own that read, "Heifer, please."

Zipporah's shoulders slumped slightly. Her head swung between Bea, standing with a look of joy on her face, and the other old woman's tiny hips swaying as though inviting a kiss.

Bea would've continued her inquisition but nature called. "Honey, where's the nearest bathroom?"

Zipporah pointed toward the bathroom. She issued another apology and walked away quickly, before Bea could respond.

Whatever was going on with those two old women, Zipporah didn't want to be in the middle. She was about to come to the conclusion that perhaps she was working in a nuthouse. Everyone seemed a little off center. And, the little snickering she'd heard coming from Mr. Lamb's office sealed the conclusion that she and he had nothing in common. And they never would.

20

Chandler finally remembered that Zipporah was waiting in the reception area and left to get her. He returned to his office giving Sister Betty an answer to a question she'd not asked. "I guess it wasn't anything too important. She's gone."

"How long has she worked for you?"

"She started about two days ago."

"And . . ." Sister Betty was almost back to her old self. "You didn't think she was a beautiful woman when you met her?"

"I meet beautiful women all the time," Chandler teased. "Look at me. You've heard the old saying, 'You attract what you are.'" They laughed at Chandler's attempt at humor.

"Do you want me to walk you down and through the casino to the exit? I don't want any aspersions cast upon your good name."

"It's too late," Sister Betty replied. "My ears are still ringing from what was probably said earlier."

"You know, folks talked about Jesus." Chandler tried again to be humorous.

"Yes, folks did. But until you've had your character assassinated by the Mothers Board, you'll never know how I feel."

"I've had my behind assassinated by you and Ma Cile on several occasions. I think I know."

"Now that's funny!"

And, it was.

While Bea was in the casino bathroom Sasha managed to secrete herself away at one of the slot machines in a far corner. A short time later she saw Zipporah walk onto the casino floor.

She was dressed in her casino outfit, which Sasha thought was completely inappropriate.

Sasha watched as Zipporah dashed about serving all sorts of drinks and whatever else the patrons wanted. Sasha's eyes narrowed as she saw the shameless way Zipporah seemed to flirt, no doubt with hopes of getting tips.

Sasha was lost in thought. She'd not placed one single nickel in the slot machine, which had not gone unnoticed by several others who waited for her to vacate. However, they also recognized her as the little old lady with the assault cane so they'd wait until she decided to move.

While Sasha continued daydreaming, the memories returned. Some were crystal clear and some were not. However, the day her life was turned upside down and she'd left the church of her youth seemed like yesterday.

Early in the morning on that dark day, she'd sat on the bed watching her sister Areal. Areal's hands kept moving across her belly as though they were trying to make something disappear. Areal had every reason to want that. She had a swollen belly with an unwanted baby. Her hands kept going back and forth for a time as she examined her belly in the bedroom mirror.

And then Sasha recalled that Deacon Jasper Epps was inside the room and he stared as well.

Deacon Jasper Epps, all six foot four inches, was a Smokey Robinson lookalike. He was a creamy-complexioned, light-eyed man with naturally straight, thick black hair born to Cree parents out of Moorehead City, North Carolina. And he could sing! Just as Smokey caused women to lose their minds and give way to fantasies that would've set confessionals on fire, Jasper Epps did, too. He'd been a heart throb ever since his youth. He was then married and just a little older than both Areal and Sasha and had known them from high school.

At the time Areal became pregnant, Sasha was in her late twenties. She'd been widowed at a young age and learned to treasure the freedom being single offered. She'd kept her married name although she'd also toyed around with the idea of returning to her maiden name of Hellraiser.

Areal Hellraiser was older by a couple of years and just as beautiful as Sasha, if not more so. She was the wild one in the family and had never married. She'd been dating Deacon Jasper for some time and they'd managed to keep it a secret. It wasn't because Areal was ashamed to date a married man. She had no qualms with it. However, Deacon Jasper's extremely wealthy wife was sure to be upset if she found out.

As most men did, Deacon Jasper had promised Areal that he was going to leave his wife, but he didn't.

It was the fourth Sunday at Financial Temple, their home church, when secrets fell out of the closet like the lock was broke.

The church was expecting a Prophet Benjamin Burning to visit. Prophet Burning went about the countryside visiting small congregations and giving them what "thus saith the Lord." Of course, according to Prophet Burning, how much information God revealed to him to dispense depended upon which money line you stood in. If you stood in the fifty-dollar line, which was almost like standing in the thousand-dollar line today, he'd tell you everything you wanted to hear. He'd solicit just enough information from the giver before he'd prophesy to make the scam work as though he'd had a one-on-one with the Almighty.

"Do you need healing and a huge financial blessing?" Prophet Burning would ask.

Everyone in the line would shout, "Yes," sometimes all at one time.

So Prophet Burning would go down the hundred-dollar line with his assistant collecting the money before he'd speak. He'd tell the giver, or the "sucker" as some called them, a word from God. And it was a corporate word that everyone received. And, although perhaps one or two out of many would get over a cold or receive some monies they'd already earned, the members would still anxiously await his return. They'd get back on the line and he'd fleece them again.

On this particular fourth Sunday, Sasha and Areal went to church. They'd not been in quite some time and no one from the church had ever bothered to visit and find out why.

Deacon Jasper had already left to pick up his wife. Earlier, he'd told his wife that he was going to attend a deacon's breakfast at another church, and he'd return to bring her to their late morning church service. Of course, what he'd told his wife was only half true. He'd had breakfast at Areal's house but he did pray a blessing over the food.

That morning, Areal's ever-enlarging belly was covered by an oversized coat. The rainy and somewhat chilly days of April provided an excuse to wear one. Sasha and Areal walked through the doors of the church and took their seats in the middle. They never sat all the way in the rear of the church, choosing to leave those seats to those who hadn't made up their minds to join and serve. They preferred to sit in the middle between the true hypocrites occupying the front pews and the ones on the fence.

Prophet Burning had called for the money lines. He'd done his routine of asking questions and doling out blessings accordingly.

All the while he did so he'd also kept his eyes on Sasha and Areal. They thought he was flirting since that's what most men did in their presence.

Instead of the prophet tending to his business, he decided to walk the aisle of the church revealing the business of those who'd not paid hush money in his offering.

"God said," he'd start off, "you need to get a job. God said, if you get in one of these lines, preferably the hundred-dollar one, He's gonna bless you with a job down at the cotton mill."

"But I don't have no money," the poor person would reply.

"Give what you can," the prophet would demand in a loud voice. "I have a layaway plan so you have no excuse."

By the time Prophet Burning reached where Sasha and Areal sat, the bucket was brimming over with paper money with not a coin to be heard.

Prophet Burning looked from Areal to Sasha and back again. He didn't bother asking for a dime. His head swung like he was about to enter a boxing ring and fight the devil.

"You having a baby and you ain't married." His steps faltered just a little as he reached for the back of a nearby pew for support. "You's a Jezebel." He hollered accusations, which, according to those who normally paid, meant he told the truth.

Sasha's eyes had rolled and she thought, *Of all the times for this fraud to get religion, why now?*

Areal, never one to mince words, stood up, and cussed him out.

Somewhere in the back of Sasha's mind she thought she heard metallic-sounding music and chimes. It brought her out of her daydream.

"Excuse me. Are you going to use that machine?" The woman peering over Sasha's shoulders pointed to the slot machine. She looked to be about the same age and was dripping in costume jewelry.

At first, Sasha didn't say a word. She turned around and stared at the woman so hard it appeared as though Sasha's face had turned to stone. Without so much as an "I'm sorry," Sasha snatched one of the Bible tracts from her Bible that she'd placed between the slot machines.

"Here," Sasha said harshly, "take one of these and read it. You're going straight to hell for gambling."

The woman looked at the Bible tract and then back to Sasha. "Aren't you gambling?"

"No, I'm not. I don't gamble. I know what I'm doing. I don't lose, so therefore it can't be a gamble." Sasha grabbed five nickels and shoved them into the machine. Sure enough the clanging sound made by the evidence of five cherries in a row rang out.

Sasha turned around and looked at the woman again. Her second look was meaner than the first. The woman silently took the Bible tract and started reading it as she walked away. What else could she do?

Sasha looked around and, to her horror, she saw Bea talking to the young woman again. Her eyes narrowed to the point of making her head hurt and her gray bun felt like it was twisting tighter. Every warning fiber of her being rubbed her nerves and she knew that Bea's butting in was never a good thing. Sasha needed to find out more about the young woman and she needed to do so before Bea did.

21

"I'll have a cup of hot tea." It was the third cup Bea had ordered from Zipporah. She'd refused to give her beverage order to any of the other casino hostesses. Every time she ordered from Zipporah she'd asked her another question.

So far Bea had found out if the young woman was telling the truth, her name, and that she only recently started working there.

Zipporah, Bea thought. *Now why does a name like that ring a bell?* She didn't have time to dwell upon it. She needed to find out if there was a connection between Zipporah and Ima Hellraiser. Maybe they were distant cousins who'd never met. But then again, why had Sasha lied about seeing any resemblance. The two young women looked so much alike that Bea was tempted to tell Zipporah to watch out. She was likely to get arrested for something Ima had done.

For the next hour or so Bea quizzed Zipporah every time she saw her. In between those times, she'd made trips to the bathroom. She'd announced that her slot machine better not be touched. And it wasn't. For even those old folks with a touch of dementia or who'd fully succumbed to it, the sight of the old woman with the red fuzzy wig and curved back was enough to keep them at bay.

And while Bea did her direct inquisition, Sasha watched. Her mood soured by the minute. Finally, she got up and left. She'd also left her cup filled to its brim with nickels. That's just how upset she'd become. The Sasha who strolled slowly out of the casino with head bowed was not the same feisty woman from Pelzer, South Carolina.

* * *

Upstairs in Chandler's office things were getting out of control. It had gone from bad to worse. He couldn't find all the papers for the report he needed. He was sure Mandy had everything organized, so it had to be his fault.

Sister Betty had left and returned with sandwiches. She didn't know anything about office work so she was of no use.

"Still no luck with getting someone to help you?" She felt sorry for him as he raced about opening and slamming file cabinets and flipping open folders.

"Most employees are on vacation. We're a bit shorthanded at the moment. I've forwarded all calls to voice mail, but I can only do that for a moment." Why hadn't he paid more attention to what Mandy was trying to tell him last night? She was probably on her vacation somewhere laughing. She knew he'd mess up, and he had.

"Is this something very important?" Sister Betty rewrapped the sandwiches. Chandler didn't appear to be as hungry as she thought.

"It's the payroll," he said hurriedly. "There will be a mutiny if I don't get it done in time."

"I don't know how much a mutiny cost but I can lend you the money for it." She'd already opened her pocketbook and prepared to write him a check.

"I'll need about two hundred and fifty thousand dollars for this week's payroll."

"That's not what you need," Sister Betty replied as she put away her checkbook and closed the snaps on her pocketbook. "You need to find someone to find what you need to type that report." As much as she loved her godson, she wasn't about to write a check for that much money. She didn't care if some called her tight-fisted, but no one would call her stupid.

During the time Chandler continued searching through papers the office phone did ring. The calls went straight to voice mail and he never attempted to retrieve the messages. In the meantime, Sister Betty felt her presence more of a distraction than a help. She left after wishing him well. He never looked up, so she didn't know if he'd heard her or not.

Zipporah finished fixing her hair and makeup inside the employees' lounge. As far as she was concerned, her lunch break hadn't come fast enough. After running relays between the bar and the gamblers, she was almost exhausted.

As soon as the floor manager had signaled for her to take her break, she'd wasted no time leaving the casino floor. She raced to her locker and threw a dress over her hostess uniform. Ten minutes later, she was at Chandler's office door. She'd calmed down and swallowed her pride, after hearing her name and the laughter that followed. She needed to see if she could talk him into changing her hours. The casino was open twenty-four hours a day. It was a part of and yet separate from the Jaeger Center in that regard.

She knew that Ms. Thompson would be returning from her short vacation and if the woman caught Zipporah arriving just one second after midnight, she'd oust Zipporah from the shelter.

She'd already rehearsed how she'd play it. Zipporah was sure despite the laughter he'd had at her expense, that he was still just a man. Changing her shift shouldn't be that much of a hassle. How many casino floor servers were needed on any shift, she wasn't certain. And she really didn't care. The bottom line: Zipporah needed to keep her job and a place to sleep. And if she'd read him wrong, well, she'd cross that bridge later.

Zipporah's soft raps on the office door almost went unheard. With the door slightly ajar, she peeked inside. It took a moment before she realized that Chandler's head was totally into trying to access Mandy's computer files.

"Excuse me," Zipporah said softly.

Her voice surprised Chandler, causing him to knock over a bowl of paper clips.

Zipporah felt embarrassed as Chandler struggled to gather the paper clips off the desk and from the floor.

"I knocked and no one answered but the door was open." She was stammering, which made it seem that she was lying. "I'm sorry. You must be busy."

"I am." He didn't mean to sound harsh but time was moving fast even if he wasn't.

"I'll come back another time." Her plan to seduce him fled with his two-word response.

He slammed his fist on the desk and followed it with a hard shove to a drawer.

"I'm not normally this frazzled, Ms. Moses."

"You're not?"

"No, I'm not. But what can I do for you? Are you not faring well on the casino floor?"

His demeanor had loosened slightly. It was enough to embolden Zipporah. She quickly expressed her desire to change her shift. She omitted the real reason why.

While she spoke, Chandler's eyes devoured her. He hadn't meant to stare but he did. Then he quickly turned away. She was pretty but not enough for him to forget the necessity of getting the report done.

Zipporah grew uneasy as she tried to pretend that she hadn't noticed his stare. Trying to avoid his eyes, she let her eyes settle upon the computer screen. She saw a column with the word *failure* repeated.

"You misspelled a word." She hadn't meant to say that but one of her pet peeves was misspelled words. She'd never been able to stomach poor grammar and misspelled words in anything printed. At one time she'd held a temporary job as a proofreader. It was only for four months, and though she was good at it, again, she didn't get hired permanently.

Chandler seemed to ignore her, so she kept quiet. She took a moment and looked around his office and then she saw it. Why she hadn't when she came for her interview, she didn't know.

Zipporah strained to read the names under several gold and platinum CDs. There were about ten of them and they were all lined up in a large frame. She recognized immediately a picture of LL Cool J and Regina Belle. She loved Regina Belle. Finally, she made out the picture of Michael Bolton and lo and behold, when she saw pictures of MC Hammer, Whitney Houston, and Yolanda Adams, her interest in Chandler grew. How did he get those? What did he know about the music business?

Zipporah stood there in awe. Before she came to Las Vegas, she'd also worked as a secretary in a marketing department at one of the large record labels in New York City. That was her day job and it kept her busy sometimes ten hours a day. But some nights and most weekends, she moonlighted. Zipporah sang wherever she found an audience. Smoke-filled clubs and studio work added money to her pocket but brought her no closer to fame. Having a manager finally helped a little. But her dreams of being discovered evaded her. It didn't matter that she was the "go-to" backup vocalist for many studios. She'd sung backup for the likes of Mariah Carey, Regina Belle, and Mary J. Blige. Her voice, they told her, wasn't unique and she'd never make it as a solo artist.

After a year of dodging unsolicited catcalls and so-called accidental touches on her body, she'd quit the record company. Because she quit she couldn't receive unemployment. Things only became worse.

"You said I misspelled a word." He could tell she'd not heard, so he repeated, "I'm asking you which word."

His eyes had locked upon her, almost pleading for her assistance.

"You typed p-a-y r-o-l-e. There's no such word, that's why it kept failing." She moved closer to the computer, slightly pushing him aside as he continued to stare in disbelief.

"Just delete the letter E and type in another L."

It took Zipporah the rest of her lunch break to guide Chandler through Mandy's files. He was amazed at her dexterity as her fingers seemed to fly over keys he'd tapped one finger at a time.

Without asking for the shift change, Zipporah received it. Chandler didn't bother to ask if she'd wanted to work different hours or another position. He was the boss and as such, he gave her Mandy's job on a temporary basis.

While they worked on another project, stopping only to have a small lunch, Zipporah and Chandler bonded. Neither of them seemed to be able to stop sharing information about their pasts.

As soon as Chandler learned she fancied herself an undiscovered singer, he asked her to sing. He didn't really expect that she would, but she did.

Zipporah didn't break a sweat as she serenaded Chandler with her pitch-perfect, soulful rendition of Aretha Franklin's mega-hit, "Until You Come Back to Me."

She'd barely pushed out the last note when she realized he was staring. His eyes were wide and his mouth had dropped. So she did what any true unknown diva would. Zipporah snagged him with one of her favorite gospel songs, "Try Jesus," just to show her versatility. She'd fallen in love with the song when she first heard Kim Burrell sing it. The full-bodied woman controlled the emotions of the crowd from her first note and Zipporah did, also.

Although Zipporah had sung the song for Chandler, she was the one left teary eyed. She fought to control any sign of a quiver in her voice when she sang the lines, "Just try Jesus, He'll never let you fall. Just try Jesus, He'll be there through it all."

Zipporah stood for what seemed an eternity, waiting for Chandler to respond. And, when he didn't, again, she thought perhaps she'd misread him.

He finally recovered his voice. "Wow!"

"If that's a good review, then I thank you." She sat down. His expression remained the same and it confused her. She added, "However, if the *wow* is because it was that bad . . ."

He put a finger to his lips, indicating that she should be quiet. "You're interrupting my thought process."

"Sorry. I was just a little . . ." She stopped speaking and fell further back onto the chair. But Zipporah being who she was started to do what she always did when nervous. She started humming.

"Are you humming Gladys Knight's 'You're the Best Thing . . . ?'"

She smiled and instead of answering, she started singing aloud again. She sang a version she loved. "Jesus, He's the best thing . . ."

"Desmond Pringle, right?" Chandler smiled. He'd almost forgotten that song. Living in Las Vegas, he was used to hearing only the original sung by Gladys Knight.

Chandler's mind raced. *She can actually sing,* he thought. He couldn't stop smiling. Her voice was like balm to his ears. Zipporah had the total package. She was still young enough to have a career. And she sang R&B as well as gospel. The best singers always could.

Chandler's interest in the business of music was revived. It was rejuvenated by the young woman he'd almost written off. He still wasn't sure if it would work. He didn't know enough about her to turn his own life around to try to make two dreams happen: hers to become a star and his to reenter the industry. But if someone could pull in crowds, she certainly could. All he needed to do was to get the right show created for her.

Both Zipporah and Chandler lay aside any preconceived notions. It seemed effortless as they shared tidbits about their lives. Neither had opened wounds and told everything, but it wasn't long before they'd learned they had much in common.

* * *

Sister Betty was on her way back upstairs to Chandler's office. She was still concerned and wanted to check up on him. She'd tried calling but his voice mail came on, so she was certain he was still working.

As soon as Sister Betty stepped off the elevator and turned the corner, she recognized Bea's profile. She walked softly, concentrating on how to approach the figure with her ear pressed up against the door, obviously listening in.

"What are you doing?" Sister Betty's voice was accusatory and she knew it. "Bea Blister, you should be ashamed of yourself."

"Hush!"

"Bea, don't you dare try and hush me." She'd started to say something further but the sound of laughter came from within the office. She recognized Chandler's voice but not the other.

Sister Betty quickly joined Bea in pressing her ear against the office door.

"I don't hear anything now," Bea said while trying to open the door a little wider.

"That's because we're trying to mind somebody's business that's not ours," Sister Betty confessed, but she made no effort to move away from the door.

The outer door to the reception area swung open so fast it almost caused Bea to fall upon Sister Betty. Sister Betty tried to keep her balance and accidentally stepped on Bea's already swollen pinky toe.

Bea screamed.

Sister Betty hollered.

And Chandler almost jumped out of his skin with Zipporah doing the same thing.

Zipporah reacted faster than Chandler. She quickly gathered her bag, prepared to flee. She thought for certain she'd been caught up in a Twilight Zone moment. Maybe Chandler was too good to be true. She ran over and unlatched the side office door to escape while she still had a chance and, hopefully, a job. She'd no sooner put her hand on the doorknob when the sound of crying stopped her. Zipporah looked back. Through the now opened door to the reception area she spied the old women who seemed to be everywhere she was.

22

Sasha had left the casino quickly and returned to her hotel room at the Luxor. She dialed Areal's number, slammed down her hotel room telephone. Three times she tried to call her sister. She left several messages, just in case Areal thought she was a bill collector trying to trick her into answering the phone.

Sasha could feel her blood pressure rise. She looked at the clock. It was almost five o'clock. In a couple of hours the Mothers Board Conference would start for the evening session. She wrestled with whether or not she'd attend. If she didn't, she'd most certainly not be able to control the votes. If she did, then she'd definitely lose control over Bea's inevitable snooping.

It was times like these when she wished she had someone she could trust, a friend who wouldn't judge her and who wouldn't talk about her business.

Sasha willed the image of the young woman from the casino from her mind. Instead, the image seemed to take on a life of its own. She saw the image pointing at her—accusing her.

And then Sasha laid aside her cane. With her arms raised she, again, implored God to listen. Words came slowly but the moans did not. It was as though every fiber of her body needed God's touch. It felt like real praying was becoming a habit for her. It wasn't that she hadn't been praying in the past. She prayed often but on her terms. And it wasn't that she hadn't prayed for others. That she most certainly had done. It was mostly to ask God to rain down His judgment on someone she perceived had slighted her. But not now.

Sasha didn't need a birth certificate or a DNA test to know who the young woman was. "Oh, God," Sasha cried. "Oh, merciful God . . ."

Sasha wept and prayed until she was drained. Her clothes were wet and her silver gray, waist-length hair, always kept neatly twisted into a bun, had become undone. Her church family would've been shocked to see her elfish figure sprawled out on the hotel room floor.

Sasha lay on the floor weeping about everything she'd kept tied up or hidden becoming exposed. What she'd done almost thirty years ago was about to become undone.

It took some effort, but she'd barely gotten off the floor when the phone rang. With energy she didn't know she still had, Sasha rushed to answer it.

"Areal! It's about time!"

Sasha plopped down upon the couch. In between sobs that flowed easier than her story, she talked to her sister.

Sister Betty and Chandler huddled together outside the casino's first-aid station while Bea had her pinky toe attended to.

"It was real nice for that young lady to go inside with Bea." Sister Betty's face showed concern. Whether it was for Bea or the young woman wasn't apparent.

"Zipporah's a very nice person," Chandler said. "I'm reading your mind, Aunt Betty. So don't you be getting any ideas with your matchmaking schemes."

"Why would I?" Sister Betty winked. She leaned over and gave her godson a kiss. "I trust you to lead your own life."

Just as Chandler started to challenge Sister Betty's false promise Zipporah stepped through the door. She was leading Bea, gently holding her by the elbow.

"I don't know how I'm gonna get around," Bea complained. "It's your fault, Sister Betty."

"What?" Sister Betty looked at Chandler, who promptly looked away. "Bea is about to make me mess up my testimony."

Just the thought of Sister Betty acting anything but overly religious caused Bea and Chandler to burst out in laughter. It was just what Bea needed to take her mind off her pain.

"What happened to your spirit of service?" Bea quipped as she winced, trying to solicit sympathy.

"I left it in Pelzer," Sister Betty responded with conviction because she meant every word. Inwardly, she felt convicted but she'd discuss that with God later. Her present state of disobedience had not ebbed when it came to doing anything for Bea and Sasha.

While the church showdown was going on between Mother Blister and Sister Betty, Zipporah watched. She was no longer offended but now fascinated by the tenacity of the old women and the look of acceptance on Chandler's face.

"We'll work something out for you, Mother Blister." Chandler interrupted what he was sure would turn into the next unholy war. "No one wants to leave you helpless."

"Thank you so much, June Bug, sweetie. I don't know how you came to have such good manners, being raised by Sister Betty and your grandma, Ma Cile." She'd tried to say the words as nice as she could but the pain made it a waste of time.

"You wouldn't say that to Ma Cile's face," Sister Betty said quickly.

The truth was that Bea most certainly wouldn't have. Chandler's one-eyed, snuff-dipping, cranky grandmother would've grabbed Bea's other pinky toe. She'd have broken it off and flipped it back at Bea while she sang "The Old Ship of Zion." Ma Cile didn't play.

For the next ten minutes or so they played ping-pong with the idea of who would assist Bea. All the while Zipporah watched as the thought of all of them being crazy returned with vigor.

She never saw it coming. No one asked if she could or would. The next thing Zipporah knew, she'd been volunteered as the one to escort Mother Blister back to the Luxor Hotel.

"Oh, thank you," Bea squealed. Having Zipporah go with her was wonderful. She'd liked her instantly and now they'd have more time to get to know one another. Of course, finding out further why Sasha had denied seeing anything familiar about Zipporah would be a plus.

Zipporah glared at Chandler.

Chandler's grin betrayed any apologies he silently tried to issue. They'd already finished the payroll, so there wasn't much else for Zipporah to do at the office.

Zipporah finally gave in to the futility of the situation. She glared again toward Chandler. She didn't care who saw her as she mouthed the words, "You owe me."

Sister Betty and Bea sat in the first-aid station side by side while they waited for Zipporah and Chandler to return from getting Bea's pain medication prescription.

"She seems to be such a sweet young lady," Bea said. If she'd noticed that Sister Betty wasn't in a talking mood, she ignored it.

Sister Betty turned and looked at Bea as if meeting her for the first time. Something was off about Bea. In all her years of knowing Bea, they'd never exchanged more than ten friendly words at a time. Unintentionally, Sister Betty spoke out, "Maybe it wasn't God speaking to me." It could've just been something I ate . . ." It was to late to take back what was supposed to be a private thought.

The confused look on Bea's face told Sister Betty that Bea probably thought she'd lost her mind. "She's very pretty," Sister Betty added, quickly.

Bea's face relaxed. "And she has such a lovely voice," Bea added.

"How would you know?" Sister Betty faced Bea. It was her turn to think Bea had lost her mind.

"I was listening at the doorway when you came along and shoved me and caused me to hurt my pinky toe."

Sister Betty was about to challenge Bea's edited version of reality when Chandler and Zipporah returned.

"You're just in time." Sister Betty had stood up faster than she'd meant. She became light-headed and couldn't finish speaking.

"She's been talking crazy ever since you left." Bea let her chubby fingers circle her head.

While they prepared to take Bea back to her hotel Chandler took Zipporah aside. He tried explaining Mother Blister's and Sister Betty's idiosyncrasies to Zipporah. "They're really sweet once you get to know them."

"And if I don't want to get to know them?"

"Please don't make me play the boss card." He tried to act stern but couldn't help but laugh.

"Please don't make me play my I-don't-give-a-crap card." She placed both hands on her hips and let her neck roll, showing she still had a little "hood" left and available.

Zipporah and Chandler were getting along like old friends. They finally made a deal. He'd take her out for a late dinner once they got Mother Blister situated. He hoped that Mother Pray Onn could handle whatever business they had at the conference alone.

*   *   *

Back at the Luxor Sasha sped around her room snatching things from the dresser drawers. She stuffed her things into her a suitcase. She hadn't been shopping and yet it seemed difficult to repack. She'd already called the airline, with the help of the hotel's concierge service, and got a flight. She'd balked at having to pay the extra fee to do so but she'd had no choice.

Five minutes after she'd finished packing, Sasha gave her suitcase to a bellhop. He explained to her that the bag would be waiting for her when she came down to the front desk.

It was completely out of character for Sasha, but she tipped the bellhop. Now, all she had to do was wait on the car service to take her to the airport.

Zipporah had finally gotten Bea into a cab. On the way back to the Luxor Bea had done nothing but chat. Zipporah wished she'd had a roll of duct tape to tape Bea's mouth. Plus, Bea had forgotten to put in her dentures and it was like looking into a cave when Bea spoke.

Zipporah stepped off the elevator with Mother Blister limping beside her. Both women focused on trying to get to the hotel room without any further damage to Bea's swollen pinky toe. Neither saw Sasha entering the other elevator.

But Sasha had seen them. She nearly had a heart attack when she spied Zipporah leading Bea off the elevator. She lowered her head and rushed inside another waiting elevator. She pressed against the back wall, trembling. "Jesus. Oh, Jesus," she repeated as the elevator descended. She thanked God for the elevator being empty and not being seen.

Zipporah felt like a suspect as Bea continued her relentless interrogation after they'd entered the hotel room. Somehow, she'd gotten Zipporah to tell her everything except her dress and shoe sizes.

"I wonder what's holding up Mr. Lamb?" Zipporah said. "I didn't think it would take him that long to take Sister Betty to her room."

"She's probably running her mouth," Bea replied. "She's kind of nosey, but she is his godmother, so she thinks she's got a right to ask about things that ain't none of her business."

Without meaning to do so, Zipporah laughed at Bea's accusation. She just hoped she wouldn't be that crazy when she reached old age.

"So tell me," Bea pressed as she tried to reposition her foot, "how long have you been singing?" She couldn't let a little thing as excruciating as pain keep her from her task.

A smile spread across Zipporah's face. The old woman had finally touched on a subject she could spend hours talking about.

Sasha raced from the elevator hoping to avoid anyone else she knew. She thought she'd gotten away clean.

The last thing Chandler expected to see when he entered the hotel lobby was Mother Pray Onn. She seemed in a hurry so he didn't bother to call out to her. Instead, he watched her as she barely used her cane, hasten to a waiting car. She carried a suitcase. By the time he'd regained his wits the car had pulled off.

I wonder where she's off to in such a hurry, Chandler thought. Mother Blister had probably worked her last good nerve.

Chandler pushed Mother Pray Onn to the back of his mind and entered the elevator. He'd promised Zipporah he'd rescue her from Mother Blister as soon as he could. Stepping inside, he recognized a familiar face. Ms. Cowing, the talent coordinator for the Luxor's musical shows.

"Hello, Alicia," Chandler said, smiling. "How are you? I haven't seen you in quite some time." A smile spread across his face as he recalled the one time they'd met for drinks. They'd laughed when each ordered a virgin daiquiri. It was pleasant but strictly business.

"Hi, Chandler," Alicia replied. She took her time smoothing an invisible wrinkle in her dress. She'd never forget their business dinner date. He hadn't tried to take it further and she was only a little grateful. She was also a bit perturbed because she'd taken time to look appealing. On that evening and even now, his good looks disarmed her. She'd never dated a black man, but for him she'd make an exception. "It has been a while. What brings you over to the Luxor?"

"I'm visiting." He gave her an appreciative wink before asking, "What floor are you heading to?"

"Oh, really, visiting?" she said, returning the wink. "I'm heading to my office." She leaned back and watched him press the button before continuing. "So, I imagine there's not enough work

for you at the Jaeger. You've got to scope out the casino competition and call it visiting."

She bent down and turned her ankle ever so slightly, running
her fingers lightly down an invisible seam. "I'm going up to my
office and attack today's trials and drama." She took her time returning her hand to her small waistline. It was another of her
feminine attributes that always caught an eye.

She'd performed the first act in her white woman's flirtation
waltz. She smiled, showing a perfect set of teeth barely covered
by red-painted thin lips as she continued the enticing dance of
possible social death, for the black man.

Chandler suppressed a smile as he leaned against the back wall
of the elevator. Her moves were transparent. He remembered
that silent taboo, the racial divide, the forbidden dance that still
existed in the twenty-first century. He also remembered from
years of living in the South that a black man never led the waltz.

"My godmother and some of her church members are visiting," he said, noticing her shocked look followed by a second of
disappointment as he expertly sidestepped her silent invitation.

But Alicia wasn't giving up without a fight. Loneliness kept
her libido ready. "Sure hope they can do something to improve
our Sodom and Gomorrah image." She puckered her lips, thinking it made her appear sexy. She, too, knew the sidestep dance.

Chandler smiled at her feeble attempt. Her sun-kissed, freckled skin and dyed blonde hair paled in comparison to the beauty
he'd just spent the afternoon enjoying. Zipporah's beauty was
hard to imitate, even by those who, like Alicia, at least had a
head start in the good looks department.

Chandler's eyes didn't totally share the conviction of his mind
as they traveled about Alicia's body. Again, he smiled. He had to
admit her legs were extraordinary. "You're gonna need special
prayer," he teased. "Thou shalt not tempt a young man." He
laughed at his feeble attempt to revise a bit of scripture.

"What I need is a special singer for tomorrow night." There
wasn't a hint of tease when she spoke. "Can you handle this?"
she asked while tossing her long hair to one side and handing
him a piece of paper.

Chandler read the paper and immediately began laughing.

"Come on, Chandler, it's not funny. I'm in trouble."

"I may have your answer." Chandler's eyes grew large.

The elevator stopped, allowing several people to enter. Chandler and Alicia moved closer and continued chatting. The move wasn't necessary because no one was paying attention to them, but they'd done it anyway.

Several floors later, the elevator was empty again. Chandler and Alicia were laughing, exchanging quick sound bites about casino and hotel drama. Her mood had changed for the better and so had his.

"I'm depending upon you," she said softly, while allowing her eyes to widen and appreciate every inch of Chandler's well-toned body.

"I got you." Chandler winked.

Alicia knew that Chandler was good for his word.

They'd first met at a casino management workshop. It'd been about two years ago. He'd walked in—no, it was more like a stroll. He'd had a quiet strength and she could tell she wasn't the only one at the workshop who noticed. There were nothing but eyes on him from both men and women. He'd worn a dark blue, pin-striped, power suit. His shoes were polished to outshine the sun, and his physique . . . She looked over and saw that he was smiling back at her. She must've looked ridiculous while lost in her thoughts.

Embarrassed, she told him, "Well, I'm gonna hold you to your promise." It was the best she could come up with and it was lame at best.

"Call me later," Alicia said softly as the elevator door opened and she stepped out. She left the invitation open to interpretation.

Chandler couldn't help but laugh as the elevator door closed. "What I won't do for success."

23

Sister Betty was unapologetic on her need for privacy as she unplugged her hotel room telephone and placed the DO NOT DISTURB sign on the knob outside. As much as she loved Chandler, the unplugged phone and privacy sign were just as much to keep him out as the others. This trip was turning out to be more of a hassle than she'd wanted.

She checked the time. There were about two hours before she was scheduled to return to the conference center for another round of battle with the Mothers Board members. She had to be honest. She really wouldn't mind avoiding another confrontation.

Lying across the bed, Sister Betty grabbed the television remote. She'd turned it on just in time to catch one of Bishop T. D. Jakes's sermons already in progress. He was speaking about Christians who'd accepted Jesus but still weren't saved.

The power of Bishop Jakes's conviction had left Sister Betty's state of mind in tatters. She'd become too comfortable. She couldn't let her salvation come under attack from her disobedience and not fight.

Reaching for her Bible, she flipped through it until she found a particular verse. She let the powerful words wash over her mind and connect with her spirit.

And, for the first time in a very long time, Sister Betty accepted the truth. She wasn't as saved as she'd thought. She'd become what she'd despised in so many religious people—a hypocrite. And it didn't matter to what degree. Her Bible told her that if she were neither hot nor cold, God would spew her from His mouth.

And then on her knobby and arthritic knees, she repented, over and over. Her regret wasn't necessary. God and most of the other occupants on her hotel floor had heard her the first time, she was so loud. There was no doubt that her sincerity and remorse had reached the throne of grace.

While Sister Betty repented in her room, down the hall Bea peppered Zipporah with more questions, and Chandler devised a plan to reenter the entertainment business. Throughout it all, Zipporah mourned the day she'd become involved with the geriatric set.

And thousands of miles away, Sasha's plane landed at New York's LaGuardia Airport, twenty minutes sooner than scheduled and thirty years too late.

As preplanned by Sasha's sister, Areal, Sasha hurried to a waiting car service that would rush her from LaGuardia Airport to the upper Bronx.

She sat in silence while her mind raced to find some rationale to her dilemma. Sasha might've been quiet but the chatty driver decided to tell her about every inch of highway they drove over.

"I would have to get a motormouth driver," she murmured, and gnawed away at her bottom lip. Her eyes rolled in aggravation as she tried not-too-subtly to ignore the driver's idle chitchat. But the driver, an enthusiastic young Puerto Rican man, had no way of knowing that it wasn't Sasha's first time in New York.

"If we were going in the opposite direction," he said with a heavy accent, "you'd be able to see the site of the old World's Fair in Queens. It's a dilapidated mess now, but it was something back in the sixties."

Sasha could take the driver's intrusion no longer. "Will you please just shut up and take me to the Bronx!"

The driver's body stiffened. He glanced quickly into the rearview mirror as though his eyes would clarify what he'd heard, but stayed quiet.

The rest of the drive to the Bronx was happily in silence. It helped Sasha to gain control of her blood pressure. She was certain it had soared to dangerous levels since she'd left Las Vegas.

Sasha did notice that the Bronx had changed since the last time she'd visited in the early seventies. There were now high-rise apartment buildings replacing the wooden structures she'd remembered. All along the Major Deegan Expressway, there were busloads of people, too many people compared to her small town of Pelzer.

By the time the car finally arrived, on the posh tree-lined street where Areal lived, Sasha's exhaustion had doubled. She saw Areal inching her metal walker down her walkway, destroying flowerbeds along the way, and dreaded what was to come.

Within an hour both Sasha and Areal sat in the living room, crying.

"You promised me that everything was taken care of." Areal reached for her walker and moved slowly toward the living room window. "All the embarrassment of being set down in front of the congregation. Was it all for nothing?"

"How was I supposed know that thirty years later the dirty laundry could air?" Sasha's voice rose in anger. "How could I know things would change?"

One thing that hadn't changed was Areal's home. The same plaid gray and brown fabric held a wooden sofa's frame a prisoner. There was the same plastic, five-foot-tall fern in a once-bright clay pot standing guard in a corner. The temperature was just as humid inside as it was out, but Areal had refused to change the blood red velvet drapes for something cooler or put in air-conditioning.

Not much had changed in the house but its occupants were another matter.

"Back then, you might've been the youngest but you definitely ran the show," Areal argued. Venom coated her words. She glared, permitting her nasty attitude to punctuate the air. Without thinking, she grabbed at strands of her long white hair that had come undone. No sooner had she managed to grasp one part, another fell. The tresses refused to return to the hairpins.

Areal let her hair fall about her shoulders and sank further back onto the sofa. "It was always your way or the highway." She stopped and pointed to a far corner of the room. "We both know what you came for. Go and get it yourself. I haven't touched it since you left."

Sasha took the verbal abuse because for once she had to admit she deserved it.

She was exhausted and struggled to make her way through the maze of ottomans and a collection of unread and unwrapped magazines. From the outside, Areal's house looked as lavish as the others in her neighborhood. Inside it was a collection of short- and long-term memories. Most of the memories were bad.

As though she'd just secreted it there yesterday, Sasha went straight toward a small nook in the bookcase. She took a small book from it. Balancing it in one hand, she shuffled, moving as if she were playing hopscotch, and then risked sitting down next to Areal.

Sasha's small mouth grimaced as she untied the fragile bow. The yellowed paper inside bore a small raised seal and was as delicate as the situation that lay before them.

Sasha looked at the paper, examining the writing several times. She then offered it to Areal.

Areal slapped Sasha's hand away as though Sasha were a small child.

Again, Sasha said nothing, knowing she probably deserved much worse. "Does Jasper still have his copy?"

Areal let the question linger in the air as she leaned back and released a sigh. "Yes," she finally answered. Her voice was sad and almost contrite. She was the total opposite of the spry old woman who'd just slapped at Sasha. "Jasper asked for it not long after his wife died. He'd contacted me only a couple of years after I'd left everything, and everyone, behind. I'd hoped he'd put it behind him, too."

"Why would he?" Sasha accidentally dropped the paper but managed to catch it before it hit the floor. "That baby was his. He had a responsibility even if he didn't have a say-so."

"Oh, now you feel he had a responsibility." Areal inched forward on the sofa and leaned on her walker. Her voice rose, seemingly two octaves at a time, with each accusation. "You took away his responsibility and his choice when you gave away that baby!"

The telephone rang. Areal stopped ranting long enough to answer by the third ring.

Sasha could tell by Areal's body language that the call would probably bring more bad news.

". . . Well, how soon can you get here? I don't give a flying hoot about what you're going through. Bring cash or a credit card, I really don't care which. I paid for Sasha to get here and you're gonna pay for her to return." Areal slammed down the receiver.

"Jasper will be here in about an hour," Areal replied to Sasha's silent question. "You may want to lie back and rest for a moment. He's putting you on the red eye back to Las Vegas."

"Thank you," Sasha said softly.

"Don't thank me. If I had to pay for it you'd be taking the train back." Areal's tone suddenly softened as she saw the drained look on her sister's face. "I'm assuming that you had enough wits about you not to check out of your hotel room."

"No, I didn't check out."

"So, what excuse will you give when they ask where you've been or why you didn't show up at that conference election or whatever it is that's going on?"

"I will have to come up with something."

"You mean to tell me that you haven't made up an excuse?"

"No, I haven't."

"You'll probably have to lie." Areal looked away. "It's not like you don't know how to lie." She turned back and looked at Sasha. "I don't go to church anymore, but even I know that God said He wouldn't judge a liar. Liars ain't worth God's time or effort."

The corners of Sasha's eyes, again, filled with tears. She was more frightened than she'd been in years. Everything her sister said was true. She'd maneuvered through life and customized her salvation to her liking. And now judgment was upon her. Her cover of well-rehearsed Bible verses and unorthodox bullying was about to be pulled back. She'd be revealed as the hypocrite. If necessary she could and would accept that indictment. But how would she explain giving away a child? And it wasn't just any child. The two-day-old baby was her niece. She'd chided and bullied Areal at a time when her sister was the most vulnerable.

Sasha and Areal started pulling small details from each other as they tried to reconstruct what had gone wrong. Each of the sisters had a piece to the puzzle and in a calm manner they tried to put it all in perspective, the good, the bad, and the ugly parts of earlier years.

They discussed how Areal was pregnant by not just any married man. She'd become pregnant by the illustrious Deacon Jasper Epps. The man sang spirituals as though he were born to do it. Areal remembered how churches for miles around bombarded him with their need for his vocal sermons. He could growl like the Mighty Clouds' Joe Ligon, or push out notes so smooth he'd make Smokey Robinson wish he could sing gospel.

After high school, Areal and Jasper had become closer when they formed a singing duet. They'd called themselves the Harmonizing Pair. Three months hadn't passed before they were taking harmony to another level. Jasper's excuse for the affair was the "my wife just don't understand me" one. Areal didn't have an excuse. She just wanted to make music whether in or out of bed.

Sasha again recalled how only a year later, Areal, Jasper, and she had returned to their home church after a long absence from being on the road. And it was at that church where the affair was uncovered. The three of them had become fearful when the traveling prophet had revealed Areal's pregnancy. Of course, Areal had hidden her swelling belly very well, so she thought, and the prophet hadn't mentioned Jasper at all.

The revelation that Sunday had jump-started an unholy pact between them. It was Sasha who convinced Areal of the unforgiving shame and humiliation that she'd bring to the family if she kept the baby.

Areal remembered arguing with Sasha in front of Jasper. "What do I care about bringing shame to this family?" Areal had declared. "That man loves me. We'll work something out."

"You're the biggest fool I know!" Sasha said, as they waited for Jasper to join in the conversation.

"You do love me, don't you?" Areal's eyes pleaded but somehow she'd known better.

Neither sister wanted to bring it up but it was time for the entire truth. They talked about the day Jasper finally revealed his true self. It'd happened on the same day Areal revealed her basement level of desperation.

Jasper had finally admitted that he'd never had intentions of ever leaving his rich wife or ruining his so-called church and public reputation or social standing. When he finally came around after a month's absence, he gave a substantial amount of money to Areal for her "troubles." As if he were doing everyone a favor by contributing financially to a situation he helped create and hoped she'd have the good sense to take care of. He'd had a lot of nerve evading blame for a mess partially created by his roaming libido.

"There ain't no more money, so don't ask for none," he'd said as he'd hurriedly peeled off several hundred-dollar bills as though each would wash away his part.

"Why are you treating me like this?" Areal finally asked him.

"It's what God would want me to do. After all, I do have a conscience." He'd answered as though he were insulted by the question.

Jasper never mentioned where God or his conscience had been when he was committing the adultery.

Soon after, Areal had no choice but to move away. She left immediately for New York, because she knew no one there. She eventually settled in the Bronx and Sasha joined her.

To make sure that no paths would lead back to them, after Sasha got Areal settled in their Bronx apartment, she suggested that the birth not take place anywhere near there.

Again, the sisters left for a place unfamiliar to them. They'd made up their minds to travel to Syracuse, New York. It was a big city and they could get lost in it. But Areal's baby had other plans. They'd made it only as far as Amsterdam, New York. Two weeks later, Areal returned to the Bronx without a swollen belly, or a crying baby.

Sasha might've orchestrated the adoption but it had also been Areal's choice, when she'd given birth, not to see her newborn or know who adopted the baby. At first, she hadn't known whether she'd given birth to a boy or a girl. Not seeing the baby meant she'd closed the door to any possible relationship with the child. And it also slammed the door to any further meaningful relationship with Sasha.

Areal found it much easier to blame Sasha for bullying her into giving up the baby. But it wasn't that easy when it came to Jasper. She'd never told him that she didn't have an abortion. She was convinced that there'd be no relationship at all with him, if she did tell the truth, so she'd taken his money without remorse.

However, just like a lot of women in her situation, common sense somehow gave way to a familiar disrespect for herself and a sexual need when a few months later, they reconnected. As soon as he'd contacted her under the guise of making sure she was all right, she was trapped.

"I thought you didn't want to have anything to do with me," she'd reminded him.

"I need you." Jasper's tone was confident and with good reason.

Three words—that was all it took to reignite their illicit affair. Areal had convinced Sasha that everything was fine and that Sasha was no longer needed.

Though Sasha initially didn't believe Areal had gotten over the baby's adoption so soon, she caved in. Sasha had returned to South Carolina thinking that she'd solved all of their problems. Of course, as fate would have it, Areal didn't have much time to mourn the baby she'd had and never seen. She became pregnant again, and by Jasper.

Sasha refused to return to New York a second time. The second pregnancy was an insult and she'd not help her sister again. She also didn't know at that time that Jasper was once more the father. Sasha reasoned that her older sister was just stupid and a slut.

Of course, Jasper hadn't changed even if Areal had. He'd stopped visiting her in New York for good once he saw her belly start to swell.

Areal, alone, gave birth to a second daughter and named her Ima. Areal never listed the father's name on the birth certificate because that would mean revealing to the world that she and Jasper had rekindled their affair and how stupid she truly was.

Areal's relationship with her daughter, Ima, went on to become problematic, but Areal was never sorry she hadn't aborted the second baby. She'd kept Ima in name only and more out of condemnation than love. It wasn't long before Areal had returned to her old nomadic ways, and by the time Ima was six, Areal had deposited her with two other cousins, and a perverted uncle. Areal's other brother and sisters wanted nothing to do with Areal.

When Sasha finally decided to forgive Areal, she repaid Sasha's kindness by depositing Ima on Sasha's doorstep.

Areal confessed to Sasha she'd finally changed her ways when one of the irate wives of one of her frivolous affairs had pointed a pistol at Areal and fired. That's when Areal decided to change courses. From that point on she only dated widowers.

The two sisters, both tired of rehashing their pasts, dozed off where they sat. They woke about the same time at the sound of heavy footsteps and a hard knock at the door. It'd been years since they'd heard those sounds, but they knew without question that it was Jasper.

24

When Chandler arrived at Bea's hotel room, he wasn't prepared for an inquisition. He was still a bit off kilter from dodging Alicia's shameless elevator flirting. So, if he'd known she would take it so bad, he'd never have told Bea that he saw Sasha leave the hotel with a suitcase.

"Sasha's a coward!" Bea hissed. "I'm sitting here with my pinky toe all busted and she leaves me. I would've stayed for her."

"Don't get so upset. I took the liberty of calling down to the desk and apparently she didn't check out of her room. She's probably just out on the town." Chandler thought his revelation had diffused the situation. He thought wrong.

"She went out on the town?" She looked at Zipporah for sympathy and dabbed at an imaginary tear. "I'm sitting here with a ruptured pinky toe and Sasha goes out on the town."

"Your toe was stepped on. It wasn't ruptured." Again, Chandler had opened his big mouth and inserted his foot. One look at Bea's face, which had turned a dark purple, told him to change paths.

Meanwhile, Zipporah's head swung back and forth between Bea and Chandler, as she tried to keep up with what appeared to be a vast difference of opinion or a conversation straight off the cartoon network.

"But, you don't really like her," Chandler reminded Bea. He managed a nervous laugh before continuing. "I'm surprised that the two of you have tolerated each other all these years."

"I thought they served on the same Mothers Board back at their home church." The words had left Zipporah's mouth before she could stop them. She looked quickly to Chandler for help.

"That little skinny Smurf doesn't take up much room on a

pew or a chair, so I do tolerate her." Bea laughed at her observation. She didn't want to talk about Sasha. She wanted to know more about Zipporah.

Bea didn't get a chance to continue her inquisition. Chandler interrupted with his news. He explained to Zipporah that an opportunity for her to sing was dropped in his lap. While Bea sat back and tried to interject more complaints, Chandler watched a wide smile creep across Zipporah's face at the news.

"You'll need to be ready by nine o'clock tonight," he explained. "You'll have to rush to have a costume fitting."

"Things are moving so fast," Zipporah gushed. "I'll have to thank your friend."

"So who's gonna take care of me if you two go running off?" Bea had started to complain again, but one look at Zipporah's face stopped her. "Don't worry. I'll be just fine. You go and sing."

Bea heard the unselfish words but had a problem believing that she was the one who uttered them. She'd never had children and never wanted any. She narrowed her eyes and looked at Zipporah and Chandler as they stood by the doorway. Her sudden feeling of curiosity was beginning to change to caring. Bea couldn't figure out why she felt she needed to take care of Zipporah. She also knew she could barely take care of her own needs as her bladder reminded her.

A short time later, Chandler was on his way taking Zipporah to Alicia's office for an official introduction. Zipporah was very chatty almost to the point of girlish giggling. Chandler couldn't take his eyes off her. The more excited she became the more he did, too. As soon as the elevator stopped and they stepped off, Zipporah thought her heart would stop, too.

"This can't be happening," she murmured. Her shoulders drooped and her smile fled, dragging the color in her face along with it.

"What's wrong?" Chandler asked, feeling as if he were watching a human chameleon in action. "Are you nervous? You shouldn't be." He tried to take her hand but she snatched it away.

Zipporah didn't have time to explain the earlier dismissal and humiliation she'd received in this same office. She'd barely gotten her heart under control when Alicia came through the office door. She slowed her walk to one that almost resembled an amateurish and comical striptease.

Even if Chandler didn't notice, which was hard to believe, none of the feminine antics displayed were lost on Zipporah. There was no doubt in Zipporah's mind. She immediately recognized Miss Cowing as the same woman who hadn't even let her sing at a recent audition after taking one look at her. She still had the same pasty complexion and that same uppity attitude. If Zipporah had any doubts, they were removed as soon as the woman walked past her without a glance and put her arm through Chandler's.

"You work fast," Alicia cooed. "But quick is good—sometimes." She lowered her eyes in appreciation of his masculinity before continuing, "And then, sometimes not."

Zipporah watched intensely. The woman had acted, again, as though she didn't exist.

Chandler gently guided his arm out of Miss Cowing's unwarranted and possessive grip. "Alicia—" he let his warm smile disarm her while he turned on the charm— "this is the answer to your dilemma."

"Who would that be?" She'd seen the young beauty but her flirtatious style required that she let the woman know who was in charge.

It only took a second for Zipporah to realize that the woman hadn't recognized her from before. With Chandler obviously the man-toy the woman wanted, Zipporah instantly relaxed. She'd recognized the game and decided she'd play along. It was also clear that there was nothing more than a business interest on Chandler's part. She'd seen the way he maneuvered out of Miss Cowing's grasp and kept to their plan.

As much as Miss Cowing would've loved to dismiss Zipporah, she couldn't. Zipporah nailed the vocals, singing a cappella effortlessly. Alicia watched her and somehow, her instinct told her that Zipporah's performance was just as much for Chandler as it was for her. As for the costumes, they'd fitted Zipporah as if they were tailor-made. Even she couldn't fit into a size 4 and look that good.

After the audition, Chandler walked Zipporah out. He showered her with praises and promises of nothing but good things happening for her.

Zipporah didn't know if she were walking or gliding, she was so high on life at that moment. But Zipporah's happiness was only on loan. Chandler suddenly offered to drive her home instead of letting her wait on a bus. He'd said he was making the offer so she could have a chance to get everything together. Zipporah panicked. There was no way she'd let him find out she lived in a homeless shelter. She didn't know how to get out of taking his offer when it made so much sense.

Chandler had just taken his keys out and was about ready for them to go to the underground garage when his cellular phone rang. He turned to Zipporah. "Just let me take this call. It won't be long."

Zipporah looked flushed but she was grateful his phone had rung. Her mind raced. She just couldn't let him discover she lived in a homeless shelter. All she needed was a few weeks of making money and then she could afford a place she'd be proud to call home and he could visit if he still wanted. Until then she needed an excuse to keep him away and not jeopardize her chance to sing at the Luxor.

"I'm sorry, Zipporah," Chandler apologized. "I'm afraid we're going to have to have a change of plans."

"Why?" She could feel her heart racing, fearing she was about to lose this precious opportunity.

Chandler saw the immediate change and concern. He prefaced his reply with a smile. "They're going to need you to come in earlier to go over the music. You're good but they can't be too careful. It's normal."

The color returned to her face. "I'd better get home and prepare." She had an idea. "I'll take a cab home."

"I've something else in mind." Chandler flipped open his cell phone as he spoke. The excitement built as he dialed a number. He spoke briefly, turning his shoulder slightly as though the conversation were private. "It's a done deal," he said.

"What is?"

"I've gotten you a room right here at the Luxor. You can relax and do whatever you need and still be ready for tonight."

Chandler read the question on Zipporah's face and answered, "It's paid for."

"Really . . . ?"

"All you need is some type of formal I.D. It's in your name. I didn't want to be too presumptuous."

"I believe I have my driver's license with me." She wasn't certain. She hadn't driven since arriving in Las Vegas and hoped it wasn't back at the shelter locked away, with her other important papers, in their office. She laughed nervously and reached inside her bag for her wallet and an excuse she'd need for not returning to the shelter by curfew.

Chandler had laughed as she dug frantically into her pocketbook. She liked that.

"There is one thing you can give me," Chandler said as his laughter ebbed but didn't entirely stop.

"And what would that be?" They were in a dark parking garage and suddenly she felt a bit leery. She just couldn't catch a complete break. She had no intention of giving him what she was sure he was about to ask for.

Before Zipporah's imagination could completely run away, Chandler saw the sudden change in her demeanor and spoke up. "I just wondered if you had a tissue in your bag?"

Zipporah's body relaxed, confirming that she'd thought the worst of him. But again, he'd put her at ease with his laughter.

"It just so happens that I do." She opened another compartment in her bag, and the first thing she noticed was that her wallet was gone.

"My wallet," she said quickly. "It's not here."

Zipporah turned the bag upside down. An almost empty packet of tissues was there, other unimportant papers, but her wallet was missing.

Being laid up didn't mean drama couldn't find Bea. She certainly hadn't wasted time while she lay around her hotel room healing.

Bea had found Zipporah's wallet. It had fallen between the cushions on the sofa. Bea was convinced that the only way to contact Zipporah to let her know that she'd left the wallet was to go through it, meticulously. And if there was something she'd find that provided more information about Zipporah, well so be it. It wasn't like she'd stolen the wallet.

Bea immediately dismissed the idea that she could've contacted Chandler and told him about the wallet, especially since he and Zipporah had left together only a short time before.

Bea was totally shocked to discover the telephone number in the wallet was for a homeless shelter. She'd called the number three times. The second time, she'd disguised her voice. The third time, she'd asked for Zipporah Moses. The woman answering seemed to be annoyed at the mere mention of Zipporah's name.

"Zipporah Moses is not in her room." The woman had almost spat out the information. "Who's calling?"

Bea was taken totally by surprise. "I'm her aunt. . . ." Bea said without giving it a second thought.

"Really," the woman had replied. "Are you local?"

"I'm right here in Las Vegas," Bea said. Her story seemed to take on a life of its own. In a matter of seconds, she'd managed to convince the woman to take her number and to have Zipporah call her. She could've told the woman that she'd found Zipporah's wallet but she didn't like the woman's tone.

Chandler offered to put the hotel room in his name to make it easier for Zipporah until she could find her wallet. Between the two, they'd retraced her steps and couldn't figure out where she'd left it. He also offered to advance her money or whatever she needed. He wanted her to be at her best for that night's performance.

"We'll find it," Chandler dished out the false hope, with a side order of a smile. He'd do whatever he could to keep Zipporah's mind on the task at hand. He added, "I'll go back inside and check with Lost and Found."

Zipporah somehow knew that he would handle things, so she asked him to wait while she used the bathroom in the lobby to pull herself together.

No sooner had Zipporah walked away than Chandler's cell phone rang, again.

He'd not recognized the number, although it did seem vaguely familiar. "Chandler Lamb," he said.

"Hi, June Bug, it's Mother Blister."

"Are you all right?" Chandler immediately asked. One day, she'd stop calling him *June Bug* and that day couldn't come soon enough.

"Well, my pinky toe done swollen up to the size of an apple." As usual she'd stretched the truth.

There was silence. Bea thought perhaps Chandler hadn't heard her. "Listen, June Bug," she continued, "is Zipporah still with you?"

"Yes. Do you need her?"

"No," Bea replied. "I found her wallet and I didn't want her to worry about it."

Chandler didn't ask nor did he care how the wallet ended up with Mother Blister. He was simply glad it had. "She's looking for it. Please hold on to it and when she returns I'll let her know that you have it."

"That's so sweet of you, June Bug." She wanted to tell him about Zipporah living in a shelter but decided against it.

Bea hung up the telephone and examined the foot. The swelling had gone down considerably but she didn't feel a need to share that information with Chandler. She certainly wouldn't get any sympathy if she did.

Bea's spirit picked up when she thought about how happy Zipporah would be when she found out that Bea not only had her lost wallet but hadn't told anyone about the homeless shelter.

Bea's foreign sense of caring grew as the swelling subsided. However, it wasn't that she'd never cared for anyone or about anything; she had. She'd just found salvation and she saw nothing but goodness in everyone.

It only took one scandalous lie from one of the church trustees to wreck Bea's trust. It was after a Thursday evening revival meeting. Several baskets of hard-earned money coerced by the preacher with threats of hellfire made their way into a back room. She'd been a member of the usher board, back then. After delivering the monies into the hands of two trustees, in the back room, she'd left.

A short time later, in between services, she'd returned to gather fans and modesty cloths. The men were so certain of their privacy they hadn't bothered to make sure the door was completely closed. It took her a moment to realize that they were dividing the proceeds among them from one of the baskets. They'd laughed as they stole hard-earned money from the congregation, "God helps them that helps themselves," she heard one of the trustees boast.

Not knowing what to do, she'd backed out. Unable to enjoy the rest of the revival, she went about her usher duty while trying to decide whether or not to inform the reverend, after the service. But when she saw the same two trustees laughing with the reverend as he was handed a thick envelope, she knew it was pointless.

Although she'd moved her membership twice since then, she'd seen the same treachery in one form or another no matter where she worshipped. As far as she was concerned, everyone had their own relationship with God. Hers had been on a day-to-day basis and some days were closer than others. But she'd never trusted or cared, completely, again.

The reason Sasha seemingly didn't like the girl still puzzled Bea. She was determined to find out. She knew Sasha liked very few people but this was a particular unspoken dislike for Zipporah, something almost akin to a fear. Bea knew Sasha feared no one, normally.

Zipporah saw Chandler's face light up when she returned. "What happened?" At that moment, she really didn't care because her mind was still on locating her wallet. She'd asked because she felt she should.

"Mother Blister has your wallet. You left it in her room."

"Really? I don't remember taking it out but I'm glad she found it."

"We'll stop by her room and pick it up later."

"I guess the free room just went out the door." Zipporah tried to smile but she wasn't convincing.

"Of course it's not. When I say I'm going to do something, I generally do it."

"But you don't really know me well enough to keep a word like that."

"I don't have to know you to keep my word." He was slightly offended by her statement but he didn't show it. "I can use the tax write off."

"I wouldn't want to deprive you of that."

The jovial mood had returned.

25

The applause at the performance later on that night was almost deafening, but enthusiastically appreciated. After the last curtain call, Alicia, watching the musicians and other background singers surround Zipporah, had to admit, inwardly, that Zipporah had stolen the show. She was about to eat the proverbial bowl of crow and compliment Zipporah before one of the other singers, bubbling over, spoke up first.

"My goodness, your singing wore me out!" The compliment rolled off the tongue from a rather large, cinnamon-colored woman who'd waited for the others to leave before approaching Zipporah. Just the night before, she'd been the one the crowd roared their approval for. At first, there was a bit of professional jealousy toward the newcomer and she'd actually waited for Zipporah to fail. But talent recognized talent and she had to give Zipporah her props.

She'd approached Zipporah swinging her large red Afro wig in one hand, leaving her salt and pepper microbraids exposed. She was a part of the oldies segment and normally received standing ovations when she imitated double-entendre-laced hits by Big Maybelle and Ruth Brown. "Gurlfriend, I'm so glad you're here."

"Thank you." Zipporah's shyness was genuine as she struggled to accept the compliment.

"You nailed Miss Aretha's 'Chain of Fools.' I almost forgot it was you singing and not the Queen." She smiled widely, showing a huge gap in her teeth that seemed to fit her personality. "Welcome aboard. They call me Miss Libido, for all the right reasons," she continued with a mischievous wink. "Now I don't have to carry this entire show by myself."

Zipporah was equally impressed with the woman's vocal styling but didn't have the nerve to cut her off to tell her.

Alicia, who'd stood off to the side and hadn't appeared to be listening, suddenly butted in. "Don't worry about carrying this entire show, Miss Libido," Alicia teased, "just make sure you can carry your own weight. . . ." She let the word *weight* linger in the air to make sure the taunt was understood.

The plus-sized woman didn't blink. She walked slowly between Zipporah and Alicia. There was no expression on her face as she passed, letting her ample bosom guide her as she brushed against Alicia and turned to Zipporah. "Let's get together after the next show. We'll chat about what singers know about."

No sooner had the woman moved away when some of the other performers gathered, again, to congratulate Zipporah and make her feel welcomed.

Earlier during the show, while Zipporah was on stage, Bea beamed. Every time Zipporah finished a song, Bea clapped louder than anyone. Normally having sat so long would've caused pain in her curved spine, but not tonight. She was thrilled that Chandler had managed to get them a table that was close to the stage.

"Too bad your godmother couldn't be so bothered as to show up and give support," Bea said, as she teetered between being grateful and her usual snippy attitude. "Even with my broken pinky toe I still came downstairs to be with you. That's what a true Christian would do. They'd come to the club."

Chandler was about to tell Mother Blister that Sister Betty wouldn't venture into a casino club ever again, even if she had to go through it to escape a fire, but at that moment, he was too thrilled with Zipporah.

"That woman can sing!" Chandler said. "The world needs to know about her!" It was as though the old music promotion juices had awoken.

Bringing the subject back to Zipporah temporarily caused Bea to forget about Sister Betty's absence. "She's a real sweetheart, isn't she?" Bea's eyes danced as she waited for Chandler to respond. She knew nothing about the music industry, but she did know about human nature and beauty.

"Yes, she appears to be so." Chandler knew where Mother

Blister was headed and he wasn't about to fall into her match-making trap. "I don't mix business with pleasure."

"Never said you had to," Bea teased. "And since this is only business, I guess it wouldn't matter to you whether she was a se-rial killer or a homeless person?"

"Couldn't care less," Chandler answered, "as long as there wasn't a warrant out for her arrest and she at least had a card-board box to sleep in, I wouldn't care."

"Really . . ." Bea moved a little closer to Chandler. "Why is that?"

"Because that singing sista is about to get herself and me paid!" Chandler laughed. "She'll make us enough money to buy the best attorney and condo money can afford."

"June Bug, you need to quit!" Bea's laughter did what it al-ways did when she put too much into it. So she needed to find a bathroom.

Bea's sudden trek to the bathroom gave Chandler an opportu-nity to go backstage and find Zipporah. He wasn't surprised to find her surrounded by the other performers. However, finding Alicia suddenly embracing Zipporah was a plus and a minus. He knew the signs of a true vulture and, tonight, Alicia Cowing was at the top of her game.

Chandler stood in the shadows and continued watching Alicia's show of sudden humility. He couldn't help but laugh quietly. The woman had chosen wisely. She knew Zipporah had to be kept happy in order to keep her. Alicia wouldn't dare continue to flirt with him, at least not in front of Zipporah. Everything from that point on would be business.

"Zipporah," Chandler called out as he rushed to her side, "you were fabulous."

"Thank you." Zipporah let her eyes drop as her mind spun trying to grasp all that was suddenly happening.

Chandler deliberately ignored Alicia's gaze as he placed an arm around Zipporah's shoulders. "Believe me," he conspired, "there are several big names from the Las Vegas entertainment scene that were clapping and about to lose their minds."

Chandler let his words rest a moment knowing that Alicia knew exactly what he meant even if Zipporah hadn't.

"Oh, Alicia." Chandler turned and smiled broadly. "I'm so

sorry. I was so excited for my artist that I'd forgotten to thank you for this opportunity to showcase her talents."

"Your artist." Alicia bit her lip to keep from telling Chandler exactly what she felt about his unexpected imposition into Zipporah's sudden fame. "I wasn't aware that you'd signed her since we spoke, only a few hours ago."

Zipporah stood by Chandler's side and watched. She knew exactly what he was doing and she approved. He was maximizing the moment and she wasn't about to spoil it.

"Excuse me," Zipporah interjected, "I'm really tired." She followed with a yawn as though bored with whatever was going on. "I imagine I can keep the hotel room until checkout tomorrow."

Now it was Alicia's turn to impress Zipporah. "You will need to be here early for an extra rehearsal. Just keep the suite and the Luxor will pick up the bill." She smiled as she saw the look of supposed surprise creep across Chandler's face. "Of course, that would include three meals and telephone for the six-week run of the show."

Chandler nodded slowly. "Of course, Alicia and I will revise the paperwork to reflect a modest pay increase and other amenities."

Even from where they stood they could still hear Zipporah's name whispered among the crowd. Alicia needed to secure Zipporah before she became too expensive.

Alicia returned the nod. She'd expected nothing less from him.

"I'm really tired." Zipporah gave a bigger yawn along with an inconspicuous wink at Chandler. "I'll let my manager handle things from here on. You don't need me." Zipporah said good night and excused herself while Chandler and Alicia's game of ping-pong negotiations continued.

Concern for whether or not she'd still have a room at the shelter lessened. It was replaced by the reality of a possible break finally happening.

The elevator was empty as Zipporah rode up to her suite. She was glad for the solitude, wanting only her thoughts as company. As soon as she entered and turned on the lights, the tiredness she'd felt disappeared in an instant. She saw roses. Long-stemmed pink, white, and red roses . . . The aroma overpowered her senses. There were more on the nightstand, the coffee table, and although she didn't drink, she appreciated the rather large bottle of champagne chilling in a gold bucket of ice.

"Not too shabby for a girl from a homeless shelter." Zipporah sang the words with a soulfulness that would become her signature sound.

She slipped out of her dress and carefully hung it in the closet. It looked perfect alongside the other outfits that Chandler had delivered to the suite earlier. She hadn't asked him for anything, but he seemed to have a sense of her personal style and they'd only met. There wasn't one outfit that she found fault with. Each outfit looked expensive but she couldn't be certain. He or someone had taken off the price tags. Either way, she wouldn't have been able to buy them. If that night was any indication of her future, she'd repay him one day.

Zipporah's eyes kept surveying her hotel suite as though if she didn't it would all disappear. She covered her mouth to muffle her laughter as she removed her makeup. And, for the first time in a long time, Zipporah fell to her knees beside a bed that didn't have the stench of the impoverished or the tear stains of desperation.

And Zipporah talked to God like He was an old friend she'd lost touch with, and then she cried.

26

Sister Betty awoke around midnight with a headache. She was almost glad she'd received the call, earlier, telling her that the Mothers Board election was postponed until further notice. She hadn't eaten since the previous morning. Her stomach growled and yet she couldn't bring herself to eat anything.

Sister Betty groped for the light on the nightstand and suddenly remembered that she'd dreamed while she slept. Whenever God dealt with her about something specific it was always through a dream.

Taking a cold, wet towel from the bathroom, she folded it and placed it upon her forehead, then lay back down. As the thumping in her head began to subside, bits and pieces of the dream returned. There were shapes, voices that surfaced slowly but without any definite revelation. She felt like a prisoner of her dream and wondered if God was still testing her. Suddenly she sat up in bed.

"Ima!" she said aloud. She snatched the wet towel that had fallen to the floor, readjusting it so that it covered her entire face as she leaned back.

She'd dreamt about Ima, Mother Pray Onn's cantankerous yet beautiful niece. Ima was a one-woman terrorist.

In Sister Betty's dream, Ima stood in two places, seemingly, at the same time. Neither of the Ima lookalikes looked directly at one another. And she remembered that Bea had her arm around one of them and Sasha, the other.

The memory ended abruptly with no resolution that made sense to Sister Betty. Perhaps God was showing her things like a television series. She'd have to go back to sleep for the next episode.

She uncovered her face, a mask of wrinkles with thin lips that pursed. She stood and tried to stretch.

One trip to the bathroom and more water on her face finally brought to Sister Betty what she thought was a rational meaning of the dream. *That girl,* Sister Betty thought, *looks too much like Ima. That's probably why I dreamed about her.*

A smile replaced the confused look as she reasoned that it wasn't Ima she'd dreamt about. She could've done a little shout right there in her hotel room if sanity hadn't decided to snatch her back to reality. Neither Bea nor Sasha was the huggable type, so why would they hug a stranger in the dream?

Sister Betty plopped back into her chair and massaged her temples. She was preparing for what she knew would be a tumultuous journey. She'd tried running from whatever it was that God planned involving Bea and Sasha. Again, she repented and decided to forgo any food. She'd need to fast and pray to deal with Bea and Sasha's particular spirits.

Sister Betty had barely a chance to embrace the idea of a possible battle with Bea and Sasha when the hotel room phone rang. For a brief moment she thought she was hearing things. She looked at the clock. It was almost one-thirty in the morning. *Who in their right mind would be calling me at this hour?* She wanted to ignore it but found she couldn't. After the third ring she answered.

"Yes." She deliberately tried to inflect her voice with irritation.

There was a pause but she could hear breathing. "Who is this?" Telephone games, particularly at that time of the morning, were definitely unwelcome. Just as she was about to pull the phone away from her ear, the voice on the other end finally spoke.

"Sister Betty," the voice said calmly, although on second thought, it seemed almost a question. "Sister Betty," the voice repeated. The voice was familiar and its eerie calmness threw her.

"Yes," Sister Betty answered. "Who is this?"

Again, the silence before the voice answered, "It's Sasha Pray Onn."

"Who did you say this was?" Sister Betty's small frame felt like folding. In all the years she'd known Sasha Pray Onn, there was never a time when she'd received a telephone call, or even a home visit, from her.

On the other end of the telephone stashed away in the corner of her hotel room, Sasha sat teary eyed as she wrung her hands. The last thing she'd wanted was to call Sister Betty but she was at her wit's end.

Just before she'd called Sister Betty in the middle of the night, Bea had called Sasha. After listening to Bea go on and on about Zipporah's performance and how she'd found out that the young woman actually lived in a homeless shelter, Sasha felt the guilt and aches of old age.

"What makes you think I care about some woman that neither of us knows?" Sasha had argued. "Shouldn't we be about the business of keeping our Mothers Board positions?"

It was as though Bea hadn't heard one word Sasha said. Instead, Bea gave Sasha line and verse of Zipporah's performance. Sasha had almost wished Bea would've blasted her about her sudden disappearance. The fact that Bea hadn't started off chastising her meant only one thing: Bea was going to be a problem, a big problem. Bea was becoming too attached to Zipporah and was unknowingly about to resurrect a secret Sasha had thought was deeply buried.

Sasha held the telephone receiver away from her ear as Bea finally began to weigh in on her earlier absence. "You got some nerve just up and disappearing without a word," Bea fumed, and without taking a breath, she changed the subject. "I'm telling you that Zipporah sang her heart out. I just met her and already I love that gal! It seems like I've known her for years."

But Bea knew how to play the crazy game when it suited her. She wasn't about to let up on Sasha. When Sasha didn't nibble on the bait, Bea added, "Don't you feel like you know her, too?" Bea wove her thoughts like a spider eager to trap her prey.

"I met her the same time you did," Sasha finally said. "You need to take something for your memory." Sasha felt Bea was fishing for something but couldn't be exactly sure what.

When Sasha could take no more of Bea's probing she hung up, without so much as saying good-bye. With no remorse, Sasha snatched the phone from its cradle and laid it on its side. She didn't want any further annoyance from Bea. Sasha also decided if Bea chose to hobble over to her room, she wouldn't let her in. Just the thought of what could happen if Bea continued to pry caused Sasha mental anxiety.

Sasha stood and dragged her aching hips over to the window. Looking over the Las Vegas skyline lit with colors of false hope, she pondered her situation. There was no way out of what she knew she had to face. Her demons had finally caught up with her. She'd rather chew on glass and chase it down with a bottle of bleach, but she had neither.

Sasha inched back to a chair and sat down slowly. At that point she really didn't have a choice for a cohort. And that's when she'd called Sister Betty.

In her hotel suite, which was to her dismay on the same floor as Sasha's, Sister Betty sat perplexed. The gnawing of another headache had started. She grabbed a handful of unwrapped peppermints that lay in a small bowl on the coffee table. Forgetting her dentures were still in a water glass in the bathroom, she chomped away. Pain sprang from her bald gums from the candy's sharp edges, but she ignored it. Her notion of fasting had disappeared as soon as she'd heard Sasha's voice. When Sasha had called moments earlier, she'd tried to talk her out of coming. With her voice laced with agitation, she'd hissed into the telephone, "Sasha, it's after midnight." But Sasha would not be denied.

Sister Betty looked at the clock again. It was almost two o'clock, the middle of the night. What was so important that Sasha had to come to her room at that hour?

Sister Betty straightened her pageboy wig, which she'd not removed since putting it on earlier in the previous day. She tugged at a stray strand of the wig as she remembered overhearing Sasha complain about her to several other Mothers Board members. Sasha had done it after a hot revival meeting, several months ago. Sister Betty had been praising God until the ushers finally sat her down so the service could conclude. She was still in the spirit but not so much that she couldn't make out Sasha's tinny voice rising above the music. "That Sister Betty is always aggravating the Lord with her shouting," Sasha had cackled. "She probably got Jesus taking Tylenol and wearing a pain patch!"

Sister Betty wasn't surprised at Sasha's nasty comments on her worship techniques. Sasha had something negative to say about most of the members. What hurt was that the other members she thought were her friends had laughed and agreed with Sasha.

Just thinking about Sasha made Sister Betty's blood pressure, diabetes, and cholesterol rise. She snatched off her wig with several bobby pins still dangling and strands of her own white hair caught in them. "Father, give me strength. Lord, please give me a sign that I don't have to deal with this." She repeated the prayer and nothing happened. There was no sudden breeze flowing through her room with its windows closed. No stiffness in her knees to alert her to God's presence. She felt as though heaven had placed her on hold because God was not pleased with her disobedience and questioning of His will.

Sister Betty ignored her better judgment and called Chandler's cell phone, knowing it was a ridiculous hour to do so. She wasn't sure how talking about her anxiety would solve anything but she had to do something. After the third ring his voice mail answered. She quickly hung up. What message could she possibly leave? "Hi, Chandler, it's your godmother. Mother Pray Onn is on her way to my room and I'd appreciate it if you could break her legs before she arrives."

Sister Betty didn't have time to think of any other foolish excuses. Several loud raps at her room door took care of that.

Before she could barely open the door, Sasha barged inside, determined. "You need to order some tea or something stronger," Sasha ordered.

"Why don't you come on in," Sister Betty snapped. "We can chat and watch the sun come up."

"I don't have time for your sanctimonious attitude," Sasha replied. She tossed her cane to the side and plopped down on the sofa.

Sister Betty was about to invite Sasha to leave but she couldn't. It took a moment before Sister Betty realized the color had drained from Sasha's face. When she saw Sasha rest her head in the palms of her hands, like a rebuked child, she softened.

"Sasha," Sister Betty said quietly and that time, sincerely, "what's going on?"

Sasha's brown eyes were wide and transfixed. Her brow furrowed. She looked as though her soul had fled, taking along Sister Betty's question and her answer to it. And just as suddenly, her thin lips fluttered, but no sound came forth. Sasha's heaving shoulders and her trembling hands tried to explain what her words could not.

Sister Betty timidly walked over to where Sasha sat shaking. She moved aside a couple of fashion magazines. "I didn't see this coming . . ." Sister Betty muttered.

She looked around the room and found her Bible. She took it from atop the desk and sat. Without giving a thought to whether Sasha needed it or not, Sister Betty decided she'd read the Twenty-third Psalm. It was as much for her benefit as Sasha's.

" 'Yea, though I walk through the shadow of death, I will fear no evil. . . .' "

Sister Betty read aloud the entire psalm before she looked over at Sasha. Sasha sat with her eyes toward the ceiling and at first she gave no indication as to whether she'd heard anything.

And then everything that could go wrong in Sister Betty's world did just that. The crying from the impish figure on the couch began almost like a muffled purr and then escalated like a rickety old roller coaster climbing toward the top.

Just as Joshua and the Israelites shouted and caused the impenetrable walls of Jericho to crumble, so did Sasha's last wall of defense, when she'd heard the Twenty-third Psalm.

In between sobs Sasha kept repeating the words *my baby, my baby*. Wringing her hands while she rocked back and forth, Sasha looked pathetic. Sister Betty had never in all the years she'd known Sasha seen her in that condition.

And while Sister Betty pondered her next move, Sasha's mouth gave up the ghosts of the past to the one person she'd have never shared it with. Too much remorse and too many ifs made her do some strange things.

Sasha alternated between confessing and excusing. She went back and forth giving Sister Betty sometimes just a piece of the story and other times, telling her everything about a particular part. And when she finished, she questioned Sister Betty as if Sister Betty held the answers.

"What if I hadn't harassed Areal into giving up the baby? What if I'd not insisted Areal not see the baby before we placed it for adoption?" Sasha's voice rose and her body rocked as the self-recrimination poured out of her. "And months later, I get pregnant by Jasper and lose the baby. Why?" Sasha's eyes lifted towards the ceiling as though expecting Sister Betty to have floated above her with the answers. But Sasha wasn't finished. She wrung her hands and quickly dropped her head. "Areal kept bragging about Jasper's bedroom skills and I was jealous. I had to try him once." Sasha raised her head, again, to the ceiling. "It was one time too many.

"Sasha!" Sister Betty had already called her name three times, and each time Sasha ignored her. She'd moved closer to where Sasha sat because she couldn't understand Sasha's mumbling.

"I don't have the answers."

"I didn't want her to have neither one of those babies." Sasha still wouldn't look Sister Betty in the eye. Everything felt like she was trapped in an old B movie. She was sitting in the hotel room of a woman she couldn't stand and revealing all her dirty secrets. Why? That's the part she couldn't figure out. She'd become the punch line to her own joke on life.

Once Sasha started releasing the secrets she'd held tight for so long, she couldn't stop. She ignored the shocked look on Sister Betty's face as more of the unadulterated truth poured from her soul. And when she finally finished recounting the sins, some of which she'd almost forgotten, she felt smaller. It was as though most of her tiny frame was made up of lies and contradictions. And then Sasha collapsed, exhausted, against the back of the sofa. Sasha looked every bit like the munchkin she'd been called so often.

Sister Betty got up and returned with a glass of water. "Here, Sasha, drink this."

Sasha refused the water. "You've got to help me stop Bea. If what I did gets out, I'm ruined. My reputation, my position on the Mothers Board." As though she'd suddenly realized that her selfishness was dominating the conversation, she quickly added, "And that poor child Zipporah shouldn't have to deal with the family. She seems to be doing just fine. It's not her fault that she looks just like Ima but it will be her undoing."

Sasha pouted to appear more convincing. "I know you probably think I'm just making all this up but you know me better than that."

Deep down Sister Betty knew Sasha was probably telling as much of the truth as she could, or would. It was still too much for her to take in and she wasn't about to become more involved than she was already. "What do you mean, I've got to help you?"

"I'm not leaving here until you do!" Truth had purged Sasha. However, her nastiness, which was crucial to her survival, hadn't completely deserted her. Sasha's eyes narrowed as she silently challenged Sister Betty's authority to rule in her own hotel room. Sasha, without blinking, kicked off her slippers to get comfortable.

And that's when Sister Betty rose and ordered a pot of strong, hot, chamomile tea, for Sasha. She needed something stronger, so she brewed a carafe of cayenne pepper tea, the extra-strength blend.

Sister Betty tried to absorb this information or as much as she could. A baby; Sasha was responsible for altering the lives of two innocent babies, Ima becoming a she-devil and Zipporah, an angel. Could it be possible?

Looking over quickly at Sasha, who sat staring down at her clasped hands, Sister Betty suddenly began to have doubts. In the past she'd known Sasha to make lives miserable. If what she'd confessed was true, that would make Sasha pure evil. Sister Betty narrowed her eyes and sighed. She concluded that Sasha had finally lost her mind and prayer might not be enough to find it.

27

It was barely after nine o'clock in the morning but Bea was determined to catch up with Zipporah before the rehearsals for that evening's performance began. She'd already tricked Chandler into giving her Zipporah's room number by telling him that she wanted to personally return Zipporah's wallet even though he'd already told Zipporah it'd been found.

When Bea had called Zipporah earlier and suggested that they have breakfast, Zipporah had tried to politely decline. Bea acted as though she didn't get the hint and wouldn't back off. Out of a sense of respect and a need to have her wallet, Zipporah accepted Bea's invitation.

Bea ambled into the hotel restaurant wearing a floral print dress, zebra-striped jacket, and large sunglasses. The sunglasses were a last minute touch in case someone wanted her autograph. She hadn't been bothered for it in the past few days but she needed to stay ready for the obligations of fame. Bea still didn't realize that it had never shown up for her.

She spotted Zipporah immediately. Zipporah had that star quality, according to Bea, that seemed to illuminate the space around her.

"Good morning, Zipporah." Bea sang the greeting as a tribute to Zipporah. She didn't seem to care or notice that her rhythm and notes were flat.

"Good morning, Mother Blister." Zipporah suppressed a smile. She really couldn't be angry with the old woman. There weren't that many people who seemed to care about her, whether she was talented or not, without wanting something in return. But she couldn't deny being curious about the reason Bea wanted to have breakfast with her.

Bea immediately handed Zipporah her wallet. When Zipporah took it, Bea noticed something she hadn't seen before. "That's a lovely tattoo on your wrist." Bea took Zipporah's hand without permission. Turning it over, she examined the small image on the inside of Zipporah's wrist.

"It's not a tattoo." Zipporah smiled and explained further, "It's my birthmark. I guess I'm accustomed to it so I don't pay it any attention."

Bea returned the smile. "Is that so?" She examined it again and for a moment thought it looked familiar, too. "What exactly is it?"

"When I was younger it looked to me like a small plant leaf." Zipporah traced the outline of the birthmark. "Now it looks like a collard green leaf."

"Really?" Bea laughed. "You ain't never had collard greens until you taste mine."

"Can I ask you a question?" Zipporah picked at the bacon and cheese omelet. She really had no intention of eating it but Bea had blurted out the order before she could stop her.

"You can ask me anything you want." Bea couldn't stop smiling. She was overjoyed by Zipporah's apparent acceptance.

"Why are you so friendly toward me? What is it that you want?"

"Say what?" Bea was truly astounded. Her face turned a deeper purple, which made her complexion look like an overripe eggplant.

"I didn't mean to insult you." The moment the question had left her mouth and she saw Bea's hurt look, Zipporah was sorry. "Why don't we just finish eating our breakfast, is that okay?"

Bea thought for a second as her normal color slowly returned. She was really impressed that Zipporah was no pushover. She just didn't expect the question to be turned around on her. "I'm not upset." She reached over and took her pocketbook from a vacant seat. While Zipporah looked on, Bea took an envelope out of her bag.

"Now, I'm really confused," Zipporah said as she dropped the wallet into her pocketbook. She didn't want to insult Bea by checking its contents, so she picked her fork up to nibble at the food.

Then Bea pushed the envelope across the table toward Zipporah. "Just open it," Bea said.

Zipporah put down the fork and opened the envelope. Curiosity was nibbling at her, yet she took an extra moment to wipe away a crumb with her napkin, almost trying to avoid what was coming.

Bea sat back as straight as she could. She locked her eyes upon Zipporah's face, daring not to look away and miss any reaction.

As Zipporah opened the envelope she tried to imagine what was in it. She opened it slowly, as though she were announcing the winner at the Grammys. And then she saw it. In the picture, standing next to what looked like the ramp of a cruise ship, was the other elderly woman, Mother Pray Onn. Standing next to Mother Pray Onn was Zipporah as a younger woman.

The questioning look crawling across Zipporah's face was not lost on Bea. She didn't say anything, preferring to watch the scene play out.

"I was never in this picture." Zipporah pushed away from the table but she didn't stand.

Bea didn't flinch. She watched Zipporah intently and said, "No, you weren't, you're right."

"Then who is this?" Zipporah was becoming suspicious, feeling tension in her stomach.

"It's not you." Bea leaned in closer and beckoned her to do the same. Nearby eyes inside the restaurant were staring.

"Take another look." Bea pointed at the picture.

Zipporah pulled her chair closer to the table and looked at the photograph again. This time, she studied it slower, letting her suspicions take a backseat. To her surprise there were some subtle differences that came into view. The younger woman wore her hair in a ponytail and her clothes were far more expensive than any Zipporah had ever worn. But those were the only differences she saw. The woman's height, weight, complexion, including the way she smirked for the camera, at first glance looked exactly like Zipporah.

Zipporah's face went blank.

Bea's face lit up. She knew it. If Zipporah saw the resemblance, then Sasha had to have seen it, too.

"That young woman in the picture with Mother Pray Onn is her niece, Ima."

"We could be twins, but I don't have any brothers or sisters." Zipporah was happy to know that the other woman had a name.

It was starting to make sense. Apparently, Mother Blister was drawn to her by the strong resemblance to her friend's niece.

Zipporah returned the photo to the envelope, pushed it back toward Bea, and then relaxed.

Bea picked up the envelope but now it was she that couldn't relax. She suddenly realized where she'd seen a similar birthmark.

Without another word uttered, Bea suddenly stood.

"What's wrong now?" Zipporah didn't like this seesaw game of emotions.

If Bea heard Zipporah, she didn't act like it. She threw down some money and dashed away, leaving Zipporah more confused than ever.

Zipporah fell back into her seat and tried to make sense of what had just happened. No matter how hard she thought about it, she couldn't. She decided she'd finish the bowl of fruit, and allow the prying eyes of the other patrons a chance to return to their own business. When she finished eating and was certain she'd avoid further embarrassment, she rose.

Zipporah took another glance around to make sure she'd not left her wallet or anything other than a couple of dollars for a tip. She was at that moment happy that no one knew who she was—or so she thought.

Someone in the restaurant did know exactly who Zipporah was, and he watched from a nearby table. He watched her as she rose from her table. And so far, he appreciated what he'd seen. She had the determination of a thoroughbred; she was a winner, he surmised.

He would've known her anywhere. It was in the way she sat and randomly pushed her food around her plate. The way her hair fell forward covering the side of her face with just the tip of her nose peeking out. When it appeared that the conversation was going wrong at her table, he'd watched her suddenly push her chair backward, ready to spring into action if she needed to do so.

A waitress appeared suddenly with his bowl of oatmeal and dry whole wheat toast. He didn't touch it. Instead he smiled, only slightly, as though doing so would hurt his sunken cheeks. He looked almost cadaverous as his eyes, sunken yet wide, fought to stay open. His bald head appeared almost misshapen, making it nearly impossible to imagine him the robust, handsome man of his youth. Rubbing the side of a lemony colored face, its skin well-worn by years of scandalous living done in the name of the Lord, he suddenly stopped smiling. It had taken a glimpse of her to fully appreciate all the time he'd wasted. The glimpse also helped him to fully appreciate that despite his paternal contribution, or lack of it, she'd seemingly inherited those positive traits that had drawn him to the older version of her—her mother.

Yes, he'd give the remaining months he had left to live to let her know that she was his child. His own ambitions, as well as threats from her mother, had kept him from claiming her or her sister, Ima. He would not leave this earth without setting things right.

His eyes narrowed and he almost snarled when he thought about Ima; that young woman was an *exact* replica of her mother. She had no remorse. From a distance he'd seen Ima display the dangerous DNA that made up the entire Hellraiser family. He wouldn't have named her Ima. He would've loved to have given her his mother's name, Hepssi. It was Cree. It meant "the natural one." But his wife would've found out. She would have put it all together and that would've been suicidal for him and his child or children.

Several years ago, other than her uncanny resemblance to Ima, he had no absolute proof that he was Zipporah's father. But he did now. He was certain she was his child with every fiber of his being, and it was without ever hearing her voice singing or speaking.

Suddenly, he could feel the onset of dizziness that often accompanied his illness. Using a technique he learned from his daughter, Gizel, a Dumas or holistic healer, he envisioned pure air entering into his lungs. He suppressed the urge to cough and began to rub the inside of his left wrist until he thought he'd rubbed away his leaf-shaped birthmark.

This time it took longer than normal for him to regain his rhythm, but he welcomed the calmness when it returned. He gave the waitress a sign that he wanted his check. While he waited, he placed a call from his cell phone. "It's me. . . . Yes, I'm positive. . . . I'll call you when I return."

He closed the cell phone quickly and looked up, expecting only to see the waitress. But he found more than he wanted and none of what he needed.

"Have you lost your mind?" Sasha had entered the restaurant thoroughly exhausted from her middle-of-the-night confessional. When she saw him at the table, she was reenergized by her hatred for him. Despite the painful arthritis in her hips, she raced over to where he sat.

"Jasper!" Her eyes narrowed, almost causing her tiny glasses to fall from her nose. "Why in the world would you come to Las Vegas now?"

"I came to see my child."

Sasha inched her aching hips onto the vacant chair opposite Jasper. "You should've stayed with my sister. I told you that I'd let you know if my suspicions were proven."

Jasper clasped his hands together and leaned forward. His stomach was again in knots and he was extremely tired. He'd flown most of the night after harassing Areal to get information about Sasha's exact whereabouts.

"I've less than six months to live, Sasha. I needed to see her." He was becoming agitated and he lost the battle to control his cough. Loudly the hacking sound came forth, bringing with it the evidence of his lung cancer. He caught the yellowish-colored sputum in his napkin, glanced away, trying to dodge the look of disapproval from Sasha and some of the other patrons.

"Sasha," Jasper finally said as his chest began to heave with exertion, "both you and Areal have had your ways for almost thirty years. I'm getting mine, now. I've only known Ima from a distance and look what a mess she became. I'll not do it to this one, and I'm not going to continue to feel guilty about the one you lost."

"You can't possibly believe that because you have all this money—inherited from the dead wife you cheated on, I might add—you're gonna step into this girl's life and be accepted." Sasha was grasping for anything that would stop Jasper. He was trying to ruin both their lives.

Sasha began to panic but she didn't want to give Jasper the pleasure of witnessing it. She was grateful that Areal finally forgave her for goading her into giving up a baby she'd never lay eyes upon. But there was no way Areal would ever forgive Sasha for becoming pregnant by a man who'd also fathered her children. It wouldn't matter that that baby didn't live.

All the emotional walls Sasha had erected were quickly crumbling. She'd sworn she'd go to her grave with her secrets. "If Jesus don't tell my business on Judgment Day, then you'll never hear it from me." That's what she always said, and of course, if she'd bothered to read her Bible, she would've known better. What she'd done in the dark was about to come out in the light.

". . . I definitely want to hear her sing." Jasper had kept talking as though Sasha was still listening, but she wasn't.

"You don't look well at all. You need to get back to New York and see your psychiatrist."

Jasper coughed again. "He's an oncologist. I see an oncologist."

"Psychiatrist or oncologist, it's the same thing."

"Only you would think so." Jasper's fatigue was almost audible.

"If I die in that girl's arms, I don't care. She's gonna know I'm her daddy. And I'm not leaving until she does."

"Having money has truly caused your stupidity to run rampant." Sasha was running out of insults and none of his resolve seemed to have lessened. "I guess you'll want to get a room here, too." She was giving in and laying all her hopes on whatever assistance Sister Betty could offer.

"That's already taken care of." He produced a hotel keycard from his shirt pocket and tossed it on the table. "I see you don't keep up with much anymore. You used to know just about everywhere I had a dime planted, so Areal could be comfortable."

Jasper shot forward, the pain evident as he did. Some days, he couldn't tell where he hurt because his entire body ached. "I keep a room in just about all fifty of the United States in case my child—" He couldn't finish because the cough started again.

Sasha turned her head to keep her stomach from churning as he deposited more of the yellowish gook into another napkin. "You've already taken a room here in Las Vegas?" Sasha feigned surprise, although nothing would surprise her from that point on.

He caught another wind and answered, "Of course, I have investments right here in Las Vegas. I've had money invested in this hotel since the first pile of dirt was removed to build it in 1991." He often had to speak quickly and say as much as he could at one time, before another coughing fit came on.

"I'm seeing my child, Sasha." He was adamant.

And as many lies as Jasper had told in the past, at that moment, Sasha knew he spoke the truth. She almost felt sympathy for him because he was about to find out much more than he'd ever wanted.

Sasha fell back against the chair and sighed. She felt something she hadn't felt in many years and she couldn't get used to accepting it. She felt defeated. Jasper had a ton of money to back his efforts and a free suite inside a luxury hotel. All she had was Sister Betty and hopefully Sister Betty's unwavering faith and favor with God. As for her relationship with the Almighty, its foundation was shaky and for that, she was truly repentant.

Jasper's cell phone rang loud and sudden. It had caused both Jasper and Sasha to flinch. Neither of them had a doubt that it was her sister, Areal.

28

Upstairs in Bea's hotel room her bladder went into overdrive because she was nervous. After meeting with Zipporah for what was supposed to be a light breakfast, it kicked like an epileptic mule on crack. Every time she tried to place a telephone call, she had to hang up and rush to the bathroom. It was on her fourth trip that she realized there was a telephone *in* the bathroom.

In between handling her business, Bea placed a call to really handle her business. After the third ring, she heard a message requesting her to leave a message.

I hate these newfangled inventions, she thought. As soon as the beep sounded for her to speak, she changed her tone.

"Sasha," Bea said as sweetly as possible. In between shifting her weight on the toilet and keeping involuntary groans and growls to a minimum, she continued. "I'm on my way downstairs to the casino. Do you want to go together? Either way, call me back."

Bea hung up and left the comfort of the bathroom. She sat down on the sofa and retrieved the envelope from her dress pocket. She vacillated between a longtime habit of trying to make Sasha's life a living hell, her need particularly at her age to stay close to Jesus, and her desire to get closer to Zipporah. Never having children meant she was on unfamiliar ground, but she felt up to the task.

Bea also needed to keep Zipporah's home situation a secret. Of course, Bea's idea of keeping a secret meant she'd only tell two or three people.

While Bea sat sipping tea upstairs in her hotel room and wrangling with deciding her next move, Zipporah sat in one of the large round chairs in the rehearsal hall of the Luxor. Holding the sheet music tightly in her hands and scanning the lyrics didn't necessarily mean she was focused. Her mind was still on Bea and the photograph. Even with the slight differences between her and the young woman, Ima, Zipporah had had to look real close to make sure the woman wasn't her.

She reasoned that she shouldn't have been too surprised. Everyone looked like someone that someone else knew. She remembered that it was only several days ago, when Mothers Blister and Pray Onn arrived in Las Vegas, some thought they were the actresses Mother Love and Irma P. Hall. She couldn't see the resemblance but that didn't matter. The crowd clamoring for an autograph had thought so. It was all in the eye of the beholder.

"I don't hear any singing." Chandler dropped down in the seat next to Zipporah. He was dressed in a light tan shirt and chocolate brown slacks. The slight five o'clock shadow from ear to ear gave him an extra ruggedness that was sexy—very sexy.

"Good morning." Zipporah was glad to see him and thankful for the interruption.

"Hmmm," Chandler said as he moved his chair closer to Zipporah, "you look well-rested and very attractive this morning. Are you wearing something new?"

"Oh, you mean this old lavender thing." Zipporah lay the sheet music aside and immediately rose. She alternated turning her ankles and twirling. Suddenly she began to strut an amateurish version of a catwalk, as she modeled the new two-piece lavender cotton pleated skirt and sleeveless blouse. "It's a gift from my new manager."

Chandler took one of her small hands in his and produced a smile that usually caused others to cave in to his whims. "He's got great taste."

"You think so?" Zipporah's face blushed as she struggled to keep from laughing like a schoolgirl. Even as she removed her hand from his, she knew at that moment, she'd given him her heart if he'd asked. When had she surrendered her heart? She didn't know and it didn't matter. Looking down at her skirt, she noticed its purple color appeared brighter as if confirming, at that moment, all she was feeling.

While they sat and waited for some of the other performers to arrive, Zipporah was able to relax and bask in the compliments

Chandler heaped upon her. She was thankful he was pleased and even more so when he announced that he had another surprise for her. It hadn't been more than twenty-four hours before that she'd wondered if she would have to sleep on the streets. Now, she was enjoying room service and an extremely handsome manager. Her only concern at that moment was when she would wake up from the dream.

"Do you mind if I join you two?" Sister Betty interrupted. Her voice was lively despite the full-sized bags under her eyes. The revelation from Sasha had completely drained her. No matter how hard she'd prayed after their gabfest, she couldn't quite get comfortable. But now she needed to put that problem aside and be supportive of her godson and seemingly, Zipporah, too.

Chandler stood and gave Sister Betty a hug and a kiss. He offered her his seat, telling her that he didn't mind standing.

Zipporah watched the interchange between godson and godmother. She also couldn't help but notice that although Sister Betty spoke primarily to Chandler, she'd kept her eyes upon her. It was though she was examining her, and it began to unnerve Zipporah. It was at that moment that Zipporah began to think that most old people were a little crazy.

While Sister Betty, Zipporah, and Chandler passed the time chatting, Zipporah spied Alicia. She'd arrived early to the rehearsal.

Alicia was dressed in a tan T-shirt that hid little and blue jeans that accented the rest. After greeting Chandler with an overzealous hug, and Zipporah and Sister Betty with a nod, she moved on to speak with a few of the musicians. For reasons of her own, Alicia seemed to alternate between keeping things with Chandler all business, and the need to be the alpha female, when Zipporah was around.

"What did you do to Alicia? She acted like she didn't know whether to kiss you like an old friend or shake your hand." Zipporah teased. The last thing she needed was her new manager and her new boss to start off wrong, but she didn't want them too close either.

"I didn't do anything," Chandler replied. . . . *And that's the problem*, he thought, *she was in the mood for chocolate and I wasn't feeling vanilla.*

Bea meant to go directly to the casino. However, with her

mind on all that was happening, she accidentally stepped off the elevator onto the same floor as the hotel restaurant.

Bea realized her mistake and was about to get back onto the elevator when she looked across the corridor. She thought her mind was playing tricks. What she now saw, right there leaning against a far wall outside the restaurant, was a vicious joke. She let her eyes roll, just ever so slightly as to not bring attention, and then she refocused. But the images were still there.

It was Sasha and she was with a man. He looked a lot older than Sasha, which meant he should've been a corpse, according to Bea. He also appeared to be annoyed, and Bea figured it was no doubt due to something Sasha had said or done. But it was something more. The man looked familiar. She looked away to gather her wits and decide which one of the current stressful situations she needed to deal with. Whether it was to be the Mothers Board election, Zipporah, her dwindling finances, or Sasha's apparent secret, she needed to choose one before she became totally stressed out.

The chatter in the corridor, along with all the sounds coming from within the restaurant, seemed to fade into the background. Her habit of not consistently taking her diabetes medication caught up with her. Bea suddenly clawed at the wall. And then she saw and knew nothing but the quietness.

29

Sasha caught sight of Bea seconds after she and everyone in the corridor heard the loud thud of flesh hitting the floor. Bea had collapsed into what looked like a purple floral print ball of putty. Items from her pocketbook were scattered close to where she lay.

"Bea!" Sasha cried out in a way that made the onlookers part and let her through. "Bea!"

There must've been about fifteen people in the hallway outside the restaurant. Not one of them was a doctor but most of the crowd, some moaning and others just pointing, had Bea either dead or dying. But Sasha wasn't about to let Bea garner all the attention. Without an ounce of remorse or shame, Sasha shook Bea by the shoulders. When that didn't wake Bea, Sasha poked her with her cane and finally pinched her hard on the meaty part of her arm.

The pinch or a combination of all the unsolicited help from Sasha brought Bea around, slowly. Bea's wig had flipped and slid to the side of her head. The buttons had popped open on her dress, exposing a coral-colored bra that was once red. Its straps were tied in knots, where the clasps were missing. Bea's taupe-colored knee-highs had enough runs in them to look like train tracks. She looked a mess.

"Wake up, Bea. You're embarrassing me," Sasha hissed. However, her words were sweet when she looked up with mock concern and told the onlookers, "She's going to be fine." Sasha slapped the wig upright onto Bea's head, which caused the last bit of consciousness to return quicker.

Bea's head rolled from side to side until her surroundings and Sasha's maniacal smirk became clearer. She popped up. Without bothering to ask how she ended up on the floor, Bea's old thug tendencies reared their ugly heads. Instead of giving thanks for the help, she laid the blame and both her hands around Sasha's tiny neck. By the time Bea fully regrouped, it was Sasha's glasses, cane, and a pair of extra dentures that claimed space on the floor. There were also two pieces of Ex-Lax, but they belonged to Bea.

"Get your hands off of me!" Bea kicked wildly at Sasha.

With all their gyrations and hand thrusts, they'd actually not gotten off the floor. At first glance, they looked like two rabid wrestlers from the GWA, the Geriatric Wrestling Association.

The entire corridor looked on in horror, although there were a few gawkers who laughed. Out of the crowd of onlookers, Jasper was the only one not surprised. Watching Sasha handle her business was nothing new. She'd always been a scrapper and definitely a risk taker. After all, she'd risked the wrath of her only sister just to have a one-night stand with him. Of course, he'd known it at the time. He'd figured that if he'd not been faithful to his wife, how could it be expected that he'd be faithful to Areal?

As for Sasha, she had other problems and right then, they didn't include Jasper. "Shut up, you old crow," Sasha whispered angrily as she slapped Bea's hands aside. "You keep fussing and they'll take your old butt back to Pelzer in an ambulance. Have you no class?"

Bea moved aside just in time to throw an evil look at a couple of strangers who'd dared to approach to help. Bea's cold and calculating look made the strangers retreat. They fled feeling confident that the old woman could handle whatever came her way.

Bea narrowed her eyes and fought to regain control of her breathing, which was coming in short puffs.

Sasha was just as winded and just as determined to get Bea to back off. "How are you going to stay on as the copresident of the Mothers Board from a sick bed?" Sasha could kill a bull with one hand and convince a jury the bull had spoken and called her a name. She was just that good.

All the fuzziness cleared as soon as Bea heard the words *ambulance* and *Mothers Board*. Suddenly she was back on task with a new plan formulating. All she had to give up was a bit of her dignity. But one more tussle with Sasha like that one and she'd have no dignity left.

While the mayhem was still going on in the corridor, Jasper determined it was a good time for him to leave. No one seemed to notice or be concerned with the elderly man hobbling along the corridor pulling an oxygen tank. And for that, Jasper was grateful.

The din from Sasha and Bea's little disagreement seemed to fade into the background as Jasper finally made it to the elevator. He could've gotten involved if he'd had the strength. He didn't and what little he had, he needed to take care of his daughter.

Age had gnawed away at his memory and every now and then a piece of his life's puzzle revisited. There was something about the woman on the floor that seemed familiar. He couldn't make out the name Sasha had yelled, but at the moment, it didn't matter. If he was supposed to remember, he would. What he was supposed to do, at that time, was to take care of his daughter. He wasn't letting anything stop him—not death, not Sasha, and not even Areal.

Of course, he hadn't counted on Bea.

30

"And she did what . . . ?" Chandler asked. He'd barely entered Bea's hotel room when she hit him with the news. He wanted to laugh but thought better of it because Bea looked so serious.

"That doggone munchkin, she tried to attack me when I was unconscious." Bea waited a second to see if there was any sympathy coming her way. But her patience was already used up, so she ranted on. "I wouldn't have fainted in the first place if I'd eaten something. And I'm not sure if I took my medication."

He wanted to remind her that they were supposed to be mothers of the church. And, even if they weren't, they were certainly too old, if not too fragile, to be rolling around on the floor of a luxury hotel. Or for that matter, any floor. But instead, he replied, "I agree. You know that you have diabetes. You've got to eat and take better care of your body and take your medicine properly."

Chandler's concern was genuine. How many times had he given that same speech to his grandmother about taking care of herself? Now, Ma Cile lay miles away, half the woman she was because of a stroke brought on by high blood pressure and diabetes. *Old folks,* he thought. *They spend most of their lives, unselfishly, taking care of others and when older, they won't take care of themselves.*

Chandler's expression softened when he saw the look of concern on Bea's face. "Well, Mother Blister. At least you don't have to pay for this suite for the rest of your stay."

"That's right."

"It's hard to believe that the reason you're getting this free suite is because you blamed the lack of security for your attack."

"Believe it."

"But you actually fainted because you hadn't eaten. It wasn't anything Mother Pray Onn did."

"And, your point would be . . ."

"How did you convince the hotel to give you a free suite when it wasn't their fault?"

"I love you, June Bug, but you are such an amateur. I gave them the name of the attorney who helped me and Sasha when we first arrived in Las Vegas. By the look on the hotel manager's face, the man is very well known. The hotel didn't say 'boo' after I threatened to call him."

"Who's this attorney who instilled fear of that magnitude in the powers that be here at the Luxor?" Chandler suppressed his urge to laugh. He couldn't imagine Bea having that much power after just arriving in Las Vegas.

"Say what?" Bea's mind had wandered onto other issues, plus she hadn't understood all the big words Chandler used.

"Who's got them scared? The hotel—whose name scared them?"

"Oh, why didn't you say that?" Bea let her shoulders heave to put emphasis on her agitation. "His name is Coch, attorney Sammy Coch."

And that's when Chandler finally understood just how dangerous Bea and Sasha could be. He'd once heard that Sammy Coch had turned down a chance to become the state attorney general because the title wasn't big enough. Chandler laughed. They were far from being pushovers.

"By the way," Chandler added, "you dropped an envelope from your pocketbook when you had your little incident. Someone in the crowd turned it in while I was standing there and I volunteered to return it to you. Actually, that's how I learned what happened between you and Mother Pray Onn." He pushed the envelope toward her.

Bea snatched the envelope, almost dislocating Chandler's finger in the process. "Did you open it?"

Chandler couldn't understand Bea's sudden change in attitude. She wasn't asking him a question as much as she was accusing him of something. "No, I didn't open it."

"Are you sure?" Bea wanted to believe him and she really didn't have a reason not to. But her conscience was pricked and she needed to relieve the pressure. Plus, if her life depended on it, she

couldn't keep a secret. "Okay," Bea blurted, "I know I shouldn't."
Slowly, she pulled the photo from the safety of the envelope and
pushed it toward Chandler.

At first glance, Chandler reacted the way Bea knew he would.
"Why are you hiding a picture of Zipporah? When did she ever
get together with Mother Pray Onn?"

Bea chuckled. "It's not Zipporah."

"Of course it is." Chandler reexamined the photograph. Satisfied he was correct, he pushed it back to her.

"It's Ima," Bea said as she flicked the picture toward him again.
"It's Ima and Sasha on a cruise we recently took."

Chandler fingered the picture as though it were either gold or
a demon as he remembered Ima. "Have mercy." If he were a betting man, he'd have lost. "They could pass for twins."

"I know," Bea replied. "Too bad Sasha can't see the similar-
ity."

"She saw the picture and didn't see that her own niece, Ima,
could pass for Zipporah's twin sister?"

"That's her lie and she's sticking to it." Bea's mind went into
overdrive. Perhaps if she leveled with Chandler, they could get to
the bottom of things. After all, he was getting close to Zipporah.

Bea suddenly smiled at Chandler. He knew that couldn't be a
good thing. She'd forgotten to put in her dentures, which made
her look like a bald mouth hawk. Why did old folks get dentures
if they weren't going to wear them? Watching her try to wink at
her own supposed genius, he prayed he wasn't the prey.

While Chandler was upstairs with Bea, Zipporah rehearsed.
The rehearsal went off without a hitch. Sister Betty had to admit
that she truly enjoyed watching and listening to Zipporah perform. There was something very magnetic about the young
woman, although Sister Betty called it an anointing.

"I wish I could sing like that," Sister Betty teased as she and
Zipporah walked out of the room. "I couldn't hold a note without it being stapled to my tongue."

"Thank you." Zipporah felt embarrassed by the attention.

"I believe June Bug did the right thing by taking you under his
wing." Sister Betty didn't try to hide her pride in her godson.

"I'm very grateful for his assistance." Zipporah stopped to let
Sister Betty enter the elevator first. "I'm also happy for yours."

Her tone turned serious as she turned and faced Sister Betty. They were the only ones in the elevator, so she thought it was a good time to ask a question that gnawed at her. "Why are you investing in me? You don't know me."

By the time Sister Betty could react to the question, they had arrived at her floor. "Do you have time to stop by my room?"

Zipporah was tired and wanted to go to her suite to rest, but her curiosity got the best of her. "I guess I can stop in for a little while."

Sister Betty was a bit surprised at how she was actually enjoying Zipporah's company. She tried to push aside the story Sasha had shared. She didn't know Areal that well, having only met her two or three times over the years. But she knew Ima Hellraiser too well. *There's no way Zipporah could be related to that demon,* she thought, *no matter how much alike they look.*

Inside her suite, Sister Betty shared with Zipporah how much she truly loved her godson. She also told her about the close sisterly relationship she had with his grandmother, Ma Cile. Laughter broke out as Sister Betty related several stories involving some of the hilarious incidents involving her and Ma Cile. It wasn't until she decided to tell Zipporah about her amazing telephone call from God, when Chandler was just a young boy, that the laughter suddenly stopped.

Zipporah's mouth gaped. She wanted to comment but decided not to. The last thing she wanted to do was tell Chandler's godmother that she thought she had lost her mind. So she nodded and appeared to accept the outrageous tale of God's telephone call.

By the time Sister Betty finished explaining why she was going to invest in Zipporah's musical career, she was euphoric. "I can't wait to hear your gospel album. Of course, first things first. You'll record God's music before you sing June Bug's worldly music. He and I have discussed it secretly, several times, but he's never had an anointed singer before you. Of course, I'm not about to put my money into some of that butt-shaking stuff. I know it will be anointed." Sister Betty fingered the large cross that hung from her neck as though it were a witness.

"You're investing in a gospel album?" Zipporah tried to hide her confusion but she couldn't. "Are you certain?"

"I sure am. June Bug, I meant Chandler, said that you were

gonna give one of my favorite gospel singers, LaShun Pace, a run for her money. Now that's another singing sista."

Before Zipporah could react to the news that she would record a gospel album in addition to having a Las Vegas show created for her, there was a rap at the door.

Sister Betty opened the door and found Chandler standing there laughing. "Godmother," he said, "you won't believe what's going on."

"There's a lot of disbelief happening," Zipporah blurted.

Chandler's surprise was real. "Hi, Zipporah. I didn't know you were here."

"That's okay," Zipporah said coldly. "Miscommunication sometimes happens."

"Excuse me . . . ?" Chandler felt the temperature plummet as confusion appeared on his and Sister Betty's face.

"We need to discuss the gospel album. The gospel album that your godmother knew about and I didn't." She stood with one foot extended and ready to widen the gap in the seat of his pants.

Chandler's mind worked overtime to perform damage control. He felt stupid for not telling Zipporah before he'd talked Sister Betty into parting with the money to record an album and invest in his business ambitions. His plan was to get Zipporah to record a gospel album for his godmother along with the Las Vegas Revue. In his mind it was simply good business. Everyone came out a winner.

Even when she was annoyed, Zipporah looked good. Chandler pretended to read the room service menu he'd grabbed to show he wasn't concerned. He was going to sail this ship of talent and confusion all the way to the front door of the bank.

"I'm over twenty-one," Zipporah said through clenched teeth. "I take my bull crap with no chaser."

Chandler let her obvious rebuke pass. Over twenty-one, she was. That was the one challenge Chandler knew he'd have to face. He knew the stage and the camera loved her. Of course, he'd rather she was younger, for a debut artist, but he was up to the test. She was beautiful and he could always adjust her age.

So while Zipporah's anger mounted and Sister Betty sat confused by the sudden change of emotions, Chandler did what he'd always done when caught in a bad situation; he simply smiled.

Smiling may have temporarily helped Chandler, or so he thought, but it didn't make things easier for Zipporah or Sister Betty.

Zipporah glanced over at her reflection in the mirror. She wore glamorous clothes and makeup, and slept in a suite provided because she had something that was bankable. She'd always had it but now it was finally given a chance to shine. She was taking her life out of layaway.

Zipporah's survival instinct suddenly went into overdrive. She'd accepted the fact that she'd needed Chandler. There was no getting around it. She needed him to keep his promise to help her fulfill her dream. Too many times she'd been led to the brink only to slip and fall because she'd let her guard down. She'd almost done that when she entertained the notion that, perhaps, there could've been something more between them. Obviously, Chandler was just what he'd said he was, when they'd first met. He was a businessman. Only a crazy woman would keep doing the same thing, the same way, and then expect a different result. Zipporah reconfirmed right then that she wasn't crazy. Whatever it was going to take, she was willing to do.

Suddenly, Zipporah walked over to where Chandler stood and took the room service menu from his hand. The look in her eyes changed from erotic to a calculated coldness, as she let them briefly sweep over Chandler before looking down at the menu. And like him, she pretended to read it.

"I'm famished," she said cheerfully. Not one word held a hint of the disappointment she felt. "I can't order anything dairy or with chocolate, though."

"I'm a bit hungry, too." Sister Betty finally entered the conversation. "Just order chicken wings and grits, if they have any." She was still confused by the sudden change in Chandler and Zipporah's body language. But if they were ordering food, she might as well eat. She'd already broken her fast and there was no need for her to be hungry and confused.

"I'm not particularly hungry but I guess I'll order an appetizer or something light." Chandler was still trying to figure out Zipporah's stare and sudden mood change. He'd seen something of himself in the way she'd switched up on him. Perhaps, he'd misjudged her naiveté as a weakness, a sweetness that he might've one day explored.

The entertainment business had made Chandler a shark. He'd learned how to pimp any situation and keep the collateral damage manageable. Yet, seeing the way she'd emotionally swam through what was obviously a sea of perceived deception was his wake-up call. The business was his excuse for being a shark. Her predatory nature seemed natural.

Zipporah looked over the top of the menu directly at Chandler. "I'll just order a garden salad with grilled chicken and a little oil and vinegar dressing on the side." She didn't return the menu to Chandler. Instead, she dropped it onto the coffee table. "I certainly wouldn't want to mess with my money-making equipment."

And while Chandler called down their food orders, Zipporah hummed a soulful version of "Jesus Is On the Main Line." She watched the more-than-pleased look upon Sister Betty's face and tossed in a few vocal acrobatics, just to show she could.

31

After her scuffle with Bea, Sasha was completely worn out and sore. Her best shawl had a snag and her cane was nicked. She was getting too old to get into fights and yet it seemed as though she always was.

She'd learned that Jasper's suite was on the same side of the hotel as hers, as well as on the same floor. That meant the suite was in the opposite direction of Bea's and Sister Betty's rooms. So she set out to find him. It didn't take much for her to sniff him out. She heard the echoes of a persistent and almost violent cough as soon as she came out of her room into the corridor.

Sasha looked around carefully, making sure there was no one else in the corridor. There wasn't. The coughing came with a hacking sound that stopped her cold. Was she imagining the echoing sound of a death rattle accompanying the cough?

Sasha continued following the coughing until she arrived at Jasper's suite. She leaned in closer, allowing her ear to rest against the door. Now that she was there, she felt torn between letting him get the rest he obviously needed, and what she needed at that moment. She stepped away from the door deciding that what she needed mattered more. She took her cane by its grip and rapped hard on the suite door.

He hadn't even asked who was at the door. He couldn't have even if he'd wanted, his strength was so sapped. Yet Jasper opened the door as though somehow he'd expected Sasha.

Sasha entered the suite without a word, watching Jasper falter slightly as he tried to return to his seat. The sound of hissing coming from the table caught her attention.

It was the sound of escaping air or something akin to it. Sasha adjusted her eyeglasses and immediately knew. Either out of respect or pity, she didn't know which, she turned away and waited until Jasper finished what was apparently a self-administered oxygen treatment.

She heard him as he inhaled air as deeply as he could into his lungs and then expelled it with difficulty. She turned back in time to watch Jasper quickly don the mask attached to the oxygen pump and inhale, again, as though his life depended upon its gift. It did.

"I'll just wait over there." Sasha pointed her cane toward a recliner near the window. While he finished sucking air she looked around the suite, which appeared twice the size of hers.

From where Sasha sat she could also see into an open closet just off to the side of the living room. There were several expensive-looking suits hanging with well-polished shoes on the shelf above them. Closer to where she sat was another table. On it she saw pictures of not only a much-younger Jasper, with his arms around Areal, but some pictures with the same pose, only with his late wife. She wore the same silly expression as Areal, probably just happy to be on the same planet as Jasper. Sasha wondered, did his wife ever realize that she and Areal were interchangeable at Jasper's whim?

Sasha saw other subtle signs of permanency about the room. Apparently, he had told the truth. He'd kept a secret suite there at the Luxor.

More than fifteen minutes had passed since Sasha's arrival. Time was something neither of them had much of and she needed to get things rolling. If Sister Betty did what she promised, and was able to get more information about Zipporah and defer Bea's snooping, Sasha could walk away from this mess pretty much unscathed.

"I hope you're not still trying to talk me out of meeting my daughter." Jasper's voice had a temporary power that was obvi-ously supplied by the oxygen treatment. "I know what time she's performing this evening. I'm going to be there."

"If there's no way I can stop you, then I guess I might as well tell you everything I know about her." Sasha had already rehearsed her words for just this moment. She suggested he listened care-fully.

Jasper's expression didn't change at all when Sasha said she was ready to tell him everything. Putting the oxygen mask back on gave him more air while giving Sasha less of a chance to read any emotions.

Sasha related how shocked she was when she first laid eyes upon Zipporah. Although the resemblance between Zipporah and Ima was undeniable, she'd played dumb when Bea asked if she noticed. She was actually retelling the same tale she'd told when she'd arrived at Areal's home in the Bronx, New York. Only this time, she was mentioning a revised version of her conversation with Sister Betty. She figured Jasper didn't need to know it all.

Jasper leaned back against a pillow that supported his back while he sat on the sofa. He listened intently as he waited for Sasha to tell him something he hadn't known. And after five more minutes, when she hadn't and he was again growing tired, he removed his mask and spoke.

"Aren't you leaving out something very important?" Jasper could feel the wheezing feeling returning. He was tired of Sasha's games.

Sasha's face feigned surprise. "I've told you all I know. She's got a promising career so it appears, and it's right here at this hotel. I even told you the part about Bea becoming too involved and threatening to blow things sky high with her nosiness. I can't think of anything more," Sasha lied. It'd barely been twenty-four hours since she'd first told him, and Areal, what she'd discovered. How could he doubt what she said? Yet, she felt he did.

"Your child, Sasha, you haven't mentioned her." Jasper reached for his mask as he waited for Sasha's response.

"Why do you care about Carrie?" She was puzzled. Her daughter, Carrie, had nothing to do with any of what was going on. Besides, Carrie was almost five years old the last time Jasper laid eyes upon her. She was now a grown, unmarried woman who was doing very well, when she wasn't husband hunting.

"I don't care about Carrie!" Jasper had snatched off the mask in frustration. "I'm talking about the baby you carried in your belly! You thought I didn't know! *My* baby. You've never once mentioned or even hinted about *my* baby."

Sasha sank lower into the chair. Was every secret she'd schemed and suffered through going to be exposed?

If silence had a sound, then the moments that passed, after Jasper's condemning accusation toward Sasha, echoed like a dynamite blast.

Sasha's head felt like a barbell. She could've sworn, as she turned it to avoid Jasper's glare, that her neck creaked. The temperature in the suite was cool, yet her tiny body felt clammy. Out of desperation she tried to mentally escape by concentrating for a moment on a single sun ray that filtered through the window. It was no use, his accusation blocked it, too.

She was becoming unglued and that was not the person she'd fought hard to show the world. By her own admission, Sasha's mind and memory had slowed down a bit since hitting her golden years. Yet, she'd spent a lot of time and enormous energy on keeping her secrets a secret.

Sasha thought she'd only sat, stunned, for a few moments. Yet when she turned back to where he'd sat, he was gone. She leaned forward, grabbing the side of the chair to see if he was standing behind her. He wasn't. She hadn't heard him move. There had been no sound of the suite door opening or of the wheels moving on his portable oxygen tank. The tank still sat by the television cabinet.

"Jasper," Sasha called out. She didn't want to call his name too loud, in case he'd only gone to the bathroom. "Jasper," she called again. This time her voice quivered.

Sasha moved forward and with more agility than she'd used in years, she almost jumped up. She searched the four-room suite and could not find Jasper. The last room she looked into was apparently the one he'd slept in. His toiletries and other items were displayed neatly on the dresser. And, again, she saw more pictures.

At that moment she didn't care if Jasper reappeared and found her in the bedroom. She moved almost in slow motion toward the dresser. Some of the people in the pictures she knew immediately. In one tall picture frame were Jasper and the famous Reverend James Cleveland. The two men were smiling broadly and dressed in skinny-leg, shiny brown suits with specks of gold thread. Jasper, his dark black hair slicked back and his face perspiring, held a microphone, and James Cleveland, a portly man at the time, sat grinning by the piano. In the background, a large audience, mostly women, was seen in various stages of appreciation.

Sasha went from picture to picture. Nearly all of them featured Jasper in some aspect of performing on stage or posing with other celebrities or with his adoring fans. She also saw that one or two pictures that he had taken with Areal were in a much smaller frame. His smile was forced and so was Areal's. The two of them looked like a pair of teenyboppers. Areal wore a high-collared white blouse and a turquoise skirt with a black and white poodle embroidered between the wide pleats. Her hair was long, past her shoulders, and she wore wide Chinese-styled bangs. Jasper's hair was long and straight; he looked almost like an Indian chief. He'd worn a dark suit with razor-sharp creases in the skinny pants legs. There was something vaguely familiar about the background, including the out-of-focus girl off to the side. Sasha couldn't quite make it all out.

Sasha didn't like being in the dark about things, so she picked up the photo and sat on the bed. She stared, concentrating on every detail. This picture was obviously from a different time and place than those she'd seen in the living room. Both Jasper and Areal looked to be in their teens. She looked at the date handwritten in the corner of the picture. It took her another few seconds to put it all together. The picture was taken several years before she'd known that Areal and Jasper knew one another in high school. She'd thought she knew Jasper first. Obviously, she hadn't.

And that's when Sasha accepted the realization that she really didn't know much.

32

Slowly, Jasper moved down the hotel corridor. He was surprised at how quickly he'd calmed down. With no regret he'd blasted Sasha's cold heart and he hadn't so much as wheezed. There was no room for sympathy when he'd gotten up and left his suite. So what if Sasha was hurt. He hadn't cared. As far as he was concerned, she could sit there in that burst bubble until the maids came and removed her, along with the other trash from the suite.

Calm he might've been, but he was still tired. Jasper clutched the small portable oxygen tank he carried in a shoulder pouch. It was an alternative he sometimes used because he could also place it in a backpack. and hide its long plastic tube under his clothes.

Jasper glanced at his watch. Zipporah should be preparing for tonight. He knew the rehearsal schedule. A smile and then almost a chuckle was followed by a quick bout of wheezing. He imagined she'd warm up her vocals with a run or two of riffs in a room void of air-conditioning. That's what he used to do. She'd avoid ice-cold water, chocolates, and anything that contained dairy. He'd done that, too.

He wanted to do right by her. That was the only thing he hadn't done. He'd do that.

Jasper shifted the pouch from one hand to the other and pulled a sheet of paper from his side pocket. He looked it over carefully and when the elevator arrived, he replaced it in his pocket, entered, and pressed a button.

Earlier in Bea's room, she'd barely started to munch on one of the expensive two-ounce bags of chips from the minibar when she'd gotten the call. *The call;* if she had to give it a name, that's the one she'd use. Yet it was so much more than that because she'd had the wind knocked out of her.

Most of the things she'd done in her past, and especially since finding God, she'd thought were hidden and forgotten. Didn't the Word say that He would make you brand new? Sure, she'd done a little time for petty crimes; she'd been no saint. She definitely wasn't before she accepted Jesus, and not afterwards, either. Did she customize her salvation needs? She admitted that she had. She'd paid tithes the best she could and when she felt that it was doable. Being on a fixed income wasn't a good excuse, but it was the one she used the most. Yet, she'd arrived in Las Vegas through a stroke of luck, so she'd reasoned, and was about to do something good for a change. This time it wasn't about her. So why now was her world so abruptly challenged?

A steady coughing outside her hotel room yanked away her thoughts. She tried to ignore the cough's persistency and concentrate on her next move. When the coughing grew more urgent and appeared that it would remain outside her door, Bea got up to see who was so thoughtless and intrusive.

When Bea opened her door she was met with a raised fist. Her instinctive nature prompted her to raise her fist as well.

Jasper had been about to knock on the hotel room door when it flew open and a chubby fist flew from out of nowhere. He didn't know he still had the strength or the sense to duck at the first sign of danger until Bea swung. If he hadn't turned aside, Bea would've knocked him out.

At the rate Bea was going, if the Luxor had security cameras running all over the hotel, she'd be on the Las Vegas Most Wanted List before the next shift came on duty.

"Jasper Epps, what the ham and cheese are you doing, you old peeping Tom?"

"Bea Blister, are you insane?"

Jasper recovered slowly and inched his way along the living room wall as Bea apologized and gathered the pouch and other items that he'd dropped in the doorway.

"I'm sorry." She knew she was repetitive but she meant every word. "I wasn't expecting you this quick." From the bluish-purplish tinge to his coloring, she knew for certain she was going to jail for *preemptive* murder. Not knowing any better, Bea found his mask and slapped it across his face to help him inhale. She almost knocked Jasper out again.

While Jasper fought literally for his life inside Bea's hotel room, Sasha lay across the bed in his suite.

She didn't know where Jasper had disappeared to nor had she heard him leave. But what she did know still had her in shock. All her years of trying to keep the left hand from knowing what the right hand did was for nothing.

It'd taken a moment but a particular memory finally returned. She turned her head aside as though doing so would give her clarity. Her eyes traveled along the pearl and pewter picture frame. It was another picture of Jasper and Areal in their youth. There was a paragraph in the bottom corner that said it was taken at the home-going service for one of the teachers named Miss Lizzie, Miss Lizzie Crow.

Rising from the bed, she felt the aches of all the battle blows life had dealt to her. She gently picked up the picture and tried to remember more details. She didn't remember Areal returning home for the funeral although they'd both had Miss Crow as a teacher. However, she did remember Jasper being there. She remembered him dressed to the tee in a gray sharkskin suit, a blinding white shirt, and a dark tie. He'd leaned on the side of a fence outside the funeral home wearing a pair of dark shades. There was no one who could compare to the way he'd embraced stardom. No one would've guessed he'd just started singing with a traveling gospel group and had returned for the funeral and would sing. As angry as she was at that moment, she smiled a bit at the memory.

Finally she figured out the identity of the blurred figure in the other photo. She almost had to hold it upside down and then sideways to get it in focus. She should've known from the start who it was. "Bea!" Sasha spat on purpose when the realization hit her. "Bea Blister!"

Sasha's head throbbed and kicked. The pain came quick, running up and down through her skull and neck, like a cheetah on speed. Each of them—Areal, Jasper, Bea—had turned and deceived the others at some point in time. And yet she'd spent most of her adult life trying to keep things hidden.

Sasha felt it was time to do it again, so she did. Sasha knelt and cried out to God. Her repentance came slowly and then accelerated. By the time she was fully into praying mode, her body lay supine on the floor. Sasha was completely at God's mercy, a place in God where she'd always been, and she had never understood or accepted it.

It hardly ever rained in Las Vegas, yet there were clouds peeking out and then hiding in the evening sky. Chandler had left almost an hour earlier, eager to complete something he'd had in mind for Zipporah. At least that's what he'd told Sister Betty. He stammered out the excuse almost immediately after Zipporah had dressed him down for not telling everything she'd felt he should, particularly about recording a gospel album. He didn't even wait around for the food they'd ordered from room service. He needed a miracle to salvage what was seen by Zipporah as a deception. He could almost feel her slipping through his hands before he'd barely closed them around her career.

Earlier, Sister Betty had floundered for a moment after Chandler abruptly left. It wasn't until Zipporah started laughing that Sister Betty felt permission to do the same. "I betcha he won't try nothing else," Zipporah said as her laughter grew stronger.

The comment was supposed to be for Chandler but Sister Betty took it as a warning, too. Over more tea, the two women chatted for the better part of an hour. When Zipporah announced that she had to leave, Sister Betty hated to see her go.

She was pleasantly surprised at how smart the young woman was and how hard she'd tried to pretend that June Bug was a manager and nothing more.

"I know you probably need to get a quick nap," Sister Betty told Zipporah. "You've got to make sure folks don't think last night's performance was just a lucky break."

"They won't." Zipporah had doubts about many things but not one about her vocals.

"The devil is tricky," Sister Betty told her. Without asking, she'd taken Zipporah's hands in hers. When Zipporah didn't try to remove them, she prayed.

Sister Betty was happy that Zipporah was agreeable to prayer. And soon after Zipporah left, she learned something else that made her even more giddy. She learned that the Mothers Board conference was, again, postponed for another day. Apparently, the conference center wasn't too forgiving about the earlier chaos brought on by Bea and Sasha. Chandler had said that a decision as to whether they'd be permitted to return had not been made and he wasn't sure how much he could influence the matter.

Sister Betty tried to read her Bible but a fourth cup of hot cayenne pepper tea that should've made her alert had caused drowsiness. She'd already found out as much information about Zipporah as she could, for Sasha. Her next move was to chat with Bea and afterward to bow out of what was certain to be a mess. God had forced her to come to Las Vegas for what she'd thought was a position on the Mothers Board. Now, she felt like she'd been tricked.

Leaning back on the sofa, Sister Betty placed a bookmark on the Bible page. Again, her mind went back to Ma Cile. Along with that memory came the pangs of guilt. Her best friend languished in a hospital with a stroke. That's where she was needed. Instead, she was in Las Vegas, Sin City, where she didn't want to be. She'd thought that God and she were on better terms.

Sister Betty needed to focus on something else. There wasn't too much to do around her hotel room since the maids did practically everything. There was nothing on the television that interested her, either. And, then she remembered Chandler had said earlier that Bea was in her hotel room resting after her little incident with passing out and fighting with Sasha.

Instead of calling Bea, she decided to just go to her room. They were all on the same floor so she wouldn't have far to go. She drained the last drop of cayenne tea. From atop the coffee table she gathered her purse and her Bible and as a precaution, she said a word of prayer.

Even with her purse, her Bible, and a prayer whispered, Sister Betty paused by the door. She looked around, hoping that God would intervene with a sudden blackout or even a burning bush right in the middle of the room. She was ready for anything that would stop her mission of becoming more involved in Bea and Sasha's messes, including the Mothers Board presidency. God had done it for Abraham just in the nick of time, too. The sacrifice of her Isaac, in her case, her peace of mind or sanity, in seconds, was about to go down.

But Sister Betty heard and felt nothing unusual outside of a sense of urgency. She opened the door to leave and came face to face with Sasha.

Sister Betty felt as though she were floundering inside a dream, or in this case a nightmare. She turned around in submission. "Okay, Lord, what's goin' on?" Neither spoke but she let Sasha gently guide her back inside the hotel room.

It dawned upon Sister Betty that she hadn't heard one word from Sasha in a while. She saw that Sasha had a glow about her that was almost angelic in nature. She couldn't even imagine angels coming into Sasha's presence to make her look like that. But something must've scared her speechless.

"Betty." Sasha finally spoke, barely above a whisper. She spoke low as though there were others listening when it was only the two of them. "Jasper already knows about the baby. He knows everything." She didn't wait for an invitation to sit down before doing so.

While Sister Betty stood gape-mouthed, Sasha revealed that Jasper was, at that very moment, in their hotel and that he planned to meet Zipporah.

Teary eyed, Sasha spoke of the pictures in his hotel suite and how she was stupid to believe all those years that she alone was the one who'd betrayed her sister by having an affair with Jasper. She almost bawled to the point of hiccupping when she told how she'd spent all that time hating Bea because she thought Bea had betrayed her. She'd let a sorry, no-good man turn her life upside down even as she'd testified, often, that she'd turned everything over to God. Right or wrong, Sasha blamed Jasper for turning her into a hypocrite.

Once she got going, Sasha wouldn't shut up. She let out every emotion she'd kept penned up inside for most of her sixty-something years. She'd released it all without cussing, and that in itself was a miracle.

"So you don't need me to do anything?" Sister Betty said quickly, when there was a short break in Sasha's tirade. She was surprised at her selfishness, but it didn't stop her from enjoying the peace it'd suddenly brought her.

"And," Sasha added, completely ignoring Sister Betty's remark, "he's got more money than you, so Zipporah won't need either you or Chandler."

Now, that part of Sasha's revelation caught Sister Betty's attention. Her eyes narrowed. "You mean that she may not record my gospel album?" She couldn't accept that.

Sister Betty knew she had to do something, plus Chandler was depending on Zipporah to launch his entertainment management company. No one was gonna mess with her godson's dreams, especially some man who'd decided to step up to the fatherhood plate on his deathbed.

The mean look that appeared and spread sardonically across Sister Betty's face scared Sasha. It was a sobering picture. Sasha had never seen Sister Betty when she wasn't talking or acting like God didn't have her on a leash or wasn't directing her every thought and deed.

It had to be a joke for Sister Betty's true nature to be revealed on the very day that Sasha felt she'd truly found God. Had Sister Betty strayed from Him, she wondered?

But Sister Betty hadn't strayed from God. She wasn't even close to doing so. The look that Sasha had taken as a mean one was just a look of determination. It was with the same tenacity that a mama bear, a mama shark, or a rabid baboon would defend its young, or in Sister Betty's case, her godson and a gospel album.

Of course, Sasha didn't know that. She got up to leave thinking that Sister Betty had crossed over to the dark side. In fact, she'd made up her mind right then that she was going to her room and pray for Sister Betty. Since she'd just opened up a prayer line of communication to God, she probably needed to use it while she could. With her salvation history, she was sure to be on a probationary sheet of thin ice.

Inside Bea's hotel room, Jasper tried to explain his side of things. Every time Jasper was able to catch a breath trying to bring Bea up to speed, Areal called. She'd interrupted Jasper three times on his cellular. Each time she'd called, she was indecisive as to whether or not she wanted Zipporah told that Areal was her mother. None of what Areal had said mattered to Jasper. He was taking responsibility as a father and that wasn't about to change.

If Jasper hadn't tired of Areal, Bea certainly had. She finally leaned over and snatched the cellular from Jasper while Areal was deep into her fourth interruption. Bea turned it off and stuffed it under the sofa pillow.

The angry yet concerned look on Bea's face stopped Jasper from retrieving his phone.

"Whatever you say is going to hurt that beautiful child," Bea said sadly, "and she doesn't deserve to be hurt any more than she's already been."

Jasper knew Bea was right but then, so was he. "I'm not about to leave this earth and not take care of my child!" Jasper had said the words *my child* with authority. He'd liked the sound of those words from the moment he'd felt for certain that Zipporah was his.

"Can't you just will her some money and let it be at that?"

"Hell no. I'm not letting it be at that!" The sudden, angry response brought about Jasper's wheezing, but he wasn't stopping, "She's . . . my . . . baby."

Bea recognized Jasper's determination for what it was—unshakeable. Neither of them really knew Zipporah but they both loved her. It hadn't been a full week, let alone a lifetime, but there was something about her that caused them to want to protect her.

"You do know Sasha will do whatever she can to stop you. She's just selfish like that." Bea was certain he was already well aware of it.

Jasper snatched off the mask he'd just donned seconds before and hissed, "I'll kill her if she does," before quickly replacing it on his face.

"You'd actually try and kill that li'l Smurf?" Bea asked before slowly adding, "I can live with that."

Inside Sister Betty's hotel room Sasha's resolve had weakened considerably since she'd arrived. It'd taken a lot but she had said what she came to say. She leaned on her cane for strength and prepared to leave. But before Sasha made it to the door, she heard the familiar bone-grinding sound of bending arthritic knees.

Sasha turned quickly, just in time to see Sister Betty shamelessly, and in obvious pain, fall to her knees. Her arms immediately spread in supplication and out of respect, Sasha stopped moving. It was not like Sister Betty to fight against what God wanted from her, so she understood Sister Betty's repentance, and it caused her to smile. She was amazed. The super saint of the church, God's right-hand woman, on her knobby knees repenting.

Whether Sasha had already gone out the door or not wasn't a concern. The spiritual knife stabbing at Sister Betty's conscience had cut deep. She heard the words repeated, "I'm sorry, Lord," but she couldn't feel them leaving her mouth. It was as though she were having another out of body experience. So she wasn't aware of Sasha's presence or the fact that Sasha had knelt beside her and was repenting for all the hurt she'd caused Zipporah.

And right there inside a suite at the Luxor Hotel in Sin City, the most unlikely of duos had come together to touch and agree. From deep within their collective spirits, each knew of God's promise. . . . "Where two or more are gathered together in My name, there will I be also. . . ."

33

Chandler raced from the Luxor parking garage. In his excitement, he wasn't sure if his feet were touching the ground. The lobby was a blur as he sprinted through, almost knocking over a huge Egyptian figure, and on toward the elevator. Fortunately, the elevator door was open and those waiting had already entered. Chandler would've run over them if they hadn't. He pounded on the elevator's "close door" button, much to the chagrin of the other riders.

Inside Zipporah's hotel room the warm, pulsating shower was refreshing enough to change her mood back from apprehension to, at best, cheerfulness. She'd done something that was certain to give her more control over her situation.

Mostly Zipporah had been worried about her living arrangements at the shelter. The encounter with Chandler still had her a little distrustful about her future and where she'd lay her head. And then, just as she was slipping out of her clothes, she'd had an idea. It was one she'd been certain would work if she executed it correctly. She'd placed a call to the homeless shelter and pretended that she was a nurse from one of the Las Vegas hospitals. She'd made certain that she'd slurred the hospital's name so the lie would work.

"This is Nurse Denton from (unintelligible) hospital. I need to confirm the address of a Miss Zipporah Moses. She's been admitted and I'm following up on the paperwork and need to contact her next of kin," she'd said.

"Is she okay?"

Zipporah recognized the voice as one of the other residents who sometimes worked the phones for an extra privilege or two.

"She'll be with us for a few days. We just need to make sure she's not penalized and her residency at your shelter remains intact."

"I can't say for certain but I will definitely give Miss Thompson the information. Can I please get your name and the hospital number?"

Zipporah hung up quickly. If she knew Miss Thompson, that woman on the phone was going to get an earful for not taking down all the information correctly. But the notice had to be logged in and if Zipporah was penalized by an eviction, heads would roll.

Zipporah combed out her wet hair. She had just begun to put several rollers in when the phone rang. She wasn't concerned that her scheme to keep the room at the shelter hadn't worked, as there was no caller I.D. on the phone. But she was curious. She waited until the fourth ring before answering. She answered with a yawn to throw the caller off.

"I'm sorry. Did I wake you?"

She recognized Chandler's voice. He spoke as though nothing had happened earlier. She decided not to hold his foot to fire at that moment. "I'm awake now. I was resting up for tonight."

"You'll be fine, I know you will. But listen, I have something to show you. Can I come over now?"

"Where are you?" She wasn't really concerned except that she needed enough time to dress.

"I'm in the room I reserved here at the Luxor." He tried to tone down the excitement in his voice as he waited for a response. She didn't give one. "Can I come over?"

Zipporah counted to ten and then answered, as nonchalantly as she could, "I don't have a lot of time before the sound check. I can spare a few minutes if you don't take too long."

Chandler detected the symptoms of a diva. He didn't know whether she was messing with him or was truly serious. He could accept that she was still a bit annoyed. He wasn't putting up with an unearned diva mentality no matter how talented she was. "I'll be there shortly." He hung up, deciding that if she still acted crazy when he got to her room, he'd keep his surprise just that . . . a surprise.

Zipporah stood with her mouth agape. *No, he didn't just hang up on me!* She smiled. He knew the game as well as she did. In one swift move of hanging up the phone first, Chandler had laid down the rules. If she wanted to succeed, and she truly did, she'd have to stop acting like a child. She ran her hands over her hips and bosom and decided that with what she had going, childlike games were useless. That's what her mind determined, but her heart knew better. There had to be a way she could have her cake and eat it too, even if Chandler weren't hungry.

Zipporah had barely changed into something a bit more appropriate than the clinging robe she'd worn moments before, when Chandler knocked on the room door.

Zipporah opened the door slowly, allowing her eyes to briefly meet his before motioning him to enter. True to her feminine nature, she'd seen and noticed everything about him in about five seconds. It was all the time she needed and that's why she was able to lower her eyes first. She then turned and walked away, not bothering to make sure he'd entered. She already knew he would and that he had.

Chandler had rehearsed the empowerment speech before he arrived at Zipporah's hotel room. He'd told himself that there was nothing she could say that would make him relinquish power. He was going to be her manager and call the shots. She would do what he said, when he said it, and be prepared to go all the way to the top of success.

But Zipporah had said nothing. Without uttering a single word, she'd turned away. She'd gathered all her feminine wiles about her, and like a she-leopard confident her kill would stay put until she was ready to eat, she'd given him a glimpse of her arsenal.

He couldn't take his eyes off Zipporah as she sauntered across the room. One glimpse trumped everything he'd planned. What he suddenly felt was not foreign. The blood raced through his body, almost making him spastic. It was a painful reminder of just how long he'd gone without being with a woman the way he'd wanted to. It'd been a while partly because he wasn't the type to be with just any woman, and partly because he'd been abstinent for the past several years.

At the height of a promising career, he'd walked away from the record industry with a lot of guerrilla marketing and promotion knowledge about the inner workings of the entertainment beast. He'd also seen too many of his peers give up promising careers and families torn apart by sex and drugs, which had often led to AIDS and ruination.

Twice, Chandler had dodged the sexual disease bullet. After getting the word that his HIV test was negative and the test for one of his best friends wasn't, he took what was happening around him as a sign that he needed to return to what he was taught in church. He figured if God was dispensing grace and mercy to him, which he certainly hadn't deserved, then he would accept it. He'd vowed to be celibate and so far he'd kept that vow. It certainly hadn't been easy and since then he'd met other women. Some of them were prettier and probably smarter than Zipporah. None of them, until that night, had moved him into reconsidering his vow of abstinence.

Chandler made up his mind to say what he had to say and get away from Zipporah—quickly.

She still had her back to him and yet she'd known how he'd reacted. Without bothering to turn around, she pretended to move around one of the sofa cushions, which meant she had to bend over slightly to do so.

Punishing him enough, Zipporah finally turned around to ask Chandler to have a seat. To her surprise, he was already seated and scanning a piece of paper held in his hands.

"What's on your mind?" Zipporah was slightly unnerved by what she took as his snub toward her not-too-subtle efforts. She buttoned the top button of her dress in defeat. "What's that you're reading?"

Chandler took every ounce of strength he had and uncrossed his legs, which released both his hands and the piece of paper. "It's a guest list for tonight's show."

"Why do I need to see a guest list?" Now she was really puzzled. Was Chandler toying with her to see if she was ignorant to the business? Was he just crazy? She was growing tired of the "is he or isn't he" game.

He smiled and laid the paper on the coffee table. He couldn't get up at that moment. After all, she couldn't tease him like that and not expect his body to react. He made it so she'd have to walk over to get it.

Curiosity got the better of Zipporah, so she surrendered. She watched him intently, while she reached for the paper on the table. She clutched the paper and with her eyes still locked on him, she backed away to sit down again.

Chandler watched her transformation. He was still fascinated by the way she confronted every situation. She was indeed an expert-in-training, when it came to mystery. He liked that.

Her body seemed to relax and tense almost simultaneously as her eyes scanned the sheet. "Are you serious?" She started giggling and couldn't stop.

"As a heart attack," he countered. Her smile was contagious. He found he'd started smiling, too. "They'll be here tonight, as a favor to me, just to see you."

Chandler fought the urge to run to where she sat and just hold her. He wanted to reassure this already self-assured woman that he was making everything all right. Perhaps at another time, he would. At that moment, he chose to sit, observe, and hope the blood stopped overflowing in his pants.

Words hovered over Zipporah like an oral balloon. She wanted to snatch the words of thanks and toss them at Chandler, but they floated beyond her reach.

Zipporah reread the sheet of paper. There were six names on the sheet. Four of the names were renowned record producers or show producers for HBO. And two of them were A&R representatives from two of New York's largest record companies. "How did you pull this off?"

"They're in town at one of the industry conferences. The big awards banquet is at the conference center this evening. They've promised to stop by and catch your second performance."

"My goodness." Zipporah blushed. "Shouldn't I be nervous?"

"I wouldn't think less of you if you were."

"But I'm not nervous," Zipporah continued. "Am I crazy? Am I overconfident?"

"Only you would know that." Chandler pointed at her. "But get back to me later about that crazy part."

They laughed at the same time and the timing of it seemed to bring them closer.

"I probably should go," Chandler said as he looked at his watch. Its plainness reminded him that when he changed for the show he needed to wear a more expensive watch. If he looked like he didn't need money he'd be shown more respect. That was something he'd learned early on in life.

It took Chandler a moment to realize that Zipporah had stopped laughing. She had a strange look. It wasn't one of fear and yet it didn't quite look like confidence, either. Just when he thought he'd broken through her mystery shield, she'd raised it again.

"I need for you to leave now," Zipporah said softly as she walked toward the door. But no matter how soft she spoke, her voice still wavered. Tears came slowly at first but by the time she'd raised her hand to wipe them away, they'd soaked the sheet of paper.

Chandler rose, not wanting to cause her embarrassment. He went to the door and opened it. He had to admit that he did expect her to be grateful and perhaps to concede that he had her best interest at heart. He never expected her to cry. But he was learning that he didn't really know what to expect from her. Tonight, he'd accept the tears.

With a quick hug and a kiss on her wet cheeks, Chandler left without saying a word, and yet his actions had said plenty.

34

Bea couldn't decide if she wanted to call for a doctor or to smother Jasper's face with a pillow. She was willing to do anything to stop his loud wheezing and coughing. She frowned again as she looked over at Jasper, as if a nasty smell had entered the room.

Back in Pelzer, when she did have male companionship with her longtime boyfriend, Slim Pickens, she called the shots and the old man would hop.

She thought about how she'd put up with Slim and his decrepit pamper-wearing butt once, perhaps twice, a month. Usually it was around the time when he'd get his pension and her money was funny. "You know I'm gonna be here for you forever," Slim had told her. She couldn't tell him that she hoped forever was a short time. She couldn't imagine, and she certainly hadn't hoped, that he would live past the time she could tolerate him.

And yet with all the ill will she harbored against some of the men she'd known and met who'd given her money or other things, she wanted nothing but the best for a strange young woman who'd given her nothing. Bea shook her head at the thought of Zipporah. She looked back at Jasper still struggling to breathe and thought of Slim again.

But Slim was a pauper compared to the money Jasper had. "Life sure is a funny thing," she muttered, pushing the unpleasant memories to the back of her mind.

Here she was with a megarich man in a hotel room. She was far from home in Las Vegas—where whatever happened here was supposed to stay here—unless one went home with some type of transmittable disease. Jasper was a man whom she'd have cut someone over, back in the day, and now he was sitting there, useless and dying.

Jasper was just coming out of one of his coughing and wheezing fits when he saw Bea coming toward him. Normally, if he'd seen a woman with a pillow in her hands, fluffing it, he'd have thought she was going to make him comfortable. But Jasper knew Bea Blister and she was no Florence Nightingale.

"Bea," Jasper managed to cry out. "What's that you got?"

"Oh, this old thing." Bea chuckled. "I was just taking it into the bedroom." She knew that he knew she was lying because he was watching when she'd brought it out of the bedroom earlier. Bea threw the pillow aside just as quickly as she had the truth.

"What time is it?" Jasper asked suspiciously.

"It's time for you to leave." Bea was about to call the concierge desk and find out if they had a luggage dolly that could wheel Jasper back to his room. She needed to be alone so she could figure out how to keep Jasper away from Zipporah. She knew Zipporah could use the financial help, but she certainly didn't need a dying daddy. At least if Bea were her, she wouldn't.

"How big is her leaf?" Jasper asked as though he were continuing a conversation instead of starting one. "Is it as big as mine?" He held out his hand with the palm up so Bea could see his birthmark.

"It's pretty noticeable," Bea answered as she gathered his belongings. "When I saw it and how much she looked like Ima, your other daughter, it almost blew me away. And that's pretty much what sealed it for me as far as you being her daddy."

"It probably sealed it for Sasha, too," Jasper stammered. His voice dropped an octave at the mention of Sasha's name.

"I told you she almost had a heart attack when I mentioned Ima and Zipporah in the same breath." She stopped and put one of her chubby arms through Jasper's free arm to help him stand.

Again, Jasper spoke as though continuing a conversation. "She ain't gonna turn out like Ima." He turned toward Bea and surrendered his other arm to her. "I mean it, Bea. That Ima, she is just plain ol' mean-spirited. All those Hellraisers are mean."

"Zipporah don't know she's a Hellraiser. And for no other reason than that, Jasper," Bea pleaded, "you shouldn't tell her that you're her father. She's gonna want to know about her mother, too."

"I don't care!" Jasper's words were starting to come forth again, in spurts, as his agitation mounted. He fell back and Bea, with her stooped back, barely caught him before he hit the floor.

"Oh, what the ham and cheese," Bea hissed, her favorite cuss phrase. She dragged him, semiconscious, back onto the sofa. "Now what?" she mumbled. He was as stubborn as she was as he continued to mumble with his eyes closed and lips barely able to move.

Bea went over to the table and picked up the phone. She wrestled with her insane idea of whether or not to call the concierge desk for a luggage dolly. She slammed the receiver down. She'd decided not to when she realized it would take more of an explanation than she was willing to give.

She covered Jasper with one of the extra blankets from the closet. It was a struggle because he kept coughing and mumbling, but she resisted the urge to place the cover over his face and mold it to the shape of his head. When she realized she hadn't given in to her urge to put him out of his misery, Bea understood that perhaps she was a bit more saved than she'd realized.

But, she thought, if he didn't shut up she'd have to take her chances and hope God would forgive her.

After Sister Betty and Sasha traded confessions, the two old women had prayed and risen with renewed vows and a greater appreciation, momentarily, for one another.

With each revelation they traded, they'd discovered how little they knew, truly knew, about one another.

"How long did you say we worshipped together?" Sasha had asked again, for the about the third time. She was almost giddy with her renewed strength in God. She felt as though she'd just gotten saved.

She had.

"I believe it's been more than thirty years if you count the time we sat on the same building fund committee. And you must know that I never, ever, wanted to be a part of the Mothers Board," Sister Betty confessed. "It was Reverend Tom who insisted that I come to Las Vegas and upset the cart."

"I'd forgotten about the Mothers Board elections." Sasha's eyes widened. "What are we going to do?"

"We don't have to do anything," Sister Betty said calmly. "We don't know when it will resume at the conference center."

"It's been cancelled? Sasha smiled. "Those folks are so unreliable." Just as Sister Betty was about to correct her and lay the blame where it belonged, Sasha winked.

The two old women laughed again. They were truly, for the moment, having a grand old time.

Sister Betty and Sasha continued to travel down memory lane, which was made up of geriatric blocks of half memories paved with arthritis. By the time they were halfway through, neither had a good enough excuse as to why they hadn't gotten along or avoided one another. They'd been at religious odds all those years, and it was all in the name of Jesus, which made it ludicrous.

"Well, I must be going. We've turned over Zipporah's situation to the Lord," Sasha announced again, as she rose. "I'm out of it."

"God will work it out for certain. All we have to do is just sit back and let Him work. I've learned not to second-guess God," she added. "I first learned that when He called me on the telephone."

And that's when Sasha stopped moving toward the door. She turned and crept back over to where Sister Betty still stood. Taking one of Sister Betty's hands in hers, she spoke. "There's something I've always wanted to ask you."

"Yes, what is it?"

"Did God really call you? I mean did He call you on a telephone that had a dial tone? Was it on a rotary phone? You weren't having a hot flash or something, were you?"

"What do you believe?" Sister Betty smiled and winked.

"I believe that you believe it," Sasha replied. "However, that's a little far-fetched to me. I don't mean to hurt your feelings, but God's touched me today, and I can't lie to you."

"It's about as far-fetched as Him finally coming into your life in a way you've never experienced before."

And that's when Sasha knew that God truly had called Sister Betty on the telephone.

Before Sister Betty could explain further, there was a persistent rap at her door. The interruption momentarily startled the women.

"Are you expecting company?" Sasha asked, raising her cane out of habit.

"Not at this hour," Sister Betty answered slowly.

She brushed past Sasha, who had moved back toward the door again. Sister Betty peeped through the peephole.

"Oh, oh."

35

"Open the doggone door, Sister Betty. This ain't room service."

Sister Betty's shoulders slumped in defeat as she opened the door.

Bea ambled in and was met with the sight of Sasha and a raised cane.

"I thought you were so saved?" Bea snapped, pointing toward Sasha. "Why you got that demon in here?"

"Come on in, Bea," Sister Betty said as she closed the door.

"You know if you resist the devil, she'll flee back to her cave in Pelzer," Sasha snapped. She gave Bea a nasty look and raised her cane a little higher.

"We've been calling on Jesus," Sister Betty told Bea, and reminded Sasha at the same time. She'd hoped Bea would calm down if for nothing more than to respect the prayers.

"There must've been a lot of static on the line," Bea said as she inched toward Sasha.

"Me and Sister Betty are best friends now," Sasha announced. "And we don't need you butting into our prayer life."

So much for Christian love, Sister Betty thought. Sasha hadn't been reclaimed for more than a good forty-five minutes and she was about to return to the devil's grip.

Before Sister Betty could pull out her bottle of blessed oil which she kept for such occasions as the one she was in, Bea and Sasha let loose.

Bea told Sasha exactly what she really thought of her, which was redundant because it was what she told Sasha every time they occupied the same space and air.

Sasha returned the favor, adding a few spicy words to her barrage. She called Bea everything that was demonic in nature as well as a reference to manure.

Sister Betty fled to a space beside the television cabinet for safety, and prayed. She was torn between trying to keep her peace and tossing Bea and Sasha out into the hallway.

What was God trying to tell her? Was He trying to tell her that she wasn't as saved as she'd thought? At that moment, she was tempted to kick their wrinkled butts and then redo her first works at the altar. She was just that fed up and needed to get off the religious roller coaster.

The confrontation lasted about two or three more minutes before it appeared it was dying down. Much to the appreciation of Sister Betty, both Bea and Sasha were becoming winded and needed to cut their insults short. At least they hadn't broken any furniture, yet.

However, leave it to Sasha to find just enough strength to light a verbal match and set off Bea, the volcano, Blister.

"... And I know it was you that was sneaking around with Jasper Epps behind my back!" Sasha accused.

"What in the ham and cheese would I want with Jasper Epps?" Bea hollered.

Neither woman remembered that up until that time they couldn't remember who they'd fought over.

"You wanted him when we were in high school because he liked *me*." Sasha was adamant as she rolled her tiny hips with her parentheses-shaped legs struggling to support her.

"Please!" Bea snapped. "That playboy liked every girl who wore a skirt and didn't have the word *no* in her vocabulary."

"I knew how to say no!"

"You might've known but that don't mean that you did. In fact, neither you nor Areal, as I recall, never said no to much, back then. How often did the two of you compare notes about Jasper?"

Sister Betty had just made up her mind to intervene and ask them to leave. The look on Sasha's face told her to mind her business even though they were in her hotel suite. So she did.

"What do you know about Areal and Jasper?" Sasha asked, remembering Bea's shadow in Jasper's picture of Areal and him.

And that's when Bea broke it down for Sasha and admitted

knowing that Areal and Jasper were lovers. Before that day her memory was a bit fuzzy. But with Jasper showing up out of the blue, he'd brought back plenty of memories, and they were becoming crystal clear.

"I'm ashamed," Sasha finally said. "Back then I didn't want to believe that my own sister would creep around like that."

"But you were creeping, too," Bea reminded Sasha. "Seems like the only one who wasn't creeping with Jasper was me."

Actually Bea had wanted to have a fling with Jasper but somehow he seemed to prefer his lemon-colored women for bed buddies and she was more a purple grape. Seeing the mess he'd made of Areal's, Sasha's and now Zipporah's life, she was glad she hadn't forced the issue.

Sometime between when Bea started and finished her story, Sister Betty felt it safe to resurface. "I'm glad that y'all got it out of your system."

Calm had returned for the moment.

It was all out in the open then. There was more than one hundred and twenty years of experience between three of the most unlikely of women to bond. Yet, to a degree, for the sake of a young woman they'd known less than a week, they'd come together.

Sasha put her things down and sat, again, on the sofa. "Sister Betty, may I use your telephone?"

Sister Betty nodded her consent and Sasha called Areal. There were accusations, tears, and a touch of profanity on Areal's end, but Sasha was persistent. She knew Areal never wanted it known that she was Zipporah's natural mother. She'd apologized and promised that she would be with Areal when she told Ima that she had a sister.

Bea and Sister Betty sat like bookends as they tried to support Sasha in her struggle to continue the conversation with her sister. Finally, Sasha hung up.

"What a mess," she moaned. "How can I undo the past? Zipporah will probably hate me."

"Don't worry, Sasha." Bea placed a fat hand across Sasha's back. She laughed quietly and added, "Everybody hates you at first."

Sister Betty almost caught a cramp as she stifled her laugh. *Leave it to Bea,* she thought.

But Bea's ridiculous sense of humor was just what Sasha needed. Sasha stopped her self-pity fest and joined Bea in the laughter.

"I could just kick my own butt when I think about how I let that man mess things up," Sasha reiterated.

"So you don't care about him?" Bea asked, "even though he's the father of your niece?"

"I couldn't care less," Sasha replied, "but I do have to love him just like Jesus does." She smiled and nodded at Sister Betty, showing that she still had her new relationship with God.

"So," Bea asked, "you won't mind if I go back to my room and have his rich, flea-ridden, asthmatic behind removed?"

"I thought he was dying," Sister Betty blurted. "At least that's what Sasha said."

"What do you mean that he's in your room?" Sasha flicked away Bea's arm from her shoulder. "Hussy, you mean to tell me that you've got me and my sister's old boyfriend in your room?"

As old as Bea and Sasha were, they learned immediately how quick they could jump if provoked. As they leapt off the sofa, the old women looked like two old Kung Fu fighters. Each had her ghetto style and neither one was about to play by the rules.

That outburst, no doubt, shook the Luxor, and it certainly shook Sister Betty. She fell back against the sofa with her arms flailing, fighting invisible demons. Sister Betty looked like an old palm tree assaulted by a tsunami as the winds of disorder tossed her from side to side.

At that moment, Sister Betty was certain that God must've been on His second bottle of Aleve for that day.

36

"Perfect pitch" was the phrase accompanying Zipporah's reviews. Everything about her that night was flawless, her makeup, cascading hair, vibrantly colored and beautiful costumes, just everything.

Zipporah took more standing ovations than she'd ever imagined possible in her life. There was no resentment or jealousy among the performers that night. There was no need. Each knew exactly who carried the show and they treated Zipporah like the star she was.

Even Alicia offered sincere accolades. What she'd seen Zipporah do at rehearsal wasn't even close to what she'd seen on the stage.

Of course, Alicia didn't know that Zipporah wasn't singing so she could just keep her new job. Zipporah wanted to ensure that the entertainment industry people who'd come to check her out weren't disappointed; no way they would leave thinking she was just ordinary.

Zipporah chatted a moment with her fellow performers, changed into a butter yellow, low-cut dress and matching shoes, and left the dressing room. Chandler was waiting by the door. She saw him beaming, obviously proud and not afraid to show it.

"Oh, my goodness," Chandler exclaimed. "I knew you were good, but you blew me away. Now I've got to act like I knew you were going to do that all along."

"We'll both be acting," Zipporah whispered. "I prayed and dug real deep to find some of those notes. I knew I was singing for my supper."

They both laughed as Zipporah allowed Chandler to embrace her and then lead her to the VIP section to meet her new fans.

* * *

As usual, upstairs in another hotel suite, all hell was still breaking out. "I wanted to hear her sing!" Bea was livid, and she was giving Sasha and Sister Betty an earful. "Y'all messed it for me."

"Shut up!" Sasha had had enough of Bea for one evening. Bea was about to make her backslide from a place in God she'd only hours ago arrived.

They'd been too tired to continue their petty fight in Sister Betty's suite. Plus Sister Betty had threatened to call security if they didn't quiet down. So they called it a ghetto draw, which meant that each had better watch her back. Sister Betty also reminded Bea that Jasper was still in her room and would probably try to get to Zipporah. So they had dashed back to Bea's suite to check up on him.

When they'd arrived back at Bea's room, they'd found Jasper half on and half off the sofa.

"He's coming around," Sister Betty said as Jasper began to mumble.

Jasper was trying to wake up but then Bea ran over to him and crimped his oxygen tube. He passed out again.

Bea, not fully trusting the other women to have her back, quickly came up with an explanation. "I thought I was supposed to do that. I saw it done on that medical show, *Grey's Anatomy*."

"I'm sure that was CPR they were giving when they did that," Sister Betty snapped.

By the time they gathered their wits and all the evidence of Jasper having been there, which included his portable oxygen pack and his cell phone, placing them by the door to discard if they had to, it was too late to see Zipporah's performance.

Each woman sat exhausted in a chair in the living room. Sister Betty clutched her Bible. Sasha held her cane by its end with the hook ready for action. Bea sat and fluffed a pillow. If Jasper woke and tried to escape, they were ready for battle, again. No one said a word. They kept their eyes trained on Jasper. A couple of times he moved, and when he did, they did, too.

"I say we kill him."

Sasha and Bea's heads turned so fast they almost got whiplash. They looked over at Sister Betty. Her mouth was twisted as she sat clutching her Bible and talking of murder. They didn't know she had it in her. Again, it broke the ice and the women giggled until each nodded off.

None of them woke when Jasper finally did.

* * *

The deejay was doing his thing as the people in the Luxor theater room danced and chatted. Chandler couldn't have planned nor asked for a better reception for Zipporah. There were men in their ultra-expensive suits and diamond-studded watches, with women glued to their sides, and they were all over Zipporah. And, to her credit, she'd refused to answer many of their questions or accept their praises without including Chandler.

"I'm so thrilled that you enjoyed the show," she'd say. "It was Chandler who secured the opportunity for me." Or she would turn the conversation around when asked about her future projects. "Chandler has that pretty much mapped out. I stay in my place as an artist and I let him handle any and *all* business dealings."

Chandler sat back and watched Zipporah do what most managers wished their artists would; she derailed any plans to separate her from him.

For barely twenty minutes Chandler and Zipporah had been entertaining the powerful group of men who'd been enraptured by her when Alicia sauntered over to their table. Her perfume was heavy, pre-announcing her arrival. She'd changed into a spectacular form-fitting chocolate brown dress that was shaped like a sarong. She'd seen the opportunistic wolves dressed in Armani and Giorgio suits surrounding Zipporah. If they were there to steal her premiere performer, she was going to stop it. It was nothing personal, just business.

Chandler rose and gave Alicia a quick peck out of respect. After introducing Alicia, he moved over to make sure she didn't try and sit between him and Zipporah.

At that moment, Alicia could care less about coming between Zipporah and Chandler. She'd already sized up her biggest threat before she'd sat. He wasn't the larger of the men, in fact, he was the smallest. She knew his face and that he was a megaplayer in the industry, but she couldn't remember exactly what he did. Alicia watched him as he watched her sit. He'd smiled showing perfectly white teeth with a small gap. So while everyone chatted, the usual industry chitchat, Alicia watched her prey.

Chandler was very good at what he did. And whether he was dealing with clients at the conference center today, or at a promotions meeting of a recording industry back then, he could smell blood in the water. His mood remained steady. His body language never gave away the fact that he knew silent deals were being made at the table. No one had to speak. With a slight nod of a head, at a particular question or remark, a deal could be secured. And, he wasn't having it.

"Alicia," Chandler said as he leaned across Zipporah. He'd touched Zipporah's hand, under the table, to let her know to remain quiet. "The hour is growing late, so I'm about to escort my artist, from this point on to be referred to as Miss Zipporah, to her suite. . . ."

"You're leaving already?" one of the men asked as he pulled a card from his pocket. "Here's where I'll be for the next two days, Chandler. You call me. Call me real quick."

Chandler took the card and without reading it, placed it in his pants pocket and not the pocket in his jacket. It was a power move that was seen by the entire table. If he'd placed it in his upper jacket pocket he'd be perceived as being too anxious. So he'd placed it in his rear pants pocket to let the man know that he'd need to come correct.

Chandler smiled at the other men knowing he'd gained more respect with that move, even from the man who'd given him the card. Laughter suddenly broke out and it permitted him to continue.

"Alicia, I'll leave you in the hands of my esteemed colleagues. I'm certain they'll be as entertaining toward you as you'll be to them."

"Thank you, Chandler." At that moment Alicia was happy that any feminine competition was removed.

"And you, sir." Chandler motioned to the smaller man whom Alicia had obviously chosen. "Behave yourself."

"God is good," the man replied and laughed.

The other men joined in the laughter and of course, Alicia had no clue as to its humor or that she was the punch line.

"Kirk, Hezekiah, John P., René, Rodney," Chandler said, offering each a firm handshake and making eye contact as he spoke, "again, I thank you for taking the time out of your busy schedules to come tonight. I'm somewhat in your debt."

Chandler then offered his hand to Zipporah to help her rise while at the same time moving to allow Alicia the chance to get closer to the others. "Alicia," Chandler teased, "watch out for

Kirk Franklin. You'll think you're getting a Las Vegas show and it'll turn out to be church."

A sign of final recognition crossed Alicia's face. That's where she'd seen the man. He was the famous artist and producer, Kirk Franklin. She had a slight dilemma. A gospel show was not something she could sell to the hotel but she didn't burn bridges, either. If she got up too quick, she'd appear to be opportunistic, which she was. And, if she sat too long, the other men at the table might get other ideas, which some already had, she was sure.

Chandler put an arm around Zipporah as she clutched a small purse to her chest to keep from laughing. She was amazed, again, at how Chandler handled situations.

"You probably play a mean game of chess, don't you?" Zipporah teased, after they'd left the table. They'd barely started walking through the room to the exit before she was nodding and accepting praises from the crowd again.

"Probably as well as you do," Chandler replied. "And I'm not above taking a risk or two."

Zipporah caught a glimpse of her reflection as they exited the room. She looked all cleaned up on the outside. But, inside she still wasn't all that confident. Despite the glamour, she was still the homeless woman who could sing. The smile came quick to cover her uncertainty, as they walked out into the corridor. In her mind she was indeed a risk, but she was also worth it. She was a walking contradiction.

They hardly spoke a word as they walked the corridor to Zipporah's suite. Chandler had playfully hugged her several times as she giggled like a schoolgirl on prom night. He liked that about her. He knew she had plenty of questions about what had happened earlier at the VIP party, but she'd had the instinct not to ask. At least, she hadn't yet and hopefully, not tonight.

Neither Zipporah nor Chandler played the usual games men and women sometimes did when they stood in front of her hotel room. She didn't linger and look adorably into his eyes. He didn't pretend that he needed to use the bathroom or ask for a drink of water. No, they didn't do any of that.

37

Chandler took the keycard from Zipporah's hand and opened her door. He entered first, as though it were his room, and then gently pulled her inside. It was almost three o'clock in the morning and yet neither felt tired. Chandler took off his suit jacket and Zipporah kicked off her shoes, revealing the tiniest feet Chandler had ever seen on a grown woman. They were perfectly arched with each toe perfectly painted. He'd not noticed she wore an ankle bracelet until that moment.

Zipporah knew her assets very well. Chandler wouldn't be the first man to notice her feet. She turned her ankle slightly and as she did she noticed the blinking light on the telephone. It only blinked when a message was left.

"Someone has left a message." Zipporah stopped her tease and reached for the telephone.

"It's probably one of your admirers from downstairs trying to see if you're serious about me as a manager," Chandler said. He was only half teasing.

"I doubt it," Zipporah said. "You were pretty clear on where our business relationship stood."

Chandler liked her answer. He pointed toward the phone as if she needed his permission to continue.

Zipporah laughed as she pressed the button for the message retrieval. She listened intently as she pressed another button to replay the message. She snapped her fingers at Chandler, indicating for him to come quickly and listen.

By the time he'd replayed the message Chandler's expression turned more sour than Zipporah's. How could such a perfect evening have such a disastrous ending?

"Does it make sense to you?" Chandler asked her the same

question repeatedly. Every time she'd answered no. But she was still adamant about getting to the bottom of it.

"I'm going to the lobby," Zipporah said. She'd already put her shoes back on and opened the door to leave. "Are you coming or staying?"

Chandler threw up his hands and accepted her decision. It seemed every time he thought he was getting to second base someone hit a foul ball.

"I don't like it," Chandler warned. "I just don't like it. It might be some sick joke."

"Are you coming or staying?" Zipporah repeated.

When they arrived downstairs, Chandler led Zipporah off the elevator directly through the mezzanine lobby toward a room to the side. He pressed the buzzer on the door, which was just under a silver-plated sign indicating that it was the on-site medical services room.

Zipporah noticed immediately that she recognized no one. Perhaps Chandler was right. Maybe this was just a sick joke.

"Zipporah Moses?" The pencil-thin man with bushy blond hair didn't wait for her to respond before turning around. "I'm Mr. Phelpson, Luxor's triage administrator. Please come with me."

The first thing that raced across Zipporah's mind was the lie she'd told the shelter to keep her room. Even though she'd lied that she'd been hospitalized, what could that have to do with this situation? Was it some type of karma?

"Can I come with Miss Moses?" Chandler asked politely, knowing he was going with her regardless.

"It's up to you," Phelpson responded as he continued walking. He still hadn't looked back to see if they'd followed. He led them to another room.

The room was completely white and sparsely furnished, giving it a transitional setting. *Definitely something temporary,* Zipporah thought as she looked around. It was also very small, but the whirr of some type of machine seemed to fill it, making it seem larger. She stood in the entrance and watched, not yet questioning aloud why she'd been summoned there. The squeeze of Chandler's hand upon hers reminded her that he was there. For a moment, she'd forgotten he was.

Chandler and Zipporah stood still. Neither of them dared to

move. They intently watched two people dressed in white uniforms who appeared to be working on something or someone. Their hands moved rapidly as though they were kneading dough. And then, the dough coughed.

He was lying down and it felt like weights had been placed on his chest. Someone was hovering over him. He saw the shape of a man. The man's face became a little clearer. He had cold eyes and cold, glove-covered hands. Jasper shivered slightly. He could barely make out whether the man was white, black, or whatever. He really didn't care. At that moment, he needed to breathe.

The woman was massaging something over his face. She was at the head of the bed and leaning over him. He could feel the massiveness of her breasts as she worked, no doubt, to save him. Her large breasts felt more like weapons to stop his breathing.

Jasper began to struggle. He heard them say, "Calm down." But he struggled more because he needed to live.

"He's a little more alert, this time," the man said. "His BP is still high."

"At least two twenty-five over one-thirty," the woman replied, lifting her heavy bosom off the patient's face. She heard him breathe in and expel air quickly, which caused her to look down. She still didn't know she'd almost, accidentally, stifled him.

"He's lucky he didn't stroke." The man squeezed the I.V. bag that hung over the bed. He straightened the line, checking it for air bubbles. "At least he was able to give his name and room number."

"He's a willful one, that's for sure. I've seen them stroke with a much lower BP." She wrote something on his chart and then laughed softly. "He wasn't in his own room. Whatever the woman laid on him must've been way too much for him to handle. At least he made it to the hallway."

If the two nurses saw Zipporah and Chandler in the doorway, they didn't act as though they had. They continued with their inappropriate conversation not caring if the patient overheard them.

"Did anyone call the next of kin?" She ran her pen across several lines on the chart before continuing. "Someone named Zip . . . I can't make it out."

"Let Phelpson handle it." The male nurse took the chart from her hand and laid it at the foot of the bed. "Let's get coffee. He should be okay."

The female nurse had just started to turn when she saw strangers—a man and a woman watching from the doorway. Her professionalism kicked in quickly. "We'd better check him again before we go."

"Mr. Epps," the man said a bit loudly over the whirring sound of the monitor, "I'll be right back. An ambulance is on its way to take you to the hospital." He eased past the couple without asking why they were there.

Zipporah looked at the man lying on the bed and pushed Chandler back out of the doorway.

"I don't know that man," she whispered. She looked away, wanting to avoid the sight of obvious distress. "There must be another patient in here."

"This is their only triage room." Chandler watched. Unlike Zipporah, he didn't try to avoid seeing the man's struggle. Instead, he watched the man's determined effort to live, even though he felt rebuked because he was staring.

Was his grandmother, Ma Cile, lying in another hospital unable to speak, trying just as hard to call out to him? Right then, he vowed that no matter what was going on in Las Vegas, he was returning with Sister Betty to Pelzer. He was going to see the only woman who'd been his rock. Ma Cile had raised him. She deserved better than what he'd given.

Compassion forced Zipporah to stay, although she'd seen enough misery in her short time to warrant her leaving. She locked her arm with Chandler's and followed his gaze to the man on the bed.

"Have you decided what you'd like to do?" Phelpson had returned. Without waiting for an answer, he placed Jasper's wallet, hotel keycard, along with a bag that contained his shoes and other personal items, at the foot of Jasper's bed. "The ambulance is here."

Chandler looked at Zipporah. He didn't want to overstep his place, but she didn't appear to be able to speak up.

"How did this happen?" Chandler didn't know why he'd asked that question when he really meant to ask, "Who is this man?"

"He collapsed outside one of the hotel rooms. Someone found him and assumed it was his room because the door was partially opened. Apparently, he'd been left alone and tried to leave for help."

"Leave for help?" Chandler looked at Zipporah. She was still studying the man on the bed, who seemed to be more alert.

"Well, there seems to be a problem," Chandler said softly, "I don't know this man."

"Zip—por—ah." Jasper's voice was weak but his words, although halting, were clear.

Jasper's head had barely risen before it fell back onto the pillow. His eyes were unfocused and his skin now a pasty, yellowed, almost jaundiced hue. The weightless I.V. tube inserted into his left wrist felt like lead. His lips moved but only a hissing sound came out. All the while he kept beckoning Zipporah with his wide-eyed stare.

Suddenly Jasper's lips appeared to snarl just slightly as he again said, "Zip-po-rah." This time there was no mistaking his words.

Zipporah and Chandler were stunned. Zipporah was not a common name and they both knew it.

"That's what he said when they brought him in. When I recorded his belongings I found your name and room number on that yellow sheet of paper. I stuffed it back into his wallet. There are a couple of other names of folks staying here at the Luxor on it, too. I guess you must be part of a group or something." Phelpson checked his pager, which had just gone off. "I have to go and sign Mr. Epps over to the EMT folks."

Zipporah flipped open the wallet, which had several one-hundred-dollar bills along with credit cards and pieces of paper crammed into it. The yellow sheet stood out.

Chandler looked over Zipporah's shoulder as their eyes scanned the numbers scrawled upon the paper. Two numbers immediately leapt out.

"Isn't this Mother Blister's room number?" Zipporah asked. She was stunned.

"I know that's her room number just as well as I know that the other number belongs to Mother Pray Onn."

"What do they have to do with this man?" Zipporah asked as she again, quickly, looked over at him. His eyes were still wide and beckoned to her. It made her skin crawl.

"My question is what does this man want with you?" Chandler

took the paper from Zipporah's grip. He looked again, that time, slower. "These are Pelzer numbers. I recognize the eight-six-four area code."

Zipporah couldn't answer any of Chandler's questions. Her need to find out more about the man was interrupted by the EMTs' arrival into the room. They asked Zipporah and Chandler to move to the side so that they could transfer the man to the hospital.

Jasper fought the EMTs. There were two of them and both outweighed Jasper. They had to finally restrain him. Although, legally, he had the right to refuse medical attention, that was not what he said. He just kept repeating Zipporah's name.

The EMTs finally began to roll Jasper out of the room. Even restrained he still tried to fight. All the while he never took his eyes off Zipporah. With tears welling up, and his breathing becoming shallower, he still twisted and turned. As they rolled the stretcher past Zipporah and Chandler, he attempted to reach out to her. He didn't seem to care that a long needle was embedded in the hand as he raised it.

If Zipporah saw it she didn't react. But Chandler did see it and he did react, inwardly. He saw the birthmark on the inside of the man's wrist. It'd been a quick glimpse but he had no doubt it was the same leaf shape as Zipporah's.

Chandler, normally cool under practically any situation, was at a loss.

38

Bea barged back into her suite with her fists balled and the arch in her back almost straightened. She hadn't remembered leaving her hotel room door ajar when she'd left. If Jasper was up she was gonna knock him back out. There was no way she was going to let him mess up Zipporah's life.

Sasha followed behind Bea with her cane raised. The two old women had left Sister Betty mentally whipped in her room and had headed back to Bea's.

Of course, Sasha had only returned with Bea to make sure that there wasn't anything happening between Bea and Jasper. She didn't care if Jasper was on his last legs, the Jasper she'd known for years would still try something.

The last thing Sasha and Bea expected to find in the room was security guards.

The last thing the security guards expected to find was two old women barreling through the hotel room door and commencing to whittle away at their manhood with nothing more than a pair of fists and a cane.

The noise brought some of the other hotel visitors on the same floor rushing from their rooms to see what was going on. It was the middle of the night and although Las Vegas was a city that never slept, they'd wanted to.

The two security guards, both well built and most certainly taller than Bea and Sasha, stood glued to a wall. Their uniforms were in tatters and one wore his flashlight dangling between his legs instead of from his belt. The other man looked as though someone had painted his lips with purple lipstick. Sasha had taken her cane and whacked him across the mouth each time he'd hollered, "Stop." Perhaps if he'd said, "please," she wouldn't have hit him so hard.

Chattering started almost immediately throughout the crowd of onlookers. Several had recognized Bea and Sasha from the day they'd arrived. So with cell phone cameras clicking away, it appeared that poor actresses Mother Love and Irma P. Hall would become innocent and mistaken fodder for the tabloids once again.

It took some time before the security guards were able to walk upright out of Bea's hotel room. They even apologized for doing their duty, hoping that the two old women wouldn't tell everything that had happened. As for Bea and Sasha, they completely forgot about finding Jasper. They were momentarily content to sign autographs for some of the onlookers.

"I knew I should've worn my shades," Bea complained after signing the last autograph and collapsing into a chair.

"Oh, you looked fine," Sasha complimented and smiled. "How did I look?"

"Like the little Smurf you are," Bea teased.

"And you looked like an energizer raisin," Sasha said with a wide grin. She didn't try to hide her snide remark behind an apology. She left it for what it was.

"I'm surprised none of that racket woke up Jasper," Sasha added as she looked around the living room. "Where is his dying, cheating behind? Do you think he called security?"

"Wait a minute!" Bea hopped around like her butt was on fire. "I left him on this sofa."

"What sofa?" Sasha asked. She certainly didn't see him stretched out on the one she sat on.

"Oh, ham and cheese," Bea hollered.

"Oh, hell no!" Sasha didn't try to mince words.

They were so scared they even looked under the sofa, which was only about two inches off the floor.

"Are you two looking for something?"

They hadn't realized they hadn't closed the door completely. It wasn't quite morning yet and there was Chandler standing in the doorway.

"Can't two old women get some exercise in peace?" Bea complained as she struggled to stand.

"One, two, and three . . ." Sasha counted as she swung her tiny arms side-to-side. "Four, five, and six." She continued as she, too, struggled to get up. "That's enough for me, Bea. I'm going back to my room and shower. All this exercising has made me sweaty."

"Chandler," Bea said with indignation, as she realized that their charade wasn't working, "what are you doing here at this unearthly hour?"

Standing in the doorway, Chandler folded his arms across his chest. He took a couple of steps forward. "Jasper Epps sent me."

39

Zipporah paced around her hotel room suite. She'd gone from room to room and still hadn't calmed down. She looked at her watch. It was almost five o'clock in the morning. It was much too early to call anyone.

She'd promised Chandler, when he'd brought her back to her suite, that she'd try to relax. It took her another ten minutes to convince herself that she hadn't dreamt the whole thing up. Holding a cup of hot tea, she willed herself to sit. With every bit of concentration she could muster, she willed her mind to recall as much of her life as possible.

Zipporah remembered bits and pieces of what she'd always called a drifting childhood. She'd lived in the Amsterdam, New York, foster care system for most of her youth. The town was small back then and was mostly a Slavic community. She'd stood out like a sore thumb, being one of a few blacks living there. She stayed with a white family that kept several foster children of all nationalities. They were a kindly middle-aged couple named Doug and Mae Teabout. They lived on Main Street in a huge house opposite the Mohawk River.

But the happy home wasn't always happy. Mr. Teabout worked long hours running a furniture store downtown. Mrs. Teabout did her charity work and accepted the praises for "taking in the orphans," six days out of the week. On the seventh day, when God ordered folks to rest, Mrs. Teabout drank. It was the town's secret that everyone knew and ignored. Even when the foster children started showing signs of abuse on the days she drank, the town people ignored it. After all, some would say, "She's taking care of kids nobody wanted. So what if she drank a little. Those brats probably deserved every beating they got."

Zipporah ran away when she was thirteen. She was picked up walking along the highway and promptly placed in another system-run house in Scotia, New York. Same situation except it was a children's shelter. That only meant that she didn't get whipped as much because it would take time to get around to her. She wasn't a bad child. If anything she was a bookworm who sang herself to sleep. By the time she was fifteen, Zipporah had discovered that she could sing herself out of most situations.

If things weren't going well in whatever home she was placed in, Zipporah sang. She soon became a showcase. She'd sing at the church, she'd sing at the school, she'd even sing in the shower and in the front and back yards. The foster parent du jour would drag her through many talent shows to win a few dollars, none of which she ever got to keep.

As a teen, Zipporah still didn't know anything about her parents but was told by every foster parent she'd stayed with that her birth mother died, from a difficult labor, when Zipporah was born. "Your mother never had a chance to lay eyes on you." She'd heard the story so often until she thought she was the blame.

While the Las Vegas sun rose, Zipporah's mind fought to retrieve some tidbit or detail to make sense of what was happening in her life. She finally dozed off with the strange man's belongings resting in her lap. Zipporah wasn't aware that what she sought was right there. Right there in her lap.

With the demonic twins gone Sister Betty had finally dozed off. She hadn't quite made it to the bed. Right on the sofa, with her feet up and resting on the coffee table, and her head thrown back with her mouth gaped and snoring, she'd slept. A damp towel covered her forehead. The towel had only cooled down her head but as usual had done nothing for the headache.

Her suite looked a mess. There were empty tea cups and candy wrappers strewn around. After she'd tossed Bea and Sasha out, she'd acted as though she'd finally lost her mind. It wasn't an act. She'd drunk more hot cayenne pepper tea and gorged on the expensive chocolate candy bars from the minibar. All the concoction did was make her edgier and send her to the bathroom, several times. By the time she'd gotten her wits together she was exhausted and collapsed on the sofa.

It took Sister Betty a few seconds to come out of her self-induced coma. She still felt as though she'd just closed her eyes. The knocking on the door and the ringing of the telephone, at the same time, just didn't seem real. She leaned forward and almost broke her legs from doing so. She'd forgotten her legs were resting on the coffee table because they'd fallen completely asleep, even if she hadn't.

"Come back later," she yelled. Sister Betty didn't want to see a maid or anyone. She started rubbing her legs trying to get the blood to cooperate but the knocking persisted. "I said I don't need my room cleaned now!" That was her first lie of the day.

"It's me, Godmother." Chandler rapped harder on the door. "I need to speak with you now!"

The sound of Chandler's voice brought Sister Betty completely around. By then the blood flow had returned to her legs and the telephone had stopped ringing. She looked over and saw the little flashing red light and decided she'd check the message later. "Hold on, June Bug."

Chandler showing up at her door was a ray of sunshine to Sister Betty. He was probably the only person in Las Vegas who could make her feel better. She walked to the door hoping that whatever happened earlier in her room was just a dream.

Sister Betty opened her door wide and found Chandler surrounded by two old nightmares.

And that's when Sister Betty did her Esther Rolle impression: "Damn, damn, damn."

Zipporah slowly replaced the phone in its cradle. It was still early but she'd hoped to speak with Sister Betty. Somehow being around that old woman gave her comfort. Perhaps, Sister Betty would return the call when she heard her message.

Zipporah's clothes felt clammy. They should have. She hadn't changed or showered since the night before.

She wrestled with whether to go through the man's belongings or to get cleaned up. Somehow going through a stranger's possessions didn't feel right, so she decided she wouldn't. She'd just return them to the front desk or whoever was in charge of such things. And, then she remembered that the man had Mother Blister's and Mother Pray Onn's hotel rooms and telephone numbers on the yellow sheet of paper. Knowing there was a possibility that the sick old man wasn't totally alone suddenly gave her a little peace. She decided to shower and rest up. When Chandler returned later, she'd give him the items to give to the women.

"Don't even try to look innocent!" Sasha declared as she used her cane to push Chandler aside and enter Sister Betty's suite again.

"You're in it, too!" Bea added her accusation and almost broke Chandler's hip as she knocked him against the side of the door frame when she entered.

"Heavenly Father," Sister Betty whispered with her hands raised. "Why Lord?" Esther Rolle was gone and she was back.

"Look at her," Sasha said to Chandler, who was still glued to the entrance. "She's trying to act like she's got God on speed dial."

"That's right," Bea chimed in. "Just last night she was talking about murder." She turned to Sasha and nodded for confirmation before turning back to Sister Betty. "Hypocrisy is such an ugly thing."

"You tell her, Bea," Sasha said as she sashayed her tiny hips to a chair to sit. "Tell June Bug, again, what she done."

"I am." Bea stopped and turned to Sister Betty and said, "I'm gonna use the bathroom, first. Make sure you don't lie and try to make Sasha and me look bad while I'm gone."

Sister Betty didn't respond. She waved Chandler in and as he closed the door, she went to the other table. She opened her pocketbook and retrieved a small plastic bottle of blessed oil.

Suddenly, Sister Betty started squirting the oil everywhere and on everyone. She started anointing chairs, windows, the sofa, and the minibar. "I rebuke you, Satan."

She raced toward Sasha squirting the oil as she went. "Be gone, Devil." Sasha started screaming like the evil witch that melted in *The Wizard of Oz.*

Chandler raced over and grabbed at his godmother, and she squirted him, too. "Back up!" she yelled.

Bea had barely gotten into the bathroom when she heard the noise and dashed back out, with her drawers still around her ankles. She couldn't get out of the way so she received a blessed-oil drenching, as well. "Back to the pits of hell, Devil," Sister Betty screamed as she chased Bea.

Almost tripping, Bea dashed back toward the safety of the

bathroom. By then, she'd hopped out of one of the drawers' legs, which had twisted and was about to bring the reality of busting one's behind to a whole new level.

By the time Sister Betty finished, there wasn't an oil-free spot or person in her suite, including her.

And, of course, security was frantically knocking on her door. "Open up! Security is here! Open the door, now!"

Chandler had barely opened the door when the security men rushed inside with their flashlights raised, ready to battle. They came to a total stop when they saw Sasha and the mess that surrounded her. It was like déjà vu. They never said one word nor took their eyes off the little oily demon with a bun and cane that stood before them. They just backed out of the room and fled.

Fortunately for her and unfortunately for them, they were the same two security guards she'd just beaten up about an hour before.

It'd taken all the soap in Sister Betty's suite and two bottles of seltzer water from the minibar to get most of the blessed oil off them. Sister Betty never apologized for the inappropriate baptism. Instead, she sat in a corner of the sofa with a second bottle, ready to repeat that morning's baptism if necessary.

Moments later, Chandler still sat fascinated as the story, or different versions of it depending on who was speaking, poured out from the old women. The one thing each of their tales had in common was Zipporah.

As Bea and Sasha bickered, again, over who was the worst slut when it came to cheating, Chandler sat trying to figure out the next move.

"As I see it," Chandler said, interrupting round ten of Bea and Sasha's championship bout, "there's only one thing that you can do."

"And what's that, June Bug?" Bea said, smiling innocently. She wasn't aware that she still hadn't put in her dentures or whether she'd put her drawers back on. Her mouth looked like a cosmic black hole every time she said a word.

Chandler wanted to grab the bottle of blessed oil from Sister Betty's clutches. He promised himself he would if either of them called him June Bug once more.

He pushed the thought to the back of his mind and continued.

"You have to tell Zipporah the truth. And no matter how much of a dog you feel her father was—"

"Still is," Sasha hissed.

"—or is," Chandler agreed, "she deserves to know her father and he certainly needs to know his child."

"And," Bea hissed, "you deserve a straitjacket if you think we're gonna let that old buzzard hurt our Zipporah!" Her smile had slid away quicker than an avalanche down a mountain.

Sister Betty leaned forward with her hand on the oil bottle trigger and aimed it at Bea. Nobody talked mean to her godson.

Bea fell back before Sister Betty went to squirting again. "I'm just saying," Bea mumbled. "That's all."

"Well, since she's actually my niece," Sasha interrupted, "I think all of you should butt out and let me handle this."

"Aren't you the main reason for this whole mess?" Chandler challenged. "By your own admission, you are."

"DNA—has anybody thought about that?" Sister Betty had finally spoken up but she hadn't relaxed her trigger finger. "If y'all are so set on butting in on this woman's life with news like this, you'd better be sure."

The room became eerily quiet as they turned toward Sister Betty.

"All of you are willing to turn this child's life upside down and the only proof you have is a matching leaf-shaped birthmark and Sasha's word." Sister Betty nodded toward Sasha. "Again, I say, only Sasha's word."

Chandler stood. He took the yellowed paper from his pocket along with two other items he'd not shown Bea or Sasha. He went over and placed them in Sister Betty's lap. "What about these?"

Bea and Sasha leaned forward but couldn't make out what Chandler had given Sister Betty. And, from the amazement on her face, they weren't about to ask, yet.

"My Lord." Sister Betty's eyes kept darting across the paper and the two pictures in her hand. She lay down the spray bottle to get a better look.

"DNA may not be necessary," Chandler said as he took the items from Sister Betty's hands. "But telling Zipporah is. She deserves to know her parents."

Sasha couldn't bare it. It took every ounce of sweetness she could gather to say the words. "What is that you're showing your godmother, Sweetie?" She should've gotten an Oscar.

Chandler looked toward Sister Betty, silently seeking her permission to share what he knew with Bea and Sasha.

"I'd like to see it, too, if you don't mind," Bea added, nicely, just as she was about to slide off the chair from trying to lean forward for a sneak peek.

Chandler laid the items on the coffee table as Bea and Sasha rose to come closer. There was an old photo of Zipporah as a child. She looked to be around seven years old and was playing in the snow in front of a store. The sign on the store read, TEABOUT'S OF AMSTERDAM FURNITURE STORE.

Chandler turned that photo over and read aloud what was written. "This is your child, Zipporah, age six. She's fine, as you can see." There was also a name written, "M. Teabout."

"Are you saying that he always knew about Zipporah?" Bea asked.

"I don't know what he knew or when he knew, but the man obviously suspected she was his." Chandler quickly turned to another piece of paper.

"This letter with a seal is sort of smudged, probably because he's carried it around so long. Anyway, it reads,

"Dear Mr. Epps,

"Many years ago, when I was initially assigned your case, I advised that I didn't think it would have a successful conclusion. The information you provided about your child, her mother, and you was not as complete as I would've wanted. You insisted upon and paid for my continued investigation and I have done my very best to give you some closure.

"This is what I have discovered, to date. The name Zipporah was given to the baby by the mother, when birthed at the Amsterdam Hospital in Amsterdam, New York. When the child was initially placed in the foster care system her first name was never changed. However, the birth mother gave her own last name as being "Moses" at the time of delivery. Although we now know that name to be false, that name was attached to this baby

*and was not changed. All paperwork, and history from
that point on, list the baby as Zipporah Moses. She was
never adopted.*

*"Now for the sad news. I've tracked Miss Moses to Las
Vegas, Nevada. Unfortunately, she has not fared well
since leaving the foster care system as a young adult. She
is now almost thirty and living in a homeless shelter in a
neighborhood certainly not of her choosing. I am enclos-
ing a most recent picture as you mentioned the urgency of
securing one because of your health issues.*

*With all facts considered and proofs retained, we are
happy to this extent to confirm that Zipporah Moses is
your biological daughter. Upon receipt of your written approval I will send a copy of this letter and all attachments
to Miss Areal Hellraiser, since she is listed as the child's
biological mother. Be reminded that I cannot forward the
necessary paperwork unless and until you remit written
approval.*

*"On a more personal note, I must add that I admire
your tenacity, as well as your willingness to dedicate substantial financial commitment to this search. Not many
men would've gone to the lengths you have to find a child
that had less than a thirty-percent chance of being a biological match. I'm sorry it took far too many years to accomplish your goal.*

"Yours truly,

"Max Reinhardt, Private Investigator"

Chandler refolded the letter and watched the astonishment on
the women's faces. He then displayed several other photos of
Zipporah at different times in her life.

"Does Zipporah have a clue?" Sister Betty asked.

"Not about this she doesn't." Chandler quickly gathered up
the items and placed them in his shirt pocket just seconds before
Sasha reached for them.

"How could she not know if she was the one they gave
Jasper's property to?" Bea asked.

"I took the liberty of going through the things when I took
her back to the suite."

"She didn't see you?" Sasha asked.

"No, I did it while she was in the bathroom."

"So there's no getting around it now," Sasha conceded. "She's gonna find out about the whole matter one way or another."

"I'm going to wait another hour so she can finish resting a little. I'll go back to her room and figure out how to tell her."

"What about her performing tonight?" Bea asked, "She'll be so upset, she might not perform well."

"And I won't get my gospel album," Sister Betty said in disappointment. When she realized her selfishness, she sprayed herself, lightly.

"Fortunately," Chandler answered, "She's not on tonight."

"How do you feel about her living in a homeless shelter?" Bea asked. "I wondered how you'd react when you found out."

"You wondered?" Chandler moved to where Bea sat looking almost ashamed. "What do you mean, you wondered?"

"I mean . . . since you read it . . . in the letter." Bea was tripping over her lie just as she had been over the drawers about her ankles earlier.

"She's lying," Sasha blurted. "I know a liar when I hear a liar. I've got experience!"

"Spit it out, Bea, or suffer the consequences." Sister Betty sprayed an oil mist in the air to remind Bea of the consequences.

"Okay," Bea confessed. "When Zipporah left her wallet behind in my hotel room, I went through it and found her shelter I.D. card. So I called the shelter and pretended to be a relative to see if it was really hers."

"And," Chandler urged.

"It was hers. I later found out that she could've been tossed out of the shelter if she has relatives, which means she has somewhere else to stay."

"You never said a word!" Sasha hissed. "You tried to get my niece put out onto the street!"

"You abandoned her in a hospital!" Bea replied. "I oughta whup your skinny behind for doing that!"

Once again, they had to stand around and dab seltzer water on their clothes after Sister Betty started spraying the blessed oil everywhere.

40

Zipporah was glad she still had enough money for a cab. As she rode she started having second thoughts. *What am I doing?* She never liked hospital smells. Why, she didn't know, but they smelled too sterile.

The cab pulled up in front of the hospital. As soon as she entered she tried to wade through the gunshot wounds, blood pouring from stabbings, urine-drenched and hallucinating druggies; yet none of that bothered her as much as the sterile odor. The fact that it tried to mask all the misery in its midst was almost laughable.

She looked out of place in her pale pink dress with a ring of red roses around the hem. She exuded innocence as she walked slowly, her footsteps silenced by a sea of chatter from white uniforms and rickety rolling medical carts.

It had taken a lot of effort and pleading to get the Luxor triage administrator, Mr. Phelpson, to release the name of the hospital. It was only after she'd lied and said that she was a relative of the patient that he did so. It seemed crazy that earlier he'd already given her the man's belongings without making her prove who she was. Now she had to almost beg him to find out where they'd taken him.

All the way over from the Luxor, she'd struggled with why she would bother to go to a hospital to see a complete stranger. She concluded that she didn't have a reason, at least not a sane one, and came anyway.

Zipporah checked the room number on her visitor's pass the information desk clerk handed to her. In a voice so monotone she almost put Zipporah to sleep after the first ten words, she instructed her to wear the sticky-back label on her dress. Zipporah wasn't about to have adhesive mess on her dress, so she carried it. She was also given the speech about not bringing live plants or foods to the intensive care unit. She hadn't thought about bringing either. Why would she?

"Can I help you?" a nurse stopped chatting on a phone to ask.

"No. I think I can find the room."

Arriving at his room, Zipporah entered and found the blinds were partially closed. But even that couldn't hide what looked like a death shadow hovering over his bed. It had crept over him and quickly disappeared. Zipporah had barely seen it, or at least she thought that's what it was. With all the beeps and the buzzing echoing from the large computer that instructed his care, she couldn't concentrate. He looked as though he was struggling, again. Had he always fought so hard? She could admire that trait if she knew him.

Zipporah crept further inside the room. Even she had not heard the door close behind her, yet he'd turned toward her as though he had.

There was nothing familiar about the figure that lay before her. Although, she was sure that if she turned her head, just a little to the side, she could picture him as a once handsome man. He was tall, she could tell that much. The soles of his feet almost touched the very end of the bed. She saw a chart hanging on a plug over the side cabinet. She was tempted to read it. But what would it tell her, that the man was extremely ill? She didn't need a nursing or medical degree to figure that out.

He moaned, which caused Zipporah to jump. He was still watching her as though she were something curious. He hadn't tried to reach out to her like he had back in the hotel's triage room. The ticking sound on one of the monitors quickened. She saw his chest heave. It was pumping rapidly but didn't seem to be doing it on its own. Zipporah's eyes followed the line from the machine to his chest. The ticking sound suddenly turned into a long hum. The man's eyes searched Zipporah's for her help. He let out another long moan. She didn't know what to do or think.

She didn't have to. Not a moment later help arrived. Three nurses raced behind the doctor. They reminded her of a horse race as they entered the I.C.U. room. The doctor, with a five o'clock shadow that looked days old, was clearly the winner. A tall nurse, Asian with both a stethoscope and glasses intertwined around her chest and wearing an ill-fitting uniform, placed second. In third place was a short brown-skinned nurse. She looked about a day past retirement age as well as a prime candidate for gastric bypass surgery. The nurse seemed to use her large belly to shove a cart filled with all sorts of gadgets. She rushed, her feet making a slapping sound on the tiles as she did.

"Wait in the hallway!" It was the nurse who placed third. She pushed the cart near the side of the man's bed while forcing Zipporah out the door.

Two other doctors sprinted toward her. They nearly trampled her as they pushed past to enter the room. One yanked his stethoscope off so fast Zipporah thought he'd get whiplash. She couldn't see inside as they'd had the professional sense to close the door. Whatever she needed to find out about him would have to wait. Or if he died, it would die with him.

There was nothing more Zipporah could do at the hospital. So she left the sterile odors that had her upset, but not before tossing the sticky-backed label back at the woman at the receptionist desk.

A few blocks away from the hospital, another Las Vegas cab weaved in and out of traffic. It was still early in the morning and yet the weather was in triple digits and distorted waves of heat emanated from the street. Everyone in traffic and on the streets moved with an urgency to get to someplace cooler or at least quickly.

However, it wasn't the heat outside that was forcing the cab driver to step hard on the gas, it was the two bickering old crones in the backseat. He almost felt sorry for the young man crushed between them with his head lowered in his hands.

If Bea and Sasha didn't stop arguing, Chandler swore that either they or he would be the next ones to end up in triage.

He hadn't slept in almost twenty-four hours, and as far as he knew, they hadn't either. Where did they get the energy? Everyone's nerves were on edge and he could imagine they would easily kill one another. He almost wished they would.

Chandler had argued with every reasonable idea he could

imagine to keep them from following him to the hospital. Only Sister Betty, probably because she was close to passing out from exhaustion, had listened.

What a mess, Chandler thought sadly. He'd taken time off from the conference center to help launch not only Zipporah's career but his own. It was going to be not only her big break but their big break. In less than a week, a mere few days, all hell had broken out, and it wouldn't be mended with apologies or even money. This woman's life was about to be turned upside down.

Zipporah would probably be a lot safer and happier, Chandler considered, if he just returned her to the shelter and made sure she never saw any of them again.

"You're crazy, Sasha," Bea snapped. "Zipporah don't have to know everything about Jasper. If you had any kind of upbringing, you'd just love her 'cause she's your kin."

"What's love got to do with anything?" Sasha said as she reached across Chandler's chest, poking him by accident. "I'm trying to look out for her. She don't need to know how messed up her DNA is!"

Chandler didn't say a word as the bickering continued. He looked up in time to see the cab driver's reflection in the rearview mirror. The man was shaking his head in disbelief.

After visiting the hotel triage room, Chandler had managed to find the administrator, Mr. Phelpson, who was still on duty. Great minds must've thought alike because Chandler told the same lie Zipporah had and that's how he knew she'd left the hotel. So getting Jasper's hospital whereabouts was the easy part. Trying to sneak out of the Luxor under Bea and Sasha's radar was impossible.

"Bea wears her Tuesday drawers on Thursdays." Sasha poked Chandler in the arm to get his attention as she tried to raise Bea's skirt with the tip of her cane. In return, Bea reached across Chandler and tried to grab Sasha's cane. There was no doubt that Bea had planned on sticking that cane in a place where it would make Sasha look like she had three legs.

Chandler could only hope that the hospital had a room for him when he checked in voluntarily.

After self-recrimination and the decision to accept everything that had happened as providence, Chandler accepted the truth. He was attracted to Zipporah on a level he didn't understand. It wasn't love as he always understood love to be; it was a connection of a different sort. He just couldn't put a name to it. There was no time to dwell on it. So, if one good thing came out of the entire fiasco, it was that Zipporah would learn the truth about her parents. He would stand by her decision as to what she wanted to do with it.

A jerk from the cab threw Chandler back against the seat. He should've been upset with Zipporah that she'd left the hotel without telling him, but she wouldn't be part "Hellraiser" if she hadn't. He'd address that issue later.

"There she is!" Bea called out. Her sudden outburst startled the others. Leave it to old eagle eyes to see her.

Chandler and Sasha yelled at the cab driver to stop at the same time. The driver hit the brakes thinking they saw something he hadn't. He cursed when his green, red, and black knitted cap flew out the window, and he almost jumped the curb avoiding Zipporah, who of course thought she was about to die.

Zipporah had seen the cab careening toward her yet couldn't move. Like everything that was going on around her, she'd simply thought it, too, was a part of the dream. Fortunately, someone from the crowd snatched her back onto the curb just in time.

Before Zipporah had a chance to even find out who saved her life or better yet, to thank the stranger, Chandler had leapt from the cab. He didn't know if she had just arrived and might've been going inside the hospital or if she were coming out.

"Zipporah!" Chandler grabbed her arm and pushed her toward the waiting cab. "What in the world are you doing here?"

Bea stuck her head out the cab's window to get a better glimpse. Once she'd seen Zipporah was all right, she chimed right in. "Zipporah, you were about to give us a heart attack!"

Sasha never said a word. She watched Chandler put a protective arm around Zipporah, and when she saw that Zipporah had not resisted, she really became concerned.

"Are we moving or what?" the cab driver asked.

Chandler opened the rear door and placed Zipporah inside, then climbed into the front seat next to the driver. "Back to the Luxor," Chandler ordered.

41

Sister Betty slowly hung up the phone. Its ringing had startled her, waking her from a deep sleep. The last person she'd hoped to hear from when she was too tired to talk or think straight was the Reverend Tom. He'd called for an update and to just chat.

She hadn't meant to tell it all but she did. Actually, she'd spilled her guts as soon as the reverend asked, "How are things going?"

It wasn't until Sister Betty had told everything that she'd wanted, and finally stopped speaking, that the reverend had a chance to talk.

"Wow!" That was about all the man of God had said. He didn't quote a scripture or whisper a word of prayer. Instead he'd finally added, "My goodness, Sister Betty." Reverend Tom was totally surprised. "You actually thought about killing someone?" It was as though that revelation trumped all the other news she'd shared.

Sister Betty had repeated the story twice before the Reverend Tom fully understood all the craziness that accompanied it.

"The way I see it," the reverend said, "we have a couple of miracles that occurred."

"What would they be?" she'd asked, because in her mind, she hadn't seen anything but confusion. Didn't God say He wasn't the author of confusion? So what was the miracle?

"The fact that it took many years to happen, but Mother Pray Onn finally got saved." He chuckled to take away his obvious implication, before adding, "And a dying man has found a daughter who obviously needed to find her family."

"I can see your point." She was actually too tired to see it but he was the pastor, so she went along. Her heavenly line to God had become somewhat static, so she wasn't about to disagree.

"Of course, the ultimate miracle is that Mothers Blister and Pray Onn have not shut down the Luxor like they almost did the conference center."

Sister Betty suddenly realized that perhaps she'd not told every detail. She'd left out the part where the two mothers nearly shut down the casino. Somehow the reverend hadn't discerned that bit of information.

They finally got around to praying. Both had accepted the fact that perhaps God had used the reverend in His ultimate plan to send Sister Betty to Las Vegas. She was somehow supposed to be a part of the glue that would hold all the situations together. And then there was the status of her spirituality. She'd discovered she wasn't quite as saved as she'd thought.

There was almost a week left before she was to return to Pelzer. Sister Betty wondered if she'd return as saved as she was before she left.

After the reverend hung up, Sister Betty turned down the air conditioner in the room. She'd worn the same clothes for the past twenty-four hours and she was beginning to smell a bit overripe. A shower was definitely in order.

Opening the closet, she took out a change of clothes. She noticed a stain on her white skirt and to her it seemed almost prophetic. She'd never worn a white outfit with a stain. And now she would. Much like her present life, where she seemed to find a rebuke at every turn, she thought her spirituality was stained with her disobedience. Sister Betty knew that obedience was better than sacrifice. All the tithing, praying, witnessing and such, they meant nothing if she would still disobey God. It seemed that lately all she did was repent.

For years, Sister Betty was so wrapped up in her own opinion of her salvation, she'd obeyed the letter of the Lord's Prayer but not its spirit. "Forgive us our debts as we forgive our debtors."

While Sister Betty was upstairs in her hotel room showering and praising God for revelation, Chandler, Zipporah, Bea, and Sasha were just arriving back at the hotel.

No one had spoken during the ride back from the hospital. Chandler had looked back every so often making sure Zipporah was all right. Bea had gently taken Zipporah's hand. When Zipporah hadn't resisted, Bea had squeezed it to comfort her.

Sasha had taken her sunglasses from her bag. She'd donned them and pretended to nod off. All the while she'd watched Zipporah, still trying to see any resemblance to the baby they'd left in Amsterdam, New York. Aside from the apparent leaf birthmark and the uncanny resemblance to her other niece, Ima, she couldn't. But Jasper had known for years, it seemed, and it was now a done deal.

Chandler helped each of the women from the cab. Weariness prevented Bea and Sasha from saying an unkind word during the ride. Everyone's common concern for Zipporah outweighed any silly arguing. When Chandler offered to escort Bea and Sasha to their rooms before taking Zipporah to hers, they declined.

"Get some rest, June Bug," Bea ordered. "Sasha and I will be just fine."

"Are you sure?"

"We'll be okay," Sasha replied and pointed to Zipporah. "You take care of Zipporah."

Sasha's reference to Zipporah surprised them. It was the first time in Zipporah's presence that Sasha had acknowledged her existence.

Zipporah shuddered a little when Sasha said her name. Why she had, other than the fact that up to that moment the old woman had ignored her, she didn't know. But she was too tired to respond. So much had happened and she had the beginnings of a migraine.

Mercifully, the elevator door opened at Bea and Sasha's floor. The two old women said their good-byes as they exited, yawning loudly as they did.

"You think he's gonna stay with Zipporah?" Bea asked.

"How would I know?" Sasha snapped. "I certainly hope so."

They watched one another closely as they started to inch toward their rooms.

"I think I'm gonna just lie down and pass completely out." Bea yawned again and tried to stretch. Her back gave out a loud crunching sound as if it snapped back into its normal C-shaped form. "Ouch!"

"You're up to something." Sasha stopped walking. "I know

you, Bea Blister. You don't try to stretch unless you getting ready to battle."

"Sasha, you're too suspicious." Bea looked away quickly to avoid Sasha's scrutiny.

"Okay, maybe I'm just too tired." Sasha moved ahead of Bea, tapping her cane as though she were using it to feel her way. "I'll see you later."

"Okay," Bea said as she again yawned. "You lie down and try to relax."

Ten minutes later, Bea and Sasha bumped into each other at a nearby corner near the Luxor. Not wanting to be seen, each had sneaked out to hail a cab. Not noticing each other in the crowd, they'd almost knocked each other down vying for the same cab.

Sasha's accusation was straight to the point. "You're a sneaky something."

"What would you call what you're doing, Sasha?" Bea asked as she slapped Sasha's hand away from the cab door.

"Handling family business, that's what I call it." Sasha grabbed at the door again and this time she made it. But before she could give the driver directions, Bea had entered through the other side.

Fortunately for the cab driver the women were going to the same place, so they didn't have to argue about that. Unfortunately, for the cab driver, it was Bea and Sasha he carried.

Chandler, for the second time that day, escorted Zipporah into her suite. This time he sat quietly, preferring she speak first if she wanted to talk. She hadn't spoken a single word since he'd placed her into the cab.

He watched her as she went into the other room. Surprisingly she hadn't closed the door completely. He could hear her moving about. There were sounds of a closet door opening and closing as well as a dresser. Perhaps she was changing out of her clothes to lie down.

Chandler took out the letter and the pictures again. He reread the letter slowly, drinking in the words as though somehow they'd nourish his mind for the next step. He didn't know how he was going to reveal all he'd discovered to Zipporah.

He thought about what Sasha had said earlier. According to Sasha, Jasper had known all about Zipporah when he'd shown

228   Pat G'Orge-Walker

up at her sister Areal's home a couple of days ago. Sasha had thought that Areal had called him to let him know that she'd discovered something disturbing in Las Vegas. But Jasper sat there and never said a word to Areal.

Sobbing came from Zipporah's room. By the time Chandler reached her room, she was balled up like a fetus. He didn't know whether to go to her or just back out of the room and let her tears flow. Perhaps, she needed to cry over what she didn't know and what she was soon to learn.

Chandler's cell phone rang out, dictating his next move. He backed out of the room, closing the door completely behind him. He looked at the phone and saw Alicia's name. He quickly pushed one of the phone's buttons, sending it directly to voice mail. Knowing Alicia probably would call Zipporah, too, he took her phone off its hook.

Chandler dragged one of the chairs over to the bedroom door and sat. Zipporah's crying tugged at him. He was so angry and frustrated. That time it truly had nothing to do with what he wanted from Zipporah.

As bad as that moment seemed for Zipporah, Chandler was grateful that he hadn't brought Sasha and Bea along. At least those two old women were asleep in their hotel rooms and out of his way, he assumed.

Chandler couldn't have been more wrong. Bea and Sasha were wide awake and entering the Las Vegas hospital at that very moment.

42

Bea and Sasha had finally agreed to call a halt to their bickering for the sake of Zipporah and because they had run out of nasty things to say. They paid the cab driver, Bea giving him a dollar for a tip.

Bea and Sasha had rehearsed their lies in the ride over and convincingly got passes to Jasper's room. They weren't aware of his earlier setback as they entered the unit clutching their Bibles and looking pious. So when one of the nurses seated at the nurses' station smiled and indicated they could enter Jasper's room, they thought their plan was working.

Though neither Bea nor Sasha was much younger than Jasper, when they entered, they were shocked. When they saw all the tubes, IV lines, and heard the persistent whirring sounds of the machines, they almost had heart attacks. Coming eye to eye to their immortality hadn't occurred to them.

And that's when they both flipped open their Bibles and started reading from the first book of Psalms. An hour later they were still standing in the middle of Jasper's room reading aloud. Neither woman planned on touching or speaking to Jasper until they'd reached the 150th psalm. They knew that David was a murderer, a liar, an adulterer, and so much more; and if he were still a man after God's own heart, then they would take their lead from reading his psalms. They didn't think there could be much of a difference between David and them.

Of course, neither of those old battling mothers thought about reading from Ephesians 6:11. "Put on the whole armor of God so that you may withstand the wiles of the devil." They'd much rather have compared their walk to that of David's, and with good reason. The only thing they hadn't done like David was to tend sheep, but they sure loved to walk in sheep dip.

Sister Betty's attempt to fall back to sleep after showering, failed. She tossed and turned, sending covers to the floor and nearly twisting her arthritic legs into pretzel shapes. Finally she gave up trying.

Looking at the clock, she realized that most of the morning was gone. Surprisingly, she wasn't hungry. She tried to push away thoughts of the mess she'd become involved in with the other mothers. She couldn't.

Sister Betty dressed, ignoring the small stain on her white dress. She drank another cup of cayenne tea, her second since she'd gotten up, and called Chandler on his cell phone. She was almost surprised that he answered, thinking perhaps he might've been busy.

"Godmother," Chandler whispered into his phone, "are you okay?"

"I'm fine, June Bug." Sister Betty wondered why he whispered. Perhaps they had a bad connection. "I was just checking in on you."

"Everything's about as good as can be expected. What can I do for you?" Chandler needed to hurry Sister Betty off the phone. The only reason he'd bothered to answer was because he thought something might've happened. His nerves were just that edgy.

"I don't need anything," She should've let it go at that, but she just had to ask. "Any further news from Bea and Sasha?"

"They're in their rooms, probably knocked out."

Sister Betty's knees started jerking as they always did when something evil was amiss. "Are you sure?"

"That's what they said when I last saw them." A feeling of heaviness started creeping into Chandler's shoulders as though a boulder had just dropped on them.

"And you believed them?" Sister Betty took her free hand and pushed hard on her knees to stop them from jerking. She couldn't.

"Oh, God," Chandler blurted, "I just hope they didn't—"

"Didn't what?" By then Sister Betty's left knee was about to knock out her right eye. It was jumping just that high.

Sister Betty quickly decided she didn't want to know anything more. She slammed down the phone hoping she hadn't hurt Chandler's eardrum. She couldn't even go to the bathroom without hopping. That's how unstable her legs became.

Chandler had shut the cover to his cell phone about the same time Sister Betty had hung up. He hoped he hadn't hurt her feelings but he'd about had enough drama. Zipporah was in the room whimpering. Alicia was trying to track him down for what, he didn't know. He was trying to keep his godmother in the dark, although if she called him June Bug once more, he was going to scream. And now he was too nervous to find out if Mothers Blister and Pray Onn were actually in their rooms.

Deep inside, he knew the old women weren't. But whatever they were up to, far too much time had passed since he'd left them, to stop it. So for the second time in two days, Chandler prayed.

Meanwhile at the hospital, Bea and Sasha kept up the charade.

Although they'd told Chandler that they thought it was best that Zipporah be told the truth, they personally weren't convinced. With that in mind, they'd decided that Jasper was in need of some personal prayer and the laying on of hands. Neither knew that Jasper was so medicated he couldn't have felt anything or hollered even if he were on fire.

With the last psalm read, they went to work on Jasper. They might've gotten away with snuffing him out if Bea's chubby paws hadn't become entangled in a mess of wires that fed his digital monitor. She wasn't really trying to kill him as much as trying to convince him to stay away from Zipporah and to remain quiet.

Sasha, in the meantime, was supposed to be the lookout. She reasoned that Bea already had her fingerprints in the penal system from her time spent in lockup for various crimes against society.

"Is he convinced yet?" Sasha asked sharply as she peered through the half-opened blinds to the room for uninvited company. It was code for "Is he dead?" Depending on who asked, should it ever come up at trial, it could be explained another way.

The old women were turning their spirituality off and on as though they only had a limited amount to use. They were trying to save their own butts and extinguish Jasper's.

But Jasper's alarm had silently gone off at the nurses' station. When Sasha saw white uniforms racing toward the room, she stepped out of the way, her tiny body hidden behind the door. In the meanwhile, when the first of several doctors arrived, they found Bea with her hand caught up in the mesh of wires and tubes feeding life to Jasper.

Sasha kept her cool. No one saw her, head bowed humbly, creep out of the room without one tap of her cane heard. She fled, leaving Bea behind and caught holding the wires.

No one but Bea Blister could've bluffed her way out of what was obviously a hot mess. As soon as the doctors burst into the room and she saw where she couldn't extricate her hand from the entanglement in time, she started babbling. She'd dropped her head pretending to be praying, but it still sounded more like babbling.

"I bind these wires that have ensnared this poor brother," Bea declared. "You shall have no power over this man." She yanked her fist to show them and the devil she meant business, and of course, it pulled out the main plug to Jasper's oxygen tank.

The alarm on the oxygen tank sent a high-pitched sound throughout the ICU. That wasn't supposed to happen because, after all, there were critically ill people there and quiet was essential.

One of the doctors had the presence of mind to rush behind the unit and push the plug back in. The other two doctors worked on releasing Bea from the grip of the tubes and wires. They hoped none of what they'd done placed the patient in more danger.

"Ouch," Bea winced, and with her free hand balled up, she accidentally hit Jasper in his chest instead of the other doctor.

Jasper's quick spurts of internal activity would've gone unnoticed because of all the noise, but the machine monitoring his vitals started beeping wildly.

"Jesus." Jasper woke and called out, "Lord, help me."

The doctors tugged at Bea's hand again. This time it came loose. They pushed her to the side and went to work on Jasper.

"Thank you, Lord." Jasper's hoarse voice grew stronger. "I thank You, Lord."

"Just hang on, Mr. Epps." The doctor was trying to keep Jasper from saying anything more while they replaced his mask.

"I healed him!" Bea screamed. "It was me that healed him."

The alarms stopped and the beeping sounds from the monitors became steady. There wasn't anyone in the room, with a medical degree or not, who could refute her. Somehow, with Bea's craziness, she'd managed to wake Jasper, who had enough drugs in him to make Rip Van Winkle jealous. They took his outcry for a good thing.

Either he'd been healed by Bea or he was just that stubborn and was going to see his child no matter what. Either way, Bea was asked, in a very polite manner, to leave so the patient could recover.

Bea said she would and as she backed out the door, she balled up her fist and then threw him a quick warning sign. Using two of her fingers, she pointed first to her eyes and then toward his.

Sick or not, Jasper couldn't misread the ghetto sign for "watch your behind." She was showing him that there was more where that came from. The alarm went off again as Jasper struggled. The way he was struggling the doctors thought that he was trying to get out of the bed to get to Bea.

"Ya'll need me to heal him again?" Bea asked sweetly, stopping just short of opening the door.

"No!" the doctors responded in unison.

"Okay," Bea replied. She threw Jasper one last eyeball-to-eyeball sign and left.

43

Sasha was lucky in finding a cab when she'd raced from the hospital. Arriving a short time later, she rushed from the Luxor elevator as quick as her tiny feet could carry her. The orthopedic Hush Puppies she'd worn since earlier that morning were beginning to pinch. That only caused her more misery. When Sasha was miserable that meant she shared it.

Sasha pounded on Sister Betty's door. "Come on and open the door."

Sister Betty had just about gotten her knees down to a half jerk per minute when Sasha appeared at the door, uninvited. By the time Sister Betty made it to her door and opened it, Sasha had taken off a shoe and was about to use it to pound on the door. She hopscotched her way into the room.

"Bea tried to kill Jasper," Sasha blurted.

"How do you know that?" Sister Betty's eyes narrowed as she waited for Sasha's response.

Sasha decided to dispense with the prepared lie and tell Sister Betty the almost-truth. It wasn't that she and Bea didn't want Zipporah to learn the truth or have a family, they just didn't think Jasper was what she needed.

"But he spent a ton of money to find his child," Sister Betty reminded Sasha. "He didn't have to do that. People do change. Didn't you change?"

"You're using me as an example?" Sasha couldn't believe her ears. Sister Betty was actually embracing her as an equal despite the evidence that she'd fallen, a few times, since they'd prayed.

"You may or may not be the best example," Sister Betty admitted. "But you tried. We all have to repent daily."

Sasha sat down and took off her other shoe, although Sister Betty had hoped it was to put it on and leave.

"So what happened to Bea?" The answer came immediately, almost like a hurricane without a warning.

"Come on, Sister Betty, open the door. I need to talk to you." Sister Betty opened the door and Bea stormed in.

Sasha, with no place to hide or run, just sat innocently as though she had no idea what the problem could be.

Bea was too winded to stomp Sasha at that moment.

"I thought you were right behind me," Sasha lied sweetly. "Are you okay, Bea?"

"I'll be right behind you, all right!" Bea wanted to move but found she was too tired. "I'll put my foot in your—"

"Bea," Sister Betty interrupted what she was certain was going to be language foul enough to fill the room with demons. "You wanna bring security here again?"

"If they come I hope they bring something to eat," Bea quipped, "I haven't eaten in hours." Bea slumped over from a low blood sugar episode.

Sister Betty ran to the minibar and retrieved several candy bars. She was about to force-feed them into Bea's mouth but stopped. Unfortunately, they were Baby Ruth candy bars with a chewy and nutty filling. Bea didn't have her teeth in, so if she swallowed them whole, she'd have choked. It took Sister Betty's conscience to mule-kick her from not giving in to the urge to push those candy bars in Bea's mouth.

Chandler looked around Zipporah's room. One box of tissues wouldn't do, so he took another from the bathroom vanity and brought it to Zipporah. She'd gone through two boxes of tissues and Chandler hadn't told everything.

He was totally surprised she had tears left. He'd sat outside her door for about thirty minutes listening to her sob. She was almost dehydrated by the time she'd stopped and fallen asleep.

But Zipporah hadn't slept for long or at least it didn't seem as though she had. Chandler had barely closed his eyes when it seemed she was up. As light as she was on her feet, Chandler instinctively knew she had crept past. There was a brief whiff of her perfume that lingered as she turned toward the kitchenette.

He hadn't said anything, at first. He preferred to see what she'd do. What frame of mind was she in? Was she all cried out?

But Zipporah knew Chandler had awakened slightly if not fully. Minutes before, she'd even heard a light snoring through the bedroom door left slightly open, and then suddenly heard nothing. When she'd passed him she glanced at him, noticing that his clothes were wrinkled. There were perspiration stains on his shirt, which was unbuttoned. A patch of dark black curly hair peeped through the shirt in a way that would force the eyes to travel its path down to the naval area. He needed a shave because his stubble had darkened, almost looking like a full beard. Some other time she'd found all that attractive, but not now.

He'd stirred again, mumbling something unintelligible, but a conversation wasn't high on her list of priorities. She'd already cried, soaking her sheets and pillow, and she'd vented, with every tear. No matter how hard she'd tried to make it go away, she couldn't get the image of Jasper Epps out of her mind. She reached for a cup and filled it with water from the refrigerator. *Old people,* she thought, *it seems they're going to be the death of me, or drive me crazy.*

Zipporah walked over to the window and looked down at the pyramid-shaped structure in the front of the Luxor. It seemed crazy for her to think of a television theme song at that time. In her head she kept hearing Janet DuBois singing the theme to *Good Times,* "Movin' on Up." She was up in the big league and yet, it felt like life had taken its bat and was beating her like an unwanted stepchild.

She could hear Chandler shifting in his seat. He was probably trying to wake. Zipporah still didn't turn around. She kept looking out over the Las Vegas skyline. It would be a while before nightfall, and she wanted to enjoy the view while she could from the top.

The water Zipporah drank suddenly had a different taste. It tasted almost bitter with a trace of salt. Without meaning to she'd started crying again. Her tears had slowly made their way down her face and dripped into the glass. How long she'd stood at the window drinking her own tears, she didn't know.

In fact, there wasn't much she knew for sure. However, one or more of the people who'd just entered into her life, bringing more chaos than she could've imagined, had answers. She just needed to figure out whom. Self-preservation took over and Zipporah took the sleeve of her robe and wiped away the tears. She needed to get a grip.

About that time she heard Chandler stir again, his footsteps on the carpet, so she knew he was fully awake. Before turning from the window to face him, she forced a smile. She'd decided that she'd play along and see how much he knew. After that, she'd play it by ear. She was tired of crying alone.

44

Zipporah took her time. Instead of bombarding Chandler with questions, she thanked him for staying and assured him that she was much better. She'd noticed that her phone had been taken off the hook, no doubt by Chandler. But she said nothing and went about ordering room service. Perhaps on a full stomach, Chandler would let down his guard.

Chandler was puzzled by the sudden change in Zipporah. Even though he'd kept his eyes closed as she moved about the living room, he'd heard everything. He knew she'd gotten water from the refrigerator and he knew she'd sobbed, again, by the window. He'd even peeped one time to see her shaking as she wept. So why was she now acting like she had total control?

Chandler got up and went to the bathroom to throw water on his face. One look in the mirror told him that he was totally out of control. He couldn't remember the last time he'd looked so unkempt. He breathed into his hands and decided he definitely needed to brush his teeth, chew on a breath mint or do something to take the edge off his breath. Thankfully, he always carried a few in his pants pocket.

Chandler thought about just going to his own room to change but then he remembered what happened the last time he'd left Zipporah alone. She'd left and he didn't want to chance it again.

"Are you okay in there?" Zipporah forced a matter-of-fact tone to her voice. "The food is here."

"I'll be right out." All of Chandler's alarms were screaming. Something wasn't right. Was she having a mental breakdown? No one could cry as hard as she just had and be so cheerful now. He quickly peered out the bathroom door and saw her start to uncover the dishes.

"Hurry up, Chandler," Zipporah called out. "I'm starving."

"I'm right here." Chandler stood behind her. He smiled as he pulled out her chair and waited for her to sit before he did.

The food did look and smell good, but everything they were doing seemed robotic. They watched every forkful and made polite conversation, avoiding any reference to what they really wanted to discuss.

During the silent moments when manners dictated that he not speak with his mouth filled with food, Chandler rehearsed his lines. Earlier, while Zipporah was in her room, he'd tried to determine how much information to share with her. He didn't want to dump every detail at once, thinking he still had to protect her.

Zipporah watched Chandler. He was thinking hard as he chewed, and his brow had furrowed. But she said nothing.

What did she need to know and when did she need to know it? Chandler thought, suddenly realizing she was watching him. "This is delicious," he said, but he'd forgotten to smile.

"I'm glad you're enjoying it."

Should he wait until after their food digested? When, what, where? At this point, in his mind, he felt as though life had tossed him into the ring without a manager or boxing gloves. But he knew that wasn't true. He hadn't been to church as much as he should have, but he did understand that God was his manager and would direct every punch.

Zipporah and Chandler finished the meal. Without meaning to do it, they sat on the sofa together. It put a crimp in both of their plans because each had wanted to sit separately. It would've given them space to think during combat.

No matter how distant Zipporah wanted to remain, Chandler's nearness disarmed her, just a little. "It's a good thing I don't have to perform this evening." She tried to make polite conversation.

"It is a very good thing," Chandler replied, while thinking that there was no way she'd be able to perform after what he was about to lay upon her. He wasn't too sure if she'd be able to make it through her scheduled performance for the next night, either.

"You look amazing," Chandler said as he slid closer to Zipporah. He didn't try to touch her, but if her body language showed he could, then he would.

She didn't move or speak.

Chandler looked around and sighed. There was nothing to do but do it. "Zipporah, I've something to tell you."

"Yes." Her eyes revealed nothing but her heart raced. "What is it?"

There were no words to open the conversation, so he pulled the envelope from his pocket. Whatever reaction she gave, he'd figure out a way to be there—if she still wanted him to.

Zipporah saw the words "Reinhardt and Levy Investigations" and fell back against the sofa. She clutched the arm of the sofa for support. Had Chandler known she was homeless all the time? Why would he have her investigated? Did he find out how she'd arrived in Las Vegas and with whom? Why had he let her taste success, only to snatch it away? What had she done to him?

Chandler couldn't judge much by Zipporah's reaction. Did she already know Jasper was her father? That didn't make sense. How could she? Had she played him all this time?

The tension was thick like syrup as they gathered their thoughts.

"Why did you do this?" Zipporah's voice was rising and she didn't care.

"I didn't do anything!" Chandler had stood without realizing it. "All I've been doing is trying to help you!"

"By investigating me . . . how's that supposed to help me?"

"What in the hell are you talking about?" He looked around for the door to leave as though he'd forgotten where it was.

Zipporah took the letter and was about to throw it at him when she saw the pictures lying under it. She threw down the letter onto the coffee table and snatched the pictures. She had to look twice but she was certain that they were pictures of her. She hadn't seen them before, but they were definitely taken by someone who knew her as a child. She shuddered as though she could feel the cold from the pictures' snowy background.

Her bewildered look caused him to stop. Chandler sat down again. If he'd been puzzled before, he was completely confused now.

"I don't understand." Zipporah's eyes stayed glued to the pictures as she scanned each. Her eyes went back and forth in disbelief. "Why would you have me investigated and what does my childhood have to do with anything?"

"I didn't!" Chandler snapped. "Your father did!"

It was out there and he couldn't take it back. Chandler hadn't meant to break it to her like that, but in the heat of his anger and confusion, he'd done it. Chandler saw the confused look on Zipporah's face as her complexion turned almost chalky. He pounded his fists out of a need to hit something. When was God going to step in and order his moves?

Chandler didn't drink but he rose, and instead of going to Zipporah, who sat stunned, he opened the minibar. He took out a bottle of wine and opened it. Instead of a wineglass, he reached for a tall glass from the cabinet and filled it to its brim. He drank the entire glass in almost one gulp. When he turned around he saw Zipporah's questioning gaze. He refilled the glass and sat it down before her.

Zipporah pushed the glass away.

Chandler took it. Like the first one, he gulped this one down, too.

"I'm sorry," Chandler finally whispered. He moved over next to where she sat like a ceramic figurine, so fragile and beautiful. He took the photographs gently from her hands. In their place he laid the letter.

45

Bea was the first one to wake. Her bladder was doing its thing even if she couldn't participate. Her legs had stiffened as had her back. She howled in pain when she tried to move.

Sister Betty and Sasha jumped. Bea's howling causing them to wake in confusion. None of them knew how long they'd been sleeping but the bright light flickering into the room from the outside was the only light.

"It's night already?" Sister Betty remarked to Sasha, who appeared to have gathered her wits.

They wiped sleep from their eyes and spittle from the corners of their mouths as they watched Bea struggling to make it to the bathroom, hopefully, in time.

"I see she's none the worse?" Sasha commented. She turned and adjusted her glasses, trying to see the clock. "What time is it?"

"It's getting dark outside. That's all I know." Sister Betty didn't bother looking at the clock. Whatever time it was, it was time for those two to get out of her suite.

Sasha ignored Sister Betty's yawning. She knew it was a not-too-subtle sign for her to leave. "So what are we going to do about Zipporah? Do you think June Bug will say anything?"

"I don't know," Sister Betty answered sharply. It was her answer to both questions.

Bea returned to the living room. She walked slowly and with her legs parted a bit more than necessary.

"She didn't make it," Sasha said as she pinched her nose to let Bea know that they knew what had happened.

If Bea got the hint she didn't take it. She plopped all her weight back onto the chair and stared at Sasha. "Drink some Listerine for that bad breath and you won't have to hold your own nose when you speak."

Sasha rose slowly. Switching her tiny hips as she approached Bea, she slowed down in front of her to give it an extra shake, then went into the bathroom.

"Well, I've had about enough," Sister Betty announced. "This craziness ends tonight!"

"How's that . . . ?" Bea shifted in her seat to face Sister Betty just in case she'd not heard her correctly." Repeat that."

"I'm ordering some food, and I'm not asking either of you what you want to eat. You'll eat whatever I order." Sister Betty's voice took on a bass tone as though she'd been possessed by an authority spirit. "We'll decide what to do about Zipporah and Jasper. Then ya'll get out of my room!"

She made no apologies to them or to God. Sister Betty determined right then and there that whatever happened, she was getting on a plane the next day. Pelzer never meant as much to her as it did at that moment. She was going home and if she had to repent, she'd do it in Pelzer.

Bea didn't often use good judgment. She decided to use some. Not saying one word would be a start.

The hospital ICU seemed a bit different at night. The staff wasn't as hurried as the ones on the day shift.

Jasper had been moved to another room on the other side of the unit. He'd be closer to the nurses' station and the room had more of the equipment he suddenly needed. That wasn't the only difference between the rooms.

There was an outer room with a sink, a cabinet, several one-size-fits-all yellow gauze material gowns, and a box of latex gloves. A sign over the next entry door ordered visitors to don the items before entering.

Jasper, having been moved into the new ICU room, seemed to have improved dramatically. There were still the tubes, the oxygen tank with its huge valve looking imposing, and monitors connected to him, but he looked more comfortable. He was.

In fact, ever since Jasper had earlier seen the strange shadows and felt the presence of his child, his discomfort had diminished. Even the threat of Bea trying, intentionally or not, to kill him hadn't retarded his progress. Was he going to die? Of course he was. He'd accepted it. Was it going to be that day? No, he would not accept that.

Jasper felt the presence of another in the room. The doctors had lowered his medication dosages, so he was a bit more alert than he chose to show, whenever he was examined. The fragrance was strange and yet familiar to him. It was dark in his room with the exception of a dimmed light over the sink on the far wall. The figure was female, of that he was certain. But who was she? He didn't think it was one of the nurses. They called him by name as they entered. He didn't see a mop or a broom in her hand, so she couldn't be a cleaner.

Jasper looked past the slowly approaching figure and saw it was dark outside. He didn't know the time or if visiting hours were still in effect. His head turned back to watch her. She walked as though she were afraid. He was the one sick. What could he possibly do to her?

A large cart sat outside Sister Betty's hotel room. All that food she'd ordered and yet they'd hardly touched a bite.

"So for the last time," Sister Betty said, "we do agree that Zipporah will be told and that Sasha should do it."

"Bea is so in love with the girl, I still don't see why I have to be the one." Sasha sat with her arms folded against her pecan-sized breasts like a stubborn child. She seemed to forget that she was the one who insisted that she do it.

"I thought you were in agreement?" Sister Betty asked. They'd discussed it at least ten times.

"I don't mind doing it but I don't want to break that child's heart," Bea said. "Sasha's her aunt and all those Hellraisers do is go around breaking hearts. She's got the experience, if nothing else."

"That's it!" Sister Betty snarled. "You two, get out of my room. I'm calling June Bug. He can tell her and let the chips fall where they may."

"June Bug ain't kin!" Sasha's hiss sounded like a rattler's rattle. "You can't just have someone tell her all willy-nilly."

"Well, you do it then." Sister Betty looked around for something to grab hold of before that something became Sasha's throat.

"Not me, I can't do it." Sasha moved out of the way just in

time to avoid Sister Betty's hands, which ended up grasping a soda can off the table.

"Why can't it be Areal?" Bea asked again. "I still say that if she's the momma, then she ought to take some responsibility, too."

"She won't have any part of it," Sasha said sadly. "I can't make her change her mind. Besides that, she still blames me for making her give up the child. She says that I have no right to now come back and involve her. She's made her peace and to her, she only has one child, and that's Ima."

"That's just ridiculous." Sister Betty still couldn't believe Areal's selfish attitude toward her own child.

"That may be," Sasha said, "but she won't let Jasper tell Zipporah about her either. That is if he ever gets the chance to tell Zipporah he's her father." She stopped and threw a conspiring look toward Bea.

"Don't look at me. I only attempt one killing per day, unless it involves removing your butt."

Sister Betty left Sasha and Bea bickering at the table while she went to the phone. She dialed a number and waited, it seemed an eternity, before an answer. She spoke a few words into the phone and returned to the table.

"Okay," Sister Betty announced. "I can't reach June Bug."

"Did you try his cell phone?" Sasha asked with annoyance. In her mind, she would've done that.

Sister Betty got up again and went to the phone. She dialed Chandler's cell phone. "He's not picking up," she said before leaving the same message as before and hanging up.

No sooner had she sat down than Bea asked, "Why didn't you try Zipporah's room?"

Sister Betty had no answer for that, so she returned to the phone. She called Zipporah's room and got her voice mail, too. She left a similar message and hung up. Before she came back to the table she put her hands on her hips and asked, sharply, "Are there any other bright ideas before I cut a path in this carpet going back and forth?"

"What's her problem?" Sasha leaned over and whispered to Bea.

"I don't know, but she sure don't know how to treat company," Bea replied in a huff.

No sooner had Sister Betty sat down than Sasha announced new business to be discussed. "Sister Betty," Sasha said, "Bea and I want you to withdraw your nomination, this time in writing, for the Mothers Board president. It'll also cover any other positions you might want to steal."

Bea had completely forgotten about that but she was glad Sasha was still on top of things. "You really don't have the experience to handle the craziness that comes along with the job," Bea added.

And that's when Sister Betty grabbed two more soda cans from the table. She symbolically squeezed them as she envisioned Bea's and Sasha's necks. And, again, she didn't apologize to them or to God.

46

There wasn't enough light inside Jasper's ICU room to see clearly, so he closed his eyes, although he could still tell that he wasn't alone. The figure seemed hesitant in its approach, but he didn't feel threatened.

"Jasper." She'd said it almost as though she questioned who lay in the bed.

Jasper slowly opened his eyes and turned toward the voice. He lifted one hand as though he were in school announcing he was present.

Even in the dimmed light and from where she stood, she saw it. The track lights a few feet up the wall and over the bed added a little more light. She saw the leaf birthmark and it stopped her dead in her tracks. Frightened, she fled from the room.

Jasper's head fell back against the pillow. No one had to tell him, he knew. It was his child. Zipporah knew who he was. Jasper smiled even as the heart monitor began to hum louder and beep quicker. He knew.

Zipporah came rushing from Jasper's room and straight into Chandler's arms. She was crying but not as loud as she had back at the hotel. It seemed all she'd done in the last few hours was cry.

"What happened?" Chandler asked. He'd been certain after all he'd told Zipporah about her father that she'd be fine when she saw him. There were some things that he didn't tell her but it didn't seem important at that moment. Zipporah didn't know about her father's wealth or the whereabouts of her mother.

"I saw it," Zipporah said as she wiped her eyes and moved from Chandler's arms. "I saw it and it's just like the one I have."

"Well, what did he say? You didn't seem to be in there long enough to talk about things."

"I didn't say anything except whisper his name."

An announcement that visiting hours were over in twenty minutes came over the loud speaker, raising Zipporah's anxiety level.

He took her by the hand. "We prayed before we left the hotel, Zipporah," Chandler reminded her. "But if you don't want to go through with it, then don't."

Zipporah gave Chandler her answer with silence. She pulled away and turned around. With her shoulders erect, she took a deep breath and reentered Jasper's outer room. Twenty minutes was not a long time but it was a start. Inside, she discarded the sterile gown and gloves, replaced them with a new set, and went back into Jasper's room.

As soon as Zipporah went inside, Chandler found a seat by the door. All he could do was pray, again. It wasn't the low, growling, prayerful voice that he'd often heard his precious Ma Cile use when she'd cry out to God. This time, he talked to God like God was one of his boys, but with more respect.

He alternated between questioning God's motives for the wreck Zipporah had as a life and thanking God for bringing her into his. When it was all said and done, he realized that like Zipporah, he, too, wasn't raised by his parents. He really didn't know his father. He'd seen him perhaps three times in his entire life and at this point didn't know if he were dead or alive. His mother, young when she had him, was too preoccupied with the bright lights of the city to raise him. He thanked God freely for Ma Cile and his cousin, Lil Bit, whom he loved like a sister.

Zipporah hadn't had a grandmother to love or care about her. She'd been moved around the foster care system like she was a chess piece, only to end up homeless. But her voice—what a magnificent instrument! It surely had to be a gift.

"Eighteen minutes until visiting hours are over." The announcement sounded prophetic to Chandler. Eighteen minutes to go before he would discover whether Zipporah would come out of that room better or worse than she'd gone inside.

He'd heard the outer door to the room open. She'd come back. Jasper could feel the change in air. It felt lighter; no doubt her presence chased away all that was negative around him. She still hadn't spoken beyond saying his name, but he held on to that. *Strange how when you know you're dying, your senses heighten,* he thought.

He could almost count how many footsteps it would take before she reached his bed. One . . . two . . . three; she was probably by the sink where the nurses washed their hands or filled the tray to bathe him.

Four . . . five . . . six; she had to be very close because he could smell his child. Her scent was wonderful and it covered the alcohol smell that made him nauseous. He never liked hospital odors. Did she dislike them, too? If he got a chance, he'd ask her.

"Jasper Epps?" she whispered softly.

His heart hastened. Again, the beeping sound from the heart monitor hurried to keep up. He liked the way she said his name. In his mind, he didn't hear "Jasper Epps." Instead, he'd heard her say, "Daddy."

Everything she'd said she wouldn't do or say, Zipporah thought about doing and saying. No matter how sick he was, she was going to give him hell. She didn't care how many years he'd searched for her; he should've been there all along. "Jasper Epps," she repeated.

Jasper struggled to remove the nose pillow insertions carrying his precious air. His child needed him. She'd called his name. They were only in his nose and yet, they felt as though they were preventing him from answering.

Zipporah watched the tube from the oxygen tank rise and collapse as the man strained to remove the nose pillows. It seemed to be keeping time with her footsteps as she neared the bed.

"Fifteen minutes until visiting hours are over." The announcement seemed to personally urge her toward the bed. Her feet picked up the pace.

Jasper's eyes widened as she neared. *Oh my,* he thought, *she's beautiful. My baby is just gorgeous. She, so much, reminds me of my own mother. Like Zipporah, she was a beautiful woman, perhaps a little thicker and darker, but a beauty no less.*

"Are you okay?" What a stupid question, Zipporah thought. It wasn't like they'd just chatted and she stopped by to see how he was doing.

Jasper weakly nodded his chin to let her know that he was fine. If "fine" meant that he knew he was dying and he was okay with it, then yes, he was fine.

There were no questions that could be asked or answered in the short time they had. But she had to accomplish something. Zipporah couldn't leave without doing that.

And, from the look on her father's face, he wasn't about to let her. If it took his last breath, he wouldn't let her leave without a part of him.

No amount of noise inside the Luxor casino could match the noise coming from the corner by the roulette wheel. Somehow or other, Bea and Sasha had hounded Sister Betty into coming downstairs with them. At first, it was under the pretense of looking for Zipporah. They'd pushed Sister Betty's buttons, and sliced up her last nerve, until she felt that if she didn't go with them, she'd have to kill them.

When the old women arrived downstairs, each of them still wearing what they'd worn the entire day, they discovered Zipporah didn't have a show that evening. And, of course, Bea had to use the bathroom. Sister Betty decided she might as well do the same since Bea was going. Sasha was okay with her toilet needs. No one could hold their water or a grudge for as long as Sasha could. However, only Bea and Sasha knew that the only way to the bathroom on that floor was through the casino.

It took more harassment but they finally got Sister Betty to walk through the den of iniquity to reach the bathroom. Somehow, in Sister Betty's sanctified mind, killing Bea and Sasha wasn't on the same sin level as a walk through the casino to pee.

Magically, as soon as they neared the roulette table and a few empty chairs, Bea no longer needed to use the bathroom. She managed to collapse into one of the seats, pulling Sister Betty down with her. Faster than a toad's sticky tongue caught a flying insect, Bea's chubby hands produced a few casino chips she'd had from her previous visit. She slammed a few dollar chips down on number twenty-two. She then announced, "This is for Sister Betty," and slammed the rest of the chips in her hand down on the green zero.

"You old hell hound," Sister Betty snapped. "You know I don't gamble."

"And the number is zero," the worker announced as he immediately started racking aside all losing chips. The ball had landed on the zero, which paid 35-to-1 odds.

Bea had placed five one-dollar chips on the zero in Sister Betty's name. Everyone at the table heard her when she said she had. But as soon as the pile of one hundred and seventy-five dollars in chips was set in front of Sister Betty, Bea caught a sudden case of amnesia.

In the meantime, Sister Betty had just reached for the chips, having already determined in seconds that she was going to give the chips to Chandler. He'd know what to do with them. But Bea had pushed her hand away and started bickering over the law of possession and insanity.

While Bea bickered with Sister Betty, Sasha watched and smiled. "It's a good thing I'm saved now," she mumbled.

And while Bea and Sister Betty argued, the roulette game continued. The man spun the wheel, flicked the ball, and again, the ball hopped several times before landing on zero. "They let it ride," the man said as he pushed another one hundred and seventy-five dollars in chips in front of Sister Betty.

And that's when Sister Betty hiked her skirt and sat down. "I'm gonna whup ya like the good Lord did when He chased out the money changers."

Bea was so shocked she stopped fussing and sat down, too. "Are you planning on betting and quoting scripture?"

"I got to get in on this." Sasha laid her cane under a seat and then climbed up on it. She peered over her eyeglasses at Sister Betty and cackled, "I never knew that being saved could be so much fun and profitable."

And while Bea, Sasha, and Sister Betty did a little recreational gambling and held a church service at the roulette wheel, a few of the other members from the Mothers Board watched from the casino doorway.

The old mothers, dressed in white, clutching their favorite Bibles, held their noses in the air. They'd just arrived from a nearby revival service. Weak bladders were common to them, and out of a sense of urgency, they'd decided to pray their way through the casino to reach the bathrooms on the other side. But every urge to tinkle was put on hold as the judgmental old women watched in horror and fascination. Each punched and pinched the other, pointing at Sister Betty, Bea, and Sasha gambling.

Neither Bea, Sasha, nor Sister Betty had realized that in an instant, they'd placed bets on more than just the roulette wheel. By the time those old mothers returned to their rooms with their revised observations, the odds on Bea's, Sasha's and Sister Betty's reputations and more importantly, their salvation would be long shots. And, forget about a presidential win.

47

Chandler was getting fidgety. He'd counted floor tiles and checked his watch so often, even the nurses were starting to watch him. He looked like he'd escaped from a psycho-ward with his unshaven and messy appearance.

Only five minutes had passed but it seemed more like an hour. He wished he could hear something from Jasper's room but he couldn't. He was tempted to rush in with or without the proper sterilized garments. But he'd promised Zipporah time to do whatever she needed to do to get things straight with her newly discovered father.

Inside Jasper's room Zipporah allowed her eyes to adjust to the low lights. Even the illumination from all of Las Vegas's nightlife, bright as it was, couldn't shed enough light on this problem.

Jasper watched Zipporah scanning the room. He liked that she was cautious. Had he been, the two of them would not be in such an uncomfortable and foreign mess.

"Ten minutes before the end of visiting hours," the announcement warned.

Zipporah willed her feet to hurry. The rubber-meeting-tile noise from her sandals sounded eerily loud as she got closer to Jasper's bed. She finally stood next to him. His face—she decided to study his face. Could she see a bit of herself in it? She looked closer, almost bending over to get a better look. He appeared to have splashes of green in his hazel eyes. She only had that when the light shone on hers in a particular manner.

Zipporah's eyes traced the outline under the sheets, all the while knowing that the man had not looked away. He was definitely a tall man, taller than she first thought. His feet reached the bottom of the bed with no space to spare. He looked very thin. Had he always been thin? She couldn't tell if he was gaunt from his illness or not. His hair was straight, thin, and a snow-white color. Under normal circumstances she'd have described his hair as a gorgeous white. It still looked healthy despite his illness.

She'd learned from Chandler that years ago he'd been a singer of some fame, in the gospel music world. She'd also learned some time ago that what you sang and how you lived didn't always match.

A sudden beep from his heart monitor caused her to jump. And when she did his eyes caught hold of hers.

"Five minutes before visiting hours are over." The announcement seemed rushed and directed at her, urging her to get on with it.

There was so much she wanted to say. So many questions she wanted to ask. She didn't realize it right away, but their eyes were still locked. Neither was willing to look away. One was unable to speak, and the other wouldn't.

Zipporah wouldn't have been able to explain her next move if paid a million dollars. She moved to the head of Jasper's bed and gently lifted his left hand. She tried to make sure that the IV needle didn't move or slip out as she did.

Zipporah examined his leaf birthmark, intently. It was larger than hers but shaped the same. She let her finger trace it, hoping it wouldn't disturb him. He didn't move. She thought he smiled.

There was a faint greenish-bluish hue to his leaf, probably because the blood didn't properly reach it. At least that was the explanation a doctor once gave her when she'd asked why hers had the same distinct coloring to it. She even counted the points on his leaf—two points on each side culminating into a wider shape. She'd always thought hers resembled a maple leaf. His did, too.

"Please be advised, the visiting hours are now over. Please be advised, the visiting hours are now over." It was as though the announcement was saying, "Zipporah, your time is up. You blew it."

The man, her father, still would not look away. He'd begun a struggle to speak. His words were urgent and mumbled. He was trying to grab Zipporah's hand, not seeming to care whether his IV came undone or not.

Zipporah saw the light brighten in the outer room. It meant that the nurse was probably coming in to order her to leave. She quickly removed her hand from his and took the envelope from her pocket. Zipporah bent over and kissed his forehead, soothing and silently urging him to calm down. She took out the pictures of her childhood and the letter and under his gaze, she placed them to her heart.

"I'm sorry, miss," the nurse said politely, "but the visiting hours in ICU are over. Please say your good-byes."

How could she say good-bye when she hadn't said hello? Zipporah fought the urge to throw the nurse out into the hallway, lock the door, and continue.

Jasper mumbled and Zipporah saw the look of desperation and sadness on his face. Again, he reached out to her. This time, she took his hand and placed it to her heart, and when she laid his hand back on the bed, she placed the pictures and the letter, too.

He could keep them so he'd know she was aware of their connection. Chandler had made copies and even if he hadn't, she'd have left these with Jasper.

"I'll come back," Zipporah promised. She'd wanted to add, "Dad." She couldn't. Perhaps, she would one day and hopefully not too late.

It was as though Zipporah's promise held healing powers. Jasper stopped struggling and the beeps from his heart monitor slowed a bit. Even the hose from the oxygen tank, when it collapsed and refilled, was slower. Somehow it seemed that Jasper Epps willed his death to slow down; he'd take his time dying. He knew his daughter needed him.

Chandler jumped up as soon as Zipporah came out of the room. She looked different, almost like some of the people he'd seen as a child after a deliverance service at church.

Zipporah hadn't cried. She'd thought she would. It was a feeling of weightlessness that crept over her. Years of not knowing who she was or where she came from had the possibility of an answer. Just that hope, alone, gave her more freedom than she'd experienced in quite some time.

Zipporah didn't say anything as she allowed Chandler to take her hand. What could she say? There were some things that only a parent and a child could share. Yet, even with all that she'd just witnessed, she was sure Chandler still knew far more than she. Even though he hadn't mentioned her birth mother, she was sure he had information. And, if he didn't, then she knew who did.

But there was time. In her soul she felt confident of it. And, whether Sasha wanted to or not, she was going to tell her the truth. *After all,* Zipporah thought as they walked to Chandler's car, *the old woman is my aunt.*

Chandler was trying to make up his mind on how much of what happened between Zipporah and Jasper he should delve into when his cell phone vibrated in his pocket.

"Please give me a moment," he said as he pulled out his phone. It was the first thing he'd said to Zipporah and the best he could come up with. Chandler checked his messages and frowned.

"What's wrong?" Zipporah finally spoke up, out of concern.

"Alicia's trying to reach me."

"That's got you upset?"

"No."

"Well, what then?" Zipporah didn't like the way his entire body had started to slump. She hadn't seen him this way before.

"It's my godmother." Chandler said. "Hotel security's holding her."

"Sister Betty!" Zipporah thought someone was surely playing a joke on him or he was teasing her.

"Yes, Sister Betty." Chandler whipped open the passenger side door, almost tossing Zipporah inside.

"Where are Mother Blister and Mother Pray Onn?"

"I'll give you two guesses and the first one won't count."

48

Chandler was moving so fast Zipporah thought she'd have to take off her sandals to keep up. He flew through the hotel lobby pushing other guests aside without as much as an "excuse me." It was Zipporah who kept issuing apologies all the way to the security office.

Chandler burst into the office and came to face to face with the head of security. He was a short, squatty man who wore an outdated Jerri Curl. He was in his fifties with brown teeth to match his brown mustache. He was walking around with one hand in his pocket, and his name tag read, "Steve Darling." Steve Darling was anything but at that moment. He stood on his tiptoes, snarling at a much taller security guard. With spittle flying like darts out the corner of his thick lips, he as much as told the guard that he was in charge and whatever he said was law. He stopped ranting immediately and gave a wide smile when he recognized Zipporah.

"Good evening, Miss Moses," spit-tossing Steve Darling said softly. "I caught your show, twice. I loved it." He motioned for the other security guard to leave while he kept cheesing at Zipporah. He offered her a seat and totally ignored Chandler. "What can I do for you?"

"Mr. Lamb and I received word that you have detained several mothers from the Mothers Board."

"Oh, really," he said. "Let me check." He scanned the clipboard. "I don't see anyone listed here that would be from a Mothers Board."

Chandler had tried to be quiet and let Zipporah handle an obvious admirer, but his frayed nerves were on a hair trigger. Steve Darling and his leering at Zipporah had just set it off.

"Where's my godmother?" Chandler stood at least a foot and a half taller than Steve Darling.

Steve Darling didn't budge. "And who is your godmother?"

"Her name is Sister Betty and she's here with Mothers Bea Blister and Sasha Pray Onn," Zipporah offered. She'd butted in, hoping that the two of them didn't get into a row over something stupid as most men would.

"Does one wear an ugly hat with a feather?"

"Yes," Zipporah answered.

"The other one, does she have a deadly weapon such as a cane?"

"That would be Mother Sasha Pray Onn," Zipporah said while watching Chandler's face turn beet red.

"Oh, they're in the back," Steve Darling answered.

"What about Mother Bea Blister?" Zipporah had thought about not bringing her up, but she couldn't just leave Bea there.

"She's in the other office."

"Why?"

"She plugged up two of the toilets and we believe she did it on purpose. That caused property damage and we can't have that here at the Luxor."

By the time Steve Darling finished explaining the circumstances of the old women's detainment, along with his shock that they were actually church women, Sister Betty, Sasha, and Bea were led out in single file by a guard. They took one look at their surroundings and dropped their heads in shame.

Zipporah rushed forward and thanked Steve Darling with a quick, a very quick, peck on his cheek and a promise to dedicate a song to him when she performed again.

Chandler on the other hand wasn't feeling the sweetness. He lit into the old women like they'd been caught shoplifting at the Family Dollar Store. "What were you thinking?" he asked Sister Betty. "Since when do you follow the likes of those two?" He pointed directly at Bea and Sasha, followed by a look that dared them to sass him back.

They didn't.

"I was trying to do the Lord's work," Sister Betty tried to explain, humbly, and even as she did, she heard how ridiculous she sounded.

"You were gambling," Chandler snapped. "How is that the Lord's work?"

"Well, Chandler." Sister Betty was so ashamed that her godson had to scold her in front of the others that she'd forgotten to use her pet name, June Bug. "In the book of Matthew, the twenty-first chapter and the twelfth verse, it talks about how Jesus went into the temple and drove out all the money changers." She stopped and smiled, still forgetting she'd not put in her partials.

But Chandler wasn't falling for her bald-gums sham. "I suppose you were placing bets to blend in and snare the other bettors?"

"That sounds good," Sister Betty replied. It wasn't quite the way she'd have explained it, but if it worked for him, fine.

"And, when you decided that it was time to chase out the money changers by snatching back your bet before the wheel stopped, were you doing the Lord's work?"

"I sure was." Sister Betty gave a nervous laugh. "When I saw that wheel slow down and that it wasn't going to come around to my number again, I simply took my money off the number. It didn't make sense to waste it. Besides, I'd already gotten paid for that zero three times. Three is a holy number and it was a sign that it was time to do the Lord's work." She turned around to Bea and Sasha for confirmation.

Chandler's mouth dropped open in disbelief.

Zipporah was then certain beyond a doubt that old people were crazy.

But Sasha and Bea had nothing but admiration for Sister Betty as they returned her smile. She'd arrived at their way of thinking. They felt so proud.

Bea and Sasha, their arms folded across their chests, inched over and stood defiant, in front of Sister Betty. It was enough to make Chandler back off before he ended up in jail for the night.

Steve Darling couldn't wait to get all of them out of the security office. He even decided that if Zipporah was a part of that nut pack, he wasn't going to her shows and she could forget they'd ever met.

While Chandler, Zipporah, and Sister Betty marched on ahead, Bea and Sasha fell back.

"Where do you think the two of them were?" Bea whispered to Sasha.

"I'm not too sure. But if they went back to the hospital, I think we'd know about it by now." Sasha caught Chandler glaring at them, meaning that they should speed things up. She returned his stare with one of hers while defiantly tugging on Bea's arm to slow her down.

"I guess you're right," Bea admitted. "There's no way she found out everything and didn't tear your munchkin butt apart."

Sasha dropped Bea's arm like it was a snake and hobbled away, trying to catch up with the others.

Chandler was still seething by the time he and Zipporah arrived at her suite. He'd almost gnawed a hole in his tongue to keep from spanking all three of those old women when he escorted them back to their respective suites. He hadn't bothered to get promises that they'd stay put because at that moment, he just didn't care.

"I've got to shower and change," Chandler finally said, standing in the doorway, after making sure Zipporah was okay. "I've only two more days off before I have to return to the conference center. I hope they will not be as crazy as this day." He caught himself. "I'm sorry. I didn't mean it to include what you're going through."

"I know," Zipporah said. "I'm not sleepy. I should be but I'm not."

Chandler smiled for the first time in an hour or so. "I'm not so much sleepy as I am funky." He raised the material from his underarm to sniff. He pretended to fall back from the odor, causing Zipporah to reach for him.

"Chandler!" Zipporah caught him by his elbow as though she were his anchor.

"Hold on," Chandler teased, kissing her hand as he lifted it from his elbow. "I really need to take a shower. I can smell me."

"You don't smell so bad," Zipporah said softly. "Not too bad, at all."

Chandler walked back into the living room and stood with both hands on his hips. "You really don't want to be alone, do you?" He laughed. "You'd suffer the smell of body odor?"

"Yes." She walked toward the television cabinet, turned the set on, and muted the sound. It was as though she were using the television as a third party in the room. Giving him a one-word answer was the best she could do despite her desire to say more. She wanted to do more, too.

She shot a quick glance over to where Chandler still stood, pretending to look past him. Her body tingled as though pins pricked her, but not in a bad way. Yes, she'd do everything except what her body suddenly felt like doing. She wasn't going to get involved in pity sex or a romp just to take her mind off unfinished business.

Zipporah, without another word, retraced her path past Chandler and went into the small kitchenette. She knew that he'd still be able to keep his eye on her from where he stood, but she wasn't concerned. She was certain that they both could use something to drink,

Chandler watched Zipporah moving about in her small kitchenette. She seemed to almost levitate as she moved. She appeared to be filling glasses or something, so he closed the door behind him. He sat down on the sofa and yawned. Watching her, he wondered, *are we both thinking about the same things?* He quickly looked away when she glanced his way. Leafing through a magazine, he thought hard about his situation. Zipporah, she was truly getting to him. He glanced over at her again, giving a half smile. If she looked any more beautiful or innocent than she did at that moment, he was going to have to reconsider his commitment to remaining celibate.

The more he moved about, the more his body odor seemed to permeate the air. Chandler imagined it hovering over them like a toxic green cloud. He became increasingly embarrassed as he continued fidgeting. If one good thing could come of funk, he thought, perhaps it would be a sexual deterrent. With his arms spread out across the back of the sofa, he leaned back and continued pretending he wasn't watching her.

Back at the Las Vegas hospital on the ICU floor, there was hardly a sound heard in or around the nurses' station. Even the hospital personnel dashing back and forth, handling one emergency after another, seemed to move in silence.

But as quiet as it was on the outside, inside Jasper's room the constant whirring from the machines had begun to grind away at his nerves. He was deep in thought and kept his head turned to the wall. Even so, he knew what was going on around him.

Every time a nurse would enter to record or check his vitals, he wanted to scream out, "Leave me alone."

He'd fought the drowsiness brought on by the medication so he could remember how she looked. He'd watched her as she'd examined their common birthmarks and he was pleased. There was an eerily sweet aura about her, unlike the disposition of her sister, Ima.

Jasper suddenly shook and coughed as he remembered his other daughter. He had never claimed Ima, either. Pangs of guilt temporarily rocked him like a direct torpedo hit. He felt like he'd had to choose between an Esau and a Jacob.

Ima was just like her mother. She was Areal reincarnate—evil to a fault like all those Hellraisers. But not his Zipporah; she was more like him. He could feel the rhythm of his heart calming down.

He coughed again, but he wasn't uncomfortable. Instead, he sighed, remembering that Zipporah had kissed him on his forehead. It was a light airy kiss she'd given him before she'd left with a promise to return. And, she'd done it after meeting him for the first time. Jasper hadn't heard her say what he'd wanted to hear, which was for her to call him "Daddy." But that would come later, he was certain.

He had a lot to atone for and he wasn't above repeatedly begging God for mercy. He'd grovel before God on his hands and knees if need be. Now, with tubes and monitors helping him to remain on this side of the grave, he could only mentally beg God, from his sickbed, for divine mercy and grace. He'd repent over and over until he was sure God heard him.

It was cool inside Jasper's ICU room. And yet perspiration suddenly broke out on Jasper's forehead. Pain came like someone had scorched him with a hot poker. He didn't know who or why, but he felt the pain tear through his arm and travel across his shoulders, causing him to almost double over in the bed.

Then there was the tunnel. Somehow Jasper found that he was in a tunnel. He knew for certain he was because every sound had an echo. The machines humming had echoes and the voices suddenly appearing out of nowhere, they had echoes, too. But then the pain disappeared. Where had the pain gone? How could he fall as fast as he was falling, without the pain that caused it?

*   *   *

At the same time, inside her hotel room, Zipporah had continued moving about the kitchenette when suddenly it began to feel smaller, as though everything in it could fit inside a dollhouse.

Zipporah heard the air conditioner in the living room suddenly kick on as though it weren't already cold enough. She hadn't touched it and she was almost certain that Chandler hadn't either. She went into the living room to check.

Zipporah's hand shook but not from the coldness in the room. She was sure about that. The shaking caused her to drop the glass she was about to set on the coffee table. She leaned her head straining to hear a low sound that kept eluding her, but she could hear her own voice and it sounded strange, as though it had too much reverb in it. Suddenly, her entire body went limp and her head just barely missed hitting the edge of the television cabinet. She tried to call out to Chandler as she fell. He wasn't there.

Moments before, frustrated from marinating in his body odor, Chandler had gone inside Zipporah's bathroom. With a pinky-swear promise to behave, he'd talked Zipporah into permitting him to use her shower as well as the extra bathrobe. Surrendering his tired body to the hot water that jabbed at his body, he'd been able to finally relax. With the sound of the bathroom's ceiling fan strumming, and the water falling, he never heard her fall.

49

Bea was panting by the time she'd arrived at Zipporah's room. She hadn't called Sister Betty or Sasha when she got the news. When Chandler had phoned her to tell her what'd happened, she rushed over, wearing only her slip and a pair of SpongeBob house shoes. She'd taken the stairs, not waiting for the elevator to take her up the two floors.

"Zipporah." Bea cradled Zipporah's head, brushing her hair aside as she called her name. "Zipporah!" Bea called her name again, slowly trying to remove the anxiety from her voice. "You want me to call you a doctor?"

"She won't let me call one," Chandler said as he paced. He was moving around in a bathrobe.

Sister Betty flew into the room through the open door with Sasha only seconds behind.

"What happened?" Sister Betty asked as she watched Bea cradling Zipporah and mumbling.

"She fell and that's all I know," Chandler said bluntly.

"Did you hit her?" Sasha asked, raising her cane at Chandler. "That's my niece and I won't let nobody abuse her!"

Chandler hadn't meant to shove his godmother so hard, but Mother Pray Onn had sucker punched him with her accusation. He rushed over to her and with all the respect he could muster, which would've filled a thimble at that moment, he blasted her.

"How dare you!" Chandler sniped as Sasha cowed. "*Now* she's your niece. Wasn't she your niece when you gave her away?"

Everything stopped. If the air flowed in that room, no one could feel it. There was a shift in the atmosphere and it wasn't healthy.

"Don't yell at my aunt," Zipporah said softly.

All heads turned to Zipporah, who was still cradled in Bea's arms.

"Say what!" Chandler snapped. He hadn't meant to use that tone when it came to Zipporah, but her sudden allegiance to Mother Pray Onn caught him off guard.

Zipporah extricated her head from Bea's grasp and sat up. Her eyes looked a bit unfocused but she spoke clearly. "Yelling at her won't get us anywhere and it won't tell me what I need."

Sasha was dumbfounded. If Sister Betty weren't standing only inches away to catch her, she'd have fallen completely out.

Chandler threw his hands up in defeat and his robe became undone.

All the women saw, but Sister Betty was the first to speak up. "My goodness, June Bug . . ." Sister Betty's eyes widened. "You've changed since you were a child."

Chandler grabbed his robe. Embarrassed, he ran into the other room.

"Now, didn't that make you feel better?" Bea asked Zipporah.

It certainly hadn't hurt things, Zipporah thought. Zipporah's old self had slowly begun to return, but she didn't answer Bea. Her words were trapped by the sight of all three women smiling at her and not one tooth showing between them. She turned her head away. *Old people are truly crazy,* she thought.

Inside Zipporah's bathroom, Chandler had finally gotten over his embarrassment and acted as if he hadn't shown the women his gift as he sauntered back inside Zipporah's living room.

"You look better," Chandler said to Zipporah, "and y'all need to be ashamed."

"Probably, we should." Bea laughed. "But I'm not."

"That's what you get for disrespecting your elders," Sasha reprimanded. "And now that I know that my niece is in good hands, I'm taking my tired butt to bed. And I mean it this time."

Sasha, her cane tapping lightly over the carpet, went over to Zipporah. Bea moved to the end of the couch so Sasha could sit.

"Zipporah," Sasha said as she took her hand, "I don't want to start off with an apology. That would take up the precious time you could use asking questions I know that you have." Sasha looked around the room and smiled. "So, for right now, you get some rest. I promise I'll tell you whatever you want to know."

"We'll come back later and have something to eat while we chat," Bea blurted.

"*I'll* come back later and perhaps over a meal, you and I will chat." Sasha turned to Bea and nodded, making sure Bea understood their need for privacy, before turning back to Zipporah. "You promise to rest up?"

Zipporah didn't promise. Instead, she took her hand from Sasha's and hugged her.

Sasha's body almost went limp. She couldn't remember the last time someone had hugged her. She breathed hard and suppressed her tears.

Sister Betty watched it all. She was amazed. So much had happened in a week and she still wasn't quite sure what it had to do with her. She started toward the door. "I've got to go. Everything here seems to be in good hands. Chandler, Zipporah, Bea, and you, too, Sasha, I'll chat with you later." And then she left.

Moments later, Bea and Sasha followed Sister Betty. Bea had secured a silent promise from Sasha's nod that they'd talk later. Bea expected a full report from Sasha about the conversation with Zipporah.

After he'd closed the door, Chandler turned to Zipporah and asked, "Are you really okay?"

"I believe so."

"What happened before you fell? Tell me again."

Zipporah repeated as best she could remember the sensation she'd felt in the kitchen and then the darkness. "That's all I can remember."

"Why don't you go and put some water on your face," Chandler suggested. "You look about as bad as I smelled."

"Okay."

While Zipporah washed her face and freshened up in the bathroom, there was a knock at her door.

Chandler thought it was probably one of the women who'd forgotten something, so he didn't mind opening it in nothing but a robe. Instead, he found Alicia. "Look at you," he said, suddenly smiling.

Alicia had her hair swept to one side with a couple of strands teasing her cheeks. An expensive diamond pin held her hair in place. She was dressed in an off the shoulder floor-length black dress that seemed destined to burst if she breathed hard.

"I've been leaving messages for you," Alicia said as she pushed aside a stray tress and stared, disapprovingly, at Chandler. She let her eyes slowly sweep across an opened part of the robe just above the knee, and then she looked up.

Chandler immediately grabbed his robe to keep it from re-opening and invited her inside.

"You didn't return my calls," Alicia continued as she entered and faced him. She switched her purse from one hand to the other, smoothing her lipstick with a tongue that darted from side to side. Her eyes pierced through him as though she were trying to read his thoughts. "I thought I would give the message to Zipporah, in person." She stopped and pulled a small envelope from her clutch purse but she didn't offer it to him. "I didn't want you to think I'd *overstepped my boundaries* since *you're* the manager." She was challenging him to explain without asking directly.

"Well, you've found me." He reached for the envelope but she sidestepped him. Chandler had tried politeness but as usual, Alicia pushed when she didn't have to.

"Where's Zipporah?" she asked almost in a whisper.

"Zipporah," Chandler called out. "We've got company."

He knew Alicia would read more into the "we've" than he meant. As tired as he was, Chandler wasn't above making Alicia uncomfortable, if that was indeed possible.

Zipporah came out of the bathroom. Her face showed surprise and puzzlement when she saw Alicia standing in the middle of her living room looking fabulous. She recovered quickly when she saw Alicia pretending not to look at Chandler.

"Good evening, Alicia. What's going on?" Zipporah came closer and stood next to Chandler. She flicked an invisible speck from his robe in a move designed to mark him as taken.

Alicia smiled. She'd played that game far too many times not to know that move. However, she'd already made up her mind that Chandler and she were not going to happen. But it didn't mean she wouldn't practice a whorish move every now and then.

"I have something for you." She waved the envelope teasingly under Chandler's nose and gave it to Zipporah.

"Thank you." Zipporah wanted to know what was in it but

she wasn't about to giggle like a schoolgirl or tear open the envelope in front of Alicia.

Alicia didn't move.

"Is there something more or do you know what's in this?" Zipporah stepped in front of Chandler. This was her suite and Alicia needed to play by her rules or better yet, leave.

"No, there's nothing more. You already know that the opening act has changed and a new costume fitting is required. It needs to happen quickly."

"No, I didn't know that," Zipporah replied, curtly.

"Really, I'm certain it was one of several messages I left on Chandler's private number. Of course, he's had time to check his voice mail. I'm sure he would've told you in time." Alicia took a moment to let the implication sink in and test the temperature change between Zipporah and Chandler. Both of them looked uncomfortable and their bodies stiffened.

"I've got a date," Alicia announced. Suddenly, it felt lukewarm and not as cozy as a moment ago. She was almost amused, noting that Chandler stood in one spot and had not commented one way or the other.

Chandler didn't wait for Zipporah to handle Alicia; he jumped right in. He took Zipporah by the hand. They both walked ahead of Alicia, leading her to the door.

"Well, you have a good evening, Alicia," Chandler said with a Cheshire cat grin. "Now Zipporah and I don't have to rush what we were doing."

"Rushing isn't your style, Chandler." Zipporah meant to get in her dig and she dug deep. "I'll get to this"—she held up the envelope again—"when I have a moment."

Alicia's face reddened. Little beads of perspiration popped like popcorn across her brow. She yanked the doorknob and dashed out.

"Was it something I said?" Zipporah spun around in Chandler's arms and laughed. She was almost happy Alicia had stopped by. Her antics had given Zipporah something to laugh about.

"What do you think?" Chandler said, smiling. "I don't wanna get on your list."

"I didn't put her on it, she volunteered."

Chandler stepped back and took a more serious tone. "Are you going to read what's in the envelope?"

"I don't know if I should." She'd answered with concern, when just a nanosecond ago she was laughing. "Envelopes seemed to come with so much drama."

"Do you want me to read it? I don't think Alicia would've made the trip if it didn't come with some importance. Whether or not she actually left a message about the costume changes tonight, I'll have to check. It wouldn't be the first time a show has been rescheduled."

"So, I'm not fired?"

"Alicia's a bit flirty but she's not crazy."

"You're right. I can sing."

"About the envelope—do you want me to read what's in it? I'm curious." He stuck out his hand, palm open.

"You might as well." Again, Zipporah forced another smile as she laid the envelope in his hand. She turned away feeling that at the speed her emotional roller coaster was moving, she was going to land in schizoid-ville soon.

Chandler patted Zipporah on the shoulder to let her know that he would handle whatever it was. He must've reread the contents five times, trying to wrap his mind around the information.

"What time is it?" It wasn't as much a question as something to utter aloud. He had to say something to keep from saying what he wanted to say.

Chandler looked over at Zipporah. He could tell by the way she was looking at him, her hands clasping and unclasping, that she was getting anxious. The words weren't spoken but he knew she definitely wanted to know what the message was about.

But there was no easy way to tell her. The time stamp on the message was only about an hour old. The message must've arrived shortly after Zipporah had fainted. How Alicia got it, he didn't know.

Chandler reread the message and for the life of him, he couldn't find a way to let Zipporah know that Jasper Epps, the father she had never known, was dead.

50

It was Chandler who'd finally gotten Zipporah to stop sobbing. She'd cried so loud he was afraid security would call the police. Zipporah had thrown things and when there was nothing left to toss, she'd thrown herself on the floor and pounded it.

When he'd first tried to hold her to keep her from harming herself, she'd clawed at him. He had two long nail slashes he hoped would heal without scarring.

Zipporah had rocked and cried on the floor for at least five minutes if not longer. He watched her the entire time and couldn't figure out how she'd not hurt herself. He decided to leave her like that until he could figure something out.

It was he who'd made the calls to Bea and Sasha. He'd seen no reason to involve Sister Betty. Obviously, Bea and Sasha had, because Sister Betty arrived half dressed in the hotel lobby with them.

Since Jasper was dead, Chandler hadn't rushed. Before calling Mothers Blister and Pray Onn, he'd called the hospital and arranged for them not to remove Jasper's body until his daughter arrived. They'd agreed to wait.

As soon as they'd stopped at a red light Chandler turned around to check on Zipporah and the other women. She looked like a zombie with her eyes still glassy and fixed. Bea, Sasha, and Sister Betty sat on both sides of her. "Is she okay?"

"She will be," Sasha replied.

Chandler watched as the old women piled their hands atop Zipporah's hand to comfort her. It seemed an odd thought, but he found himself comparing her to a painting he'd once seen. It was of the Hindu goddess Saraswati, playing a sitar with several pairs of hands that protruded from her body.

The path to the ICU seemed awkward. There was a supply cabinet overflowing with yellow and blue gowns and a shelf containing paper shoes. The sign read that they were to don them whether or not they were there to see a patient. They didn't and no one stopped or chastised them.

Jasper's room seemed a long way off. It hadn't seemed that far earlier. "Have you waited long?" The question came from out of nowhere. Everyone turned around to meet the voice except Zipporah. She had to be steered.

"Miss Moses, I'm sorry for your loss." The woman kept speaking as if she'd met them all before. "Let's sit down." She pointed to a small room that had a desk and several chairs.

Ms. Diaz was one of the hospital's social workers who dealt with bereavement cases. She appeared to be in her mid- to late forties and wore long dreadlocks pulled back into a ponytail that peeked out from the center of a huge head wrap. Her rimless glasses perched upon a short, cinnamon-colored and freckled stubby nose.

Miss Diaz sat and waited for Chandler and the other women to sit as well. Zipporah, her eyes red and swollen, was seated next to him. "Again, please accept our condolences." She immediately adopted a motherly demeanor as she turned and addressed Zipporah. She pulled several forms from her folder and handed them to Chandler, thinking he was Zipporah's husband.

The meeting with Miss Diaz didn't last too long. She gave permission for Zipporah, and the others if they'd wanted, about five to ten minutes to find closure with the deceased. And then she'd need information as to what was to happen with the body. Neither Zipporah nor the others had a clue as to how his remains would be disposed of.

"Mr. Epps had a stage-four lung cancer that had apparently spread to other parts of the body rather quickly. We haven't had an autopsy, naturally, since he only died earlier this evening. However, according to the medical charts he also had congestive heart disease. If one thing hadn't killed him the other did." She flipped through the file, removed her glasses and quickly read one of the pages. "Apparently, Mr. Epps's attorney faxed over some instructions. We'd notified all interested parties about the same time but I hadn't realized someone, other than his immediate family, had responded so quickly."

Miss Diaz, seeing how distraught Zipporah remained, handed several sheets of paper to Chandler. "I must return to my office on the second floor, social services division. If you should need me before I return, just call." She handed Chandler her business card and explained the next steps he should take.

Every word Miss Diaz had spoken sounded like background noise to Zipporah. If she didn't wake from this nightmare, she would scream. Zipporah didn't notice when Miss Diaz had stopped talking. She barely remembered Bea and Chandler literally lifting her from the chair and walking her to Jasper's hospital room.

Chandler walked away and returned moments later to give Zipporah a cup of water. He watched her sip from the plastic cup and then took her hand and squeezed it.

All the while neither Sister Betty nor Sasha had said a word. If Chandler or Bea noticed that Sister Betty and Sasha held hands as they walked, they said nothing.

Sasha and Sister Betty were praying. They dropped back a little from the others as they walked to Jasper's room. It was Sasha who had suggested they pray. Sister Betty agreed and together the most unlikely of old church women walked together, praying their most unselfish of prayers. They were praying for Zipporah.

Again, they thought about how Zipporah had been in their lives barely a week. And already she'd become the common thread that wove the blanket of love now covering them.

Although she'd drunk the water and walked down the corridor, her mind was still clouded. Standing in front of Jasper's hospital room, Zipporah began to mutter, showing that she was beginning to come around. She then stood for a few moments, staring at the door to the outer room, as though it should open automatically.

"You want me to go inside with you?" Chandler asked. He'd never been comfortable with the dead and funerals were occasions he tried to avoid when he could. And yet, he'd have gone in her place had she asked him.

"I'll do it," Zipporah said before entering cautiously into the small preparation area that led into Jasper's room.

Zipporah was surprised at how quickly she'd calmed down. There was no reason to continue the self-exiled state her mind had escaped to a short time ago. She'd accepted her father's death, in her own way, but among all the questions she needed answered, suddenly only strange ones entered her mind.

Was she supposed to put on one of the sterile yellow gauze gowns still clinging to the hook? Did she need to wear the plastic gloves? Looking through the narrow venetian blinds that covered the door window into his room, she could see his outline. What was she supposed to do while looking at the body of the man she'd just discovered was her father? What could they have shared in less than twenty-four hours that would offer her the peace she needed?

Zipporah decided that she would put on everything she'd worn earlier when she'd seen her father for the first time. She didn't know why but she closed the venetian blinds completely once she entered Jasper's room.

The first thing she noticed was the sounds. There were none. No beeps, no whirring, no alarms, no bells or whistles. Nothing but complete silence occupied a room where life once had. In fact, all the equipment that had struggled against all odds to keep him alive was already gone.

Zipporah cautiously crept to the side of the bed, as if she'd wake him if she didn't. Someone had already wrapped a sheet tightly around him as though they'd tucked in a sleeping child. The sheet also covered his head, leaving only his face exposed.

Zipporah reached for a nearby chair and sat down by his bed. There was a small space by his knee where the sheet hadn't been tucked in tight, so she reached over and pushed it in.

Zipporah fought the urge to cry. Jasper had a sheet covering him in his death. Where were the sheets she needed in her life?

All the things she'd wanted to come back to say to him suddenly began to flood from her mouth. They weren't as much angry words as they were just questions. She didn't expect answers but she had to ask anyway.

"Jasper," Zipporah whispered as though she'd only wanted him to hear, *"you have a sheet covering you, but over the years whenever the internal need for your paternal covers arose, there were none to cover me, no fitted sheet of fatherly love, no flat sheets of warmth, and no blanket of protection and respect."*

* * *

Zipporah rose from her seat and leaned in closer to Jasper. She gently poked at one cheek and noticed, for the first time, that his mouth was still wide open. He looked like he wanted to answer, and Zipporah found herself shushing him so she could continue.

"I was left to lie naked on this worldly bed covered instead with a fitted sheet of secondhand love, often bought on sale and overpriced. I needed it, so I paid using my body as currency."

"Visiting hours in the ICU unit will be over in ten minutes." It was the announcement over the loudspeaker that again dictated how much time she had to spend with Jasper. Once more, she was at time's mercy. Zipporah strolled to the foot of Jasper's bed, finding another small place where the sheet had not been properly tucked in.

She continued speaking, fighting to keep deep-rooted anger from turning her sharp words of reproach into knives, *"I had to settle for the flat sheets of warmth. They, too, often came with a price far beyond my means. It was a mental struggle, Jasper. But I worked through a hellish existence every day to pay for it. I fought with every fiber I had to keep it, though I knew its fabric consisted of never-meant-to-be-kept promises and unreliable threads of moral heat."*

Zipporah surrendered to the anger. *"That's right, Jasper. Your little girl might as well have been a whore, because I was tossing it out the front and back door just to hear the word* love.*"*

Zipporah pounded the bed, just barely missing one of Jasper's elbows, which lay crosswise over his chest. There was no stopping her. By then she didn't care who heard her outside or inside that room, she wanted Jasper to know what his negligence had done to her.

"Knowing I had no blanket of protection and respect of my own, when the harsh cold winters of truth came, I needed and accepted sold as is, discounted protection and respect." She stopped and pointed at him, adding, *"Did you know its warranties often expired before the dawn came?"* She circled the bed and checked for any signs of the sheet becoming undone before

continuing. *"Miss Diaz, she's the social worker here at the hospital, Jasper, in case the two of you hadn't met. Anyway, she says that around the same time I fainted back at the hotel, you'd suffered a massive heart attack and died."*

Zipporah didn't mean to do it but suddenly she put her hands on Jasper and started shaking him, almost violently. *"Were you thinking of me? Did you somehow get a clue how totally uncovered I was?"*

Zipporah's body froze. What had she done? Her shaking Jasper had caused the sheet to become undone and his arms now lay by his sides. *"Oh, God, I'm so sorry."* She wasn't so concerned with stopping the tears that were surely coming as she was with apologizing to her father. Zipporah cradled Jasper's head, feeling the softness of his hair, now lying exposed where the sheet had fallen away.

"I'm sorry. I know you tried to find me. But I'm still hurt and angry. You were supposed to spend all that time loving me instead of looking for me. I should've said something before and I didn't. But I make you a promise now."

It wasn't a flood of tears but more like small droplets, and they almost ran onto Jasper's face. Zipporah moved so they wouldn't, but she didn't let go of him. *"I'm making you a promise,"* she continued. *"I want you to know this; also buried with you, so that you won't be cold during your sleep, will be my blanket of undying, unspoken love and respect. I can give that to you because I've managed to find and hopefully to keep a real love."*

Zipporah touched the body. It was still warm and the skin on his face pliable. She kissed his forehead. *"Rest in peace, Dad."* And though she'd never share what she saw next, she'd never forget it. Jasper's gaping mouth seemed to turn into a smile, or so she imagined. . . .

51

As Jasper had requested, his remains were flown back to Belton, South Carolina, which wasn't too far from Pelzer. So it'd been up to Zipporah to decide whether or not she'd accompany her father's body. It surprised no one that she did. She'd barely slept or eaten since finally allowing the morgue to retrieve Jasper's body from his room. The attendants almost had to bring Zipporah down to the morgue with Jasper. She wouldn't let go of his body. She fought them with every bit of Epps and Hellraiser strength she possessed.

Surprisingly, neither Bea nor Sasha seemed disappointed they'd have to miss the Mothers Board election. While they were on the plane returning home the election was being held back in Las Vegas. As for Sister Betty, she was just happy to be back home.

A waiting limousine picked them up at the Greenville-Spartanburg Airport. Sister Betty insisted Zipporah stay with her and Chandler stay at his grandmother Ma Cile's house, which was only two doors away from Sister Betty's home. If he was needed, he wouldn't be far away.

As they drove along highway 85, Zipporah took note of the countryside and how it was so calm and different from Las Vegas. She was blocking out most of the polite chitchat among Chandler and the others, preferring to watch the moving scenery. Finally, she turned when she heard Chandler speaking directly to her.

"Zipporah, are you okay?" He knew it was a stupid question and one he seemed to ask every few minutes. This was all new to him. He didn't like death and funerals. And he wasn't really sure if he was just her manager or becoming something more. Had it already progressed to that level? "Just let me know if you need something," he added.

"I'm fine, Chandler," Zipporah replied, and winked. What would she have done if he hadn't been there for her? She'd met him while looking for a job and now she'd become his job. The term *life-changing* had taken on a whole new meaning to her.

As usual Chandler had stepped up to the plate and taken care of everything for Zipporah. He'd talked to Jasper's attorney the day after Jasper died because she was still inconsolable. Between him and the attorney, all the necessary paperwork was completed, and funeral arrangements were made.

Jasper's death had made Chandler think about his grand-mother, Ma Cile. He hadn't told Zipporah but the speed with which everything had happened over the past week or so had only made him more determined to see Ma Cile. Not that he would've returned to Pelzer and not seen her. Whether the stroke would allow her to communicate or not, he intended to see his grandmother. He looked over at Sister Betty and remembered how close she and Ma Cile were. Between his godmother and his grandmother, they'd taken him to church more often than he would've liked, but it did help him to become the man he was. And his grandmother, she dipped her snuff, which made her act crazy at times, and she'd put a switch to his behind more times than the present law allowed. Even so, he loved Ma Cile more than life. Whatever he had to say to her, he meant to say on this side of the grave.

Zipporah stared at Chandler and as was her habit sometimes, she forced a smile. Back in Las Vegas, she had been a little miffed with Chandler and Sasha when they'd finally told her about Jasper's wealth and her mother, Areal. It wasn't the money or the fact that she had a birth mother that was alive and still didn't want to be in her life; it was more the fact that, again, someone had held out on her. She'd grown tired of being a puppet. She fussed so much that they'd promised to never withhold anything again, no matter how good or bad it was.

Zipporah felt a touch on her hand. Of course, it was Bea. Despite her rough exterior and her curved spine the woman had nothing but straight-up unconditional love. Without judging,

Bea had shown more love toward her than anyone she'd ever met, except Chandler.

Bea squeezed Zipporah's hand again. "I'm here for you, sweetie. That's what godmothers are for." Bea let out a small giggle hoping it was not too inappropriate.

"And, I'm so happy you agreed to be my godmother." Zipporah smiled. She truly was. She'd seen how close Sister Betty and Chandler were—godmother and godson. She admired that. Bea had shown that same closeness to her and didn't have a title or a good reason. At the airport Zipporah had asked her if she'd consider being her godmother. Bea had almost done a church dance after saying yes. Zipporah could tell it'd meant more to Bea than money. An ecstatic Bea had confirmed it by telling anyone who'd listen or couldn't get out of earshot, including flight attendants and the pilot, that she was Zipporah's godmother.

The limo dropped Bea off first and then Sasha. Sister Betty lived in another part of Pelzer that was more upscale. Zipporah was amazed at the mansions and their well-kept acres of lawn. And when the limo finally pulled into the winding driveway to Sister Betty's house, Zipporah's mouth dropped open. She'd have never thought Sister Betty lived so richly, even though she knew she had money. The old woman was so modest in apparel and her demeanor. Zipporah's respect level for Sister Betty rose.

"Are you coming inside, June Bug?" Sister Betty asked and yawned. Again, she hadn't realized just how exhausted she was.

"No, Ma'am," Chandler answered. He'd almost gotten used to the fact that he'd always be her little June Bug no matter how much of a man he'd become. "We have to meet with the funeral director." His eyebrows arched in surprise when he realized a look of concern suddenly spread across Sister Betty's face. His first thought was that his own must've looked like he was in pain at the mere thought of going to a funeral parlor.

"You don't have to be involved in everything," Sister Betty said to Chandler. She knew he didn't like funerals. "I can handle things with Zipporah."

"You should get some sleep," Zipporah added. She wasn't sure what the problem was, but Chandler looked like he was about to throw up.

"No, I'll go with you." Chandler stifled a desire to yawn and hold her both at the same time. He looked away and kicked at a pebble much like a shy kid would. At the first opportunity he was going to have to find a way to get his mind, and his heart, in check. Certainly, each was out of control.

"Okay, June Bug." Sister Betty turned to let the limo driver inside the gate so he could take her luggage to the house. "I'll go on inside and rest up. You two go ahead and take care of things, but you make sure you don't wear Zipporah out."

Chandler smiled. He knew exactly what Sister Betty hinted at. Translation: Bring Zipporah right back here and don't even think about taking her back to Ma Cile's empty house.

Chandler shook his head and laughed as he led Zipporah back to the limo. With the way those old women were circling Zipporah's beautiful "wagon," he'd never get a chance to ride, even if he wanted.

And he did.

52

Jasper had done more to make things run smoothly in his death than he had in life. There wasn't one stone left unturned. The trip to the funeral home had been a formality. Zipporah signed a few papers and that was all. He'd planned his entire funeral including the casket, flowers, and guest list. He'd even chosen the preachers. Jasper had wanted two just to cover his bases.

Apparently, by the time Jasper's attorney had left Las Vegas, the legal wheel had already started turning. He gave Zipporah power of attorney. Chandler had been amazed at the simplicity of the matter. Long before he'd returned to Las Vegas determined to meet her Jasper had made sure Zipporah was declared the executor of his estate. According to the attorney, Jasper had filed all the necessary papers as soon as the private investigator confirmed Zipporah was indeed his natural child.

Jasper had made certain that neither Areal nor even his other daughter, Ima, could touch his estate. But he wasn't completely cold-hearted toward Ima. He'd left it up to Zipporah whether or not to share with her sister. Unlike Zipporah, he'd not declared, confirmed, or even legally made Ima his child. But he did believe that it would make Ima more loving toward her sister if she knew Zipporah controlled the purse strings, at least that's the reason he'd given his attorney. Clearly, in keeping track of his two daughters, Jasper had found Zipporah to be the most deserving.

On the morning of Jasper's funeral, held at his old church, Financial Temple, there wasn't a cloud in the sky. It was as though Jasper was still running things, or God had truly forgiven him. And apparently most of the congregation had also. They turned out three deep just to take a look at the celebrity who was once a member.

Zipporah had almost forgotten that her father had not only been a rich man but also quite the superstar. The gospel world had turned out in full force. Many of them did not know Jasper personally but were familiar with his music and his incredible talent for songwriting. There were a few who'd shared the stage with him when he'd sung with Sasha and Areal many years ago.

Huge floral sprays of gladiolas, snapdragons, carnations, daisy poms, lilies and tree ferns adorned the entire pulpit. Jasper had requested his gold and bronze casket be place front and center. Many of his old songs were played through the church's sound system; he didn't want a choir messing up his music. He'd even planned the menu for the after-burial repast.

Jasper hadn't wanted anything long and boring so he'd planned his viewing and funeral, one to follow the other, with a bit of entertainment in between to add levity to the occasion.

Specifically, he'd requested a well-known Christian comedian by the name of Brotha Smitty out of Manhattan to give a fifteen-minute laugh fest. Brotha Smitty, a dark-skinned, rotund man in his forties, brought the house down in laughter when he'd threatened that if folks didn't laugh they'd have to carry him around. Folks took one look at Brotha Smitty's four-hundred pounds and laughed until they'd cried. In fact, many had cried so much there weren't too many tears left for Jasper.

A white stretch limo had brought Zipporah, Chandler, Bea, and Sister Betty to the church just a short time before the funeral began. Just when they thought Sasha had changed her mind about coming, she showed. And, of course, she and Bea showed out.

Each old woman tried to outcry and outshout the other. If Brotha Smitty's performance was funny, then Bea and Sasha's was just downright hysterical. And they'd planned it to be so. They were a little disappointed that Jasper hadn't included them in the funeral plans, so they did what they'd always done. They did it their way.

No funeral would be legit if there weren't some family drama happening. The news spread quicker than wildfire that Jasper had an illegitimate rich daughter. People who wouldn't have spat on Zipporah had she been on fire stepped on toes and broke all sorts of funeral protocol to get a look at her or shake her hand. Even the two preachers kept leering down at the front pew. They tried to get her attention by invoking her name every chance they got.

Sister Betty, on the other hand, had been designated the look-out by Chandler. Her job was to pray and if necessary get a couple of burly teenagers from the youth choir to put a choke hold on Ima or Areal should they show up.

If both Areal and Ima did show up, they must've hidden among the crowd and behaved. But Sister Betty saw no evidence of their attending, and anyone who knew those Hellraisers knew behaving was not an option. So she was able to relax, welcoming the opportunity to do so.

The burial and the repast went as well as could be expected. Those who'd wanted to see Zipporah cry and scream at the gravesite were as disappointed as they'd been when she'd calmly sat through the funeral. This was her father's funeral and she wasn't about to upstage him by sobbing, no matter how much she'd wanted to do just that and more.

The day after Jasper's funeral Zipporah decided that she needed to be of assistance to someone. She couldn't just sit around doing nothing, so that meant she had to think and make decisions. But decision-making—she wasn't ready for that yet.

Zipporah overheard Sister Betty telling Chandler that she would go to see his grandmother with him. Zipporah decided that she'd go, too. He hadn't asked her to come along, but she figured it was because he, as usual, was trying to protect her. In his mind, he'd probably thought she'd had enough of hospitals for a while.

But Zipporah gathered her strength, determined that she would be there for Chandler whether it was at a hospital or anywhere else.

It was her turn to watch Chandler as they rode to the hospital. She sat between him and Sister Betty. Both were looking out their windows thinking about what, she didn't know. Not knowing Ma Cile or how to comfort either of them, Zipporah took each one's hand. She held it and she prayed. In her mind, her prayer was a bit awkward but she knew God would get her meaning. Somehow, although she hadn't mentioned her own anxieties, and only prayed for God to strengthen Chandler and Sister Betty, Zipporah felt better.

In fact, Zipporah felt so much better that she allowed herself a moment to lie back and let her thoughts come freely, as she held on to Chandler and Sister Betty's hands.

She closed her eyes and moments later had a vision. It was a vision where there fell a mist of fresh-smelling rain, and balls of light flickered as though they wanted her to follow them. And then she saw her father, Jasper. He was beckoning her to come to where he was, standing by a four-poster bed. She went to him, and then she and Jasper continued their conversation from the hospital. They were laughing as she crawled into the bed. He covered her with the whitest sheets she'd ever seen. He kept laughing and talking while he tucked her in. She began giggling. Here she was a grown woman and her father was tucking her in like a baby, making sure the sheets were tight. She saw and could feel Jasper smoothing the sheets. He tucked them quickly as though he were trying to regain time. In the vision, he'd started singing. She could hear the lyrics and without realizing it, she began to sing a melody out loud.

"If fire came today, I'd not leave you.
If water rose above my head, I'd not leave you.
If death called me home, I'd not leave you.
There's nothing that can separate me from you.
You're covered with my sheets of love.
You're protected by my sheets of love.
You're warmed by my sheets of love.
Uncovered, my baby, you'll never be."

"That's a beautiful song," Sister Betty whispered.

Zipporah's eyes fluttered and then opened. "I didn't realize anyone heard me."

"I don't think I know that song," Chandler said. "It's got a beautiful melody. I wasn't able to catch all the words."

"Thank you."

"Sounds like something you should record for my gospel album." Sister Betty hadn't forgotten about the album but since the opportunity had presented itself, she brought it up.

"Who recorded it first?" Chandler asked, trying to avoid the look from Sister Betty. She obviously wasn't going to let him off the hook.

"It hasn't been recorded."

"Really," Chandler said, surprised. "It's got a beautiful melody and I think you could do something with the hook, perhaps tweak a word here and there."

Zipporah gave Chandler a disapproving look. "I'm not recording it."

"Why not?"

"My father *just* gave it to me moments ago and you're already talking about recording it." Zipporah laid her head back and, again, she sang her new song, the one her father had just given her.

Sister Betty and Chandler looked at each other with both concern and amazement.

It was obvious that Zipporah wasn't ready to let go, or perhaps she had a way to deal with her grief that they didn't understand. Either way, Jasper had and probably always would play a huge part in her life. After all, he'd already flipped it.

A light rain had fallen since their arrival back at Sister Betty's from the hospital visit to see Ma Cile. The quick sprinkle seemed calming as Chandler stood at the window with his arms folded, listening to the drops gently tapping the shutters on the house. He inhaled deeply, breathing in the rain's tranquility as though it were precious air.

"I didn't realize it could still be so lovely even at sundown and especially during a rain," Zipporah said, trying to sound as cheerful as her words. She'd pulled her long hair into a plain ponytail, changed into a comfortable red denim pants suit and entered the living room moments earlier. She'd stood at the entrance to the living room and watched Chandler unobserved. Zipporah didn't want to interrupt what seemed like a moment of reflection and despite how she was feeling, she was happy to see him at peace.

The welcomed intrusion had caught Chandler off guard. He turned slowly, smiling to show his pleasure at her appearance. "I see you've changed." He held out his hand, indicating she should join him.

"I see you haven't," Zipporah whispered, as she joined him by the window.

"I haven't." He gave a sheepish grin hoping it would hide his confusion. "Why would you say that?"

"I'm not sure. It's really not what I meant to say." Zipporah turned her head thinking she'd seen a dark shadow streak across the room. The last time she'd seen such a thing was in her father's room on the night he'd died.

Chandler's eyes followed her gaze. He couldn't tell what she was looking at. "What did you mean to say?"

Zipporah nodded her head, sighed and turned back to Chandler. She didn't speak. Instead, she suddenly laughed and began to sing.

If fire came today, I'd not leave you. If water rose above my head, I'd not leave you. If death called me home, I'd not leave you.

Zipporah stopped singing, choosing instead to hum the melody. She removed the clip holding her ponytail, allowing it to fall around her shoulders. She kept humming. From her jacket pocket she took a piece of paper and placed it in Chandler's hand and she continued humming.

Chandler's mind raced. He was caught totally unaware. Without saying a word or questioning what she wanted, he joined in and sang the words completing the song, as Zipporah continued humming Jasper's melody.

There's nothing that can separate me from you. You're covered with my sheets of love. You're protected by my sheets of love. You're warmed by my sheets of love. Uncovered, my baby, you'll never be.

With the soft rain as their background music they sang. They sang the words they couldn't speak—Jasper's words.

From inside her room Sister Betty listened to the music made by Zipporah and Chandler. "Well, Jasper, you finally did it. You old rascal, you left a dowry with your daughter that will flourish forever."

Sister Betty quietly closed her bedroom door to give Zipporah and Chandler privacy. And even with the rain bothering her old arthritic knees she raced to the phone. She called Ma Cile's hospital room and had the nurse place the phone next to Ma Cile's ear. With the cordless phone in one hand she crept to the bedroom door and opened it. As the sound of the beautiful duet sung by Zipporah and Chandler travelled through the phone line, she could only imagine the healing it was giving to Ma Cile, who managed to emit quick gasps to show she'd heard the music.

And then Sister Betty called Bea and Sasha. Over the telephone the three women wee beside themselves as they secretly listened in on Zipporah and Chandler's "private" declaration of love.

Of course, the three old women's camaraderie only lasted as long as the song. Within five minutes they were back to arguing. Each blamed the other for the failed conference. But since it had been cancelled, Bea and Sasha retained their positions as president and vice president. However, no matter how many times Sister Betty promised she'd never run against them, they still wanted it in writing.

Epilogue

It took Sister Betty a long time to get over just how close she *wasn't* to God. Choosing whom she would or not bear witness to was not an option she was supposed to have. Judging was God's work and not hers. She'd become so comfortable, God had had to shake her up.

And He shook her good! The pastor and congregation at Crossing Over Sanctuary Temple were shaken as well. Because the first thing Bea and Sasha did, when they had a chance, was to testify about how Sister Betty crossed over onto the dark side in Las Vegas. They regaled the congregation with their version of how Sister Betty had to be dragged from the casino and placed into the hands of hotel security. And the dramatic way they told of Sister Betty's determination to commit murder, without remorse, should've been taped and televised on CNN.

Of course, Sister Betty hadn't been at church that night so Bea and Sasha felt free to embellish and omit a lot of details. Sasha particularly didn't mention that she hadn't been saved or as saved as she'd claimed, all those years.

But on the bright side, Bea now had a family. The way Bea told it, not only was Zipporah her "godbaby" but she'd actually gotten her vocal talent from her.

To try and keep Bea out of trouble because of her inherent need to add to her fixed income, Zipporah started a day care in Pelzer and hired Bea to run it. She wanted Bea to not only make extra money but to put that huge heart of hers to some good use. And, of course, Bea loved the idea because she loved babies. But before Zipporah knew it the day care was losing money. Bea was taking in babies for either half the fee or no fee at all. So it became both a job for Bea and a tax write-off for Zipporah.

Miracles were the order of the day. No sooner had Chandler and Zipporah returned to Las Vegas than Ma Cile started regaining her strength. Whatever Chandler had said when he'd visited his grandmother, according to the doctors, had been just the medicine she needed. Secretly, Chandler thought Ma Cile had taken one look at Zipporah and, stroke or no stroke, had seen the possibility of some beautiful great-grandchildren. As stubborn as Ma Cile was, she wasn't about to leave earth and miss out on that.

Sasha did what she'd promised. She sat Zipporah down and told her the good, the bad and the ugly side of the Hellraiser clan. Sasha also had to let her know that Zipporah's sister, Ima, had found out about Jasper. At that time, Ima was in South Africa with her fiancé, the Reverend Lyon Lipps, doing missionary work. Sasha warned Zipporah that Ima would return soon and that perhaps Zipporah might want to hire security to watch her back. But definitely not the wimps that she'd dealt with at the Luxor.

Sasha had also tried to talk Areal into meeting with Zipporah, but Areal wouldn't do it. Perhaps, one day she would but not then. Sasha had bullied Areal once before and it'd led to nothing but heartache.

Surprisingly, Zipporah calmly accepted Areal's decision but left the door open if her birth-mother ever wanted to meet her. Secretly, in her heart, Zipporah hoped her mother would do it before it was too late.

Life sometimes had a strange, and perhaps less than kind way of leading a person into providence. And it seemed it didn't just lead Zipporah, it dragged her over cactus thorns to get there.

Zipporah's path had been littered with abuse and mistrust. And it didn't matter that she was gorgeous or had a good heart and even less that she could outsing most of those who'd seemed to regularly receive recognition and fame. But just like the forging of steel, she'd become a force of nature, and Daddy was still helping from the grave.

Details of Jasper's funeral had hit several newspapers, including a few in New York, Las Vegas, and California. Pictures of him and Zipporah ran side by side in celebrity columns, on television, and even in a few music magazines. He'd left her not only wealthy but well connected. She'd be able to greet and meet with anyone of power, and they were knocking down her door already.

There were some who were not happy about the way Jasper hadn't owned up to his responsibility, but they were the ones who didn't know the entire story. They were also the ones who soon learned that if it hadn't bothered Zipporah, it certainly shouldn't bother them. Business was business and the newly formed Las Vegas, Nevada, Moses and Lamb Entertainment Agency was all business.

Chandler and Zipporah had the buzz going about their company within six months of Jasper's death. Many of the bigwigs at the record companies had flown in personally to check out his roster of exceptional talent. There wasn't a genre in the business he couldn't supply talent for.

And, as he'd promised Zipporah, Chandler found the brightest and the best to create a Las Vegas show just for her. It was spectacular and she looked and sounded amazing. In no time she was pulling crowds away from Celine Dion and Toni Braxton. And to show that there were no hard feelings, Zipporah hired Alicia to comanage the show. She knew it was better to keep Alicia where she could watch her; after all, Las Vegas wasn't that big.

Zipporah also found time to record Sister Betty's gospel album. Zipporah had written every song with the exception of the one Jasper had given her in the vision. She titled the album *Sheets of Love*. The album hadn't cost a lot of money because only one copy was pressed. The hardest part was finding a plant that still pressed vinyl. Sister Betty didn't have a CD player and balked at having to purchase and learn how to use one.

One of the proudest moments for Zipporah came when she was able to present a sizable check to a kinder and gentler Miss Thompson and the homeless shelter. She even apologized for her little "white lie" about being hospitalized. The check helped the forgiveness.

Two years after Jasper entered and left Zipporah's life, forever changing it, another change occurred. Chandler and Zipporah exchanged wedding vows. It was a new and adventurous time for the two of them.

For the first time Zipporah and Chandler shared a gift that

was unmistakably blessed. On their wedding night they finally got to know one another the way the Bible had meant for a husband and wife to. Each had kept their vow of abstinence.

And not only was their wedding night amazing and exhausting for them, but Zipporah happily wrote a new song the next morning. Almost a year later it became a hit. Just around the same time they became parents to baby Jasper Chandler Lamb.

This list of questions has been created to encourage a group or an individual to dig deeper—explore the heart of the book's content. The questions are designed to encourage interaction and discussion.

DISCUSSION QUESTIONS

1. It's often preached that Christians are supposed to have all their needs met by God. If that is true, why would you think Bea and Sasha gambled? Was it a habit?

2. What about grudges? Have you released yours?

3. God often has to move us out of our comfort zone. What caused Sister Betty to fall temporarily out of favor?

4. Have you ever been placed in a situation that seemed as though God abandoned you? Did you repent? Did you question God?

5. Are you obedient to God's commands as they pertain to you? Do you know God's voice?

6. Would your Christian walk be compromised by a location, such as Las Vegas?

7. Zipporah is a Biblical name. Who was Zipporah in the Bible?

8. How important do you feel it is to have a healthy, God-fearing relationship with your father?

9. Would you accept a father that you felt abandoned you? Could you forgive him?

10. Zipporah had an amazing voice and yet she had to go through so much difficulty before it was discovered. What gift do you have that is hidden?

11. Bea Blister had a criminal past and yet she was able to accept Zipporah and show love without hesitation. Do you

believe our pasts can hinder our futures? What does love have to do with it?

12. Chandler had a preconceived notion when it came to the type of woman he would date. Zipporah, with the exception of her beauty, did not fit. He almost missed what God had in store for him. Have you ever dismissed a blessing based upon your preconceived ideas? What was the outcome?

13. Sasha's attempt to hide an embarrassing situation set off a series of events that impacted drastically upon the lives of those she thought she was helping. Was she truly trying to avoid embarrassment or was she simply jealous? How did she reconcile what she'd done with her Christian walk? How could she have claimed salvation for so many years while not acknowledging such an act?

14. Sister Betty, unknowingly, became a modern day Jonas after she became wealthy. She became too relaxed and did not continue her mission as she'd done before. Have the embers of your fire for God begun to fade? How do you rekindle it?

15. Sister Betty was placed in a situation where she supposedly should have been the moral compass. Instead, she became a follower when she knew better. Have you had the same experience?

16. Jasper Epps, a gospel celebrity and a "daddy-come-lately," finally tried to do the right thing, or did he? Should he have totally claimed one child and disclaimed the other? Why couldn't he see that Ima was as much a product of her upbringing as Zipporah? Whether you are a celebrity or not, when you're involved in Kingdom work, shouldn't you be held accountable when you lead others astray?

17. Has there ever been an instance in your life where someone has appeared or reappeared in such a manner that only God could've worked it that way?

18. The craziness brought about by the mothers Bea and Sasha continued to gain momentum as they aged. Were they doing more harm to themselves or their church positions? Why? Do you know seniors such as these women?